WEB OF
DECEPTION

WEB OF
DECEPTION

Misinformation on the Internet

Edited by
Anne P. Mintz

CyberAge Books

Information Today, Inc.
Medford, New Jersey

First printing 2002

Web of Deception
Misinformation on the Internet

Library of Congress Cataloging-in-Publication Data
Web of deception : misinformation on the Internet / [edited by] Anne P. Mintz.
    p. cm.
Includes bibliographical references and index.
  ISBN 0-910965-60-9
 1. Internet fraud. 2. Electronic information resource literacy. 3. Computer network resources--Evaluation. 4. Internet searching. I. Mintz, Anne P.
 ZA4201 .W43 2002
  025.04--dc21

                  2002004687

Printed and bound in the United States of America.

Publisher: Thomas H. Hogan, Sr.
Editor-in-Chief: John B. Bryans
Managing Editor: Deborah R. Poulson
Production Manager: M. Heide Dengler
Cover Design: Jacqueline Walter Crawford
Book Design: Kara Mia Jalkowski
Copy Editor: Robert Saigh
Indexer: Sharon Hughes

DEDICATION

*This book is dedicated to our colleagues
—librarians and other information professionals—
the unsung heroines and heroes
who synthesize data into information
and weave information into knowledge.*

TABLE OF CONTENTS

FOREWORD

This book, ably edited by Forbes Director of Knowledge Management, Anne P. Mintz, could not be more timely. The Internet burst upon the scene a decade ago and grew exponentially. The high-tech bust is a temporary detour. Hundreds of billions of equity dollars were lost when numerous computer and telecommunication companies crashed. And the politicians still have not sorted out the Net's increasing impact on television, radio, telephony, and cable. But the technology is moving forward just as it did in the mid-1980s when the personal computer bubble burst. Remember Atari and Commodore? Remember the founder-head of Digital Equipment, then an independent and consequential company, who said, "The PC is a passing fad?" That prophecy was followed by breakthroughs in graphics (the mouse) and more powerful chips. Soon, PCs could be connected to each other, and our homes and offices haven't been the same since.

Today, most hotels, homes, and small offices still try to get by with only 50,000 bits of information per second. An enhanced subscriber line might get you 400,000 bits. But we will have over a billion bits per second within a few short years. Then the Net will truly obliterate the once strong walls that separated cable, television, and telephones. These carriers of information and a whole lot of others will find their worlds destroyed or turned upside down by this infinitely more powerful Internet. Instead of going to the doctor or clinic, for instance, health providers will be coming to you via the Internet. The promise of the Net is truly awe inspiring. The microchip and its off-shoots are indeed enhancing the power of the human brain the way machines expanded the human muscle during the industrial era.

But all this is precisely why this book is so important. Progress does not come without price. The automobile gave unimaginable mobility and freedom to hundreds of millions of people around the world. You could personally go by your own timetable rather than the railroad's or the stagecoach's. It generated immense wealth and job creation. But the automobile also meant carnage, pollution, and congestion. It meant creating rules of the road, highway patrols, more courts and judges to adjudicate disputes emanating from accidents, more insurance adjusters, not to mention more insurance companies.

The Internet's very ease of communication has manifestly not exempted it from the underside of human nature—misinformation, libelous gossip, child pornography, fraud and thievery (including theft of your very own identity), assaults on privacy, disruptive viruses, global terrorism networks, and a whole array of other crimes. In fact, these shortcomings are frighteningly magnified because of the Net.

Experts here walk you through the risks and traps of the Web world and tell you how to avoid them or to fight back and remedy wrongs done to you.

Consumers getting essential information they can act on is crucial for a vibrant free market. *Web of Deception* will also be an instrument to prod lawmakers and regulators to provide essential protections as the Net develops. Otherwise the pitfalls this book speaks of will undermine and prevent the eventual full flowering of the Internet.

Anne Mintz and her collaborators have done us a genuine service.

Steve Forbes

ACKNOWLEDGMENTS

Obviously, the authors of the individual chapters deserve most of the credit for bringing the subject of intentional misinformation on the Internet front and center. Each is an expert in his or her field and I am honored that they considered tackling such a difficult task. Professionals in the information arena are familiar with this expertise: Steve Arnold's vision and grasp of new technologies, Susan Detwiler's expertise in the medical information world, Helene Kassler's work in competitive intelligence and business information, Lys Chuck's evaluations of the world of e-commerce, Sue Feldman and Liz Liddy's work in natural language processing and search engine functionality, and Carol Ebbinghouse's legal mind and writings about legal information online. Paul Piper added his wonderful sense of humor to his contribution on counterfeit sites and hoaxes, and LaJean Humphries demonstrates the professionalism of the law librarian in assessing the accuracy and quality of information. Sandra Tung, Business Information Manager at Boeing Space and Communications, contributed to the chapter on misinformation in the corporate universe. I thank them for their willingness to share their expertise and understanding of the pitfalls of using the Internet for research, as well as their fine advice on navigating around them.

Barbara Quint conceived the idea for this book, convinced me to take it on, and worked with me to flesh out what it might contain. Light years ahead of me (and everyone else I know), she guided me through the process.

John Bryans, the Editor-in-Chief of the book division of Information Today, Inc., liked the proposal immediately and then trusted our collective judgment completely to make it happen as we envisioned it. He is a wise editor as well, guiding us to make it even better. He has honored us by publishing what we delivered. I thank him for his role in making this work come to life.

Deborah Poulson, Managing Editor, and Heide Dengler, Production Manager, at Information Today, Inc., have contributed enormous professional expertise that is invisible to the reader but shows on each page to the authors. The care they brought to the production of the book is truly appreciated.

Tom Hogan, President of Information Today, Inc., a good friend (still), believes in me (still) and was willing to take a risk. He disproves the cliché that one should never do business with friends.

To other friends and colleagues: Elinor Hoffman, Dennis Kneale, Dr. Mindy Seidlin, and Peter Silverman reviewed sections of the manuscript, red-flagged what to avoid, and added significant suggestions on how to enhance the text. Their contributions are greatly appreciated. I thank Helen Goldberg for her wisdom and good judgment. Much appreciation to Dr. Nina Wacholder for waking at 4 A.M. one morning with the title (and remembering it). Thank you to my professional colleagues, from whom I learn something every day. And thanks to the rest of my friends for still speaking to me. It's been a very long year.

Anne P. Mintz
May 2002

INTRODUCTION

Lies, Damned Lies, and the Internet

Anne P. Mintz

When you log onto www.martinlutherking.org you expect the site to be sponsored by an organization with official connections to the family of Dr. Martin Luther King, Jr. You expect factual information that a schoolchild could use in a homework assignment. You expect information about his life and his work. You do not expect to find a page alleging that King plagiarized his doctoral thesis. You do not expect to find a speech entitled *The Beast as Saint: The Truth About "Martin Luther King, Jr."* that refers to him as a "modern-day plastic god." You do not expect the site to suggest purchasing books such as *My Awakening* by David Duke or *Holiday for a Cheater* by Michael Hoffman.

This book is about information on the Internet that is intentionally wrong or misleading. It is about deception on the Web, dangerous data in your future, the age of misinformation to come. Intent is the focus of this book. What does the sponsor of a Web site intend for you to see, intend for you to think, or intend to host? Information is no longer inviolate just because one can view it on a computer screen. We can no longer count on its legitimacy because the technology tools for giving created works the imprimatur of appropriateness are in the hands of millions of computer owners. The Internet has made self-publishing possible for anyone with a computer and a modem, requiring no editing or checking for factual accuracy.

This situation is especially alarming when children and other students use the Internet for their education needs. People of all ages, but particularly kids who don't have training in evaluation and criticism, become targets for organizations or individuals with deception in mind. The absence of an authority on the presented facts can pose dangerous problems to kids and teenagers who may come to believe things to be true that are not. Intermediaries such as editors, teachers, or librarians usually fill those roles in the world of bricks and mortar, but in cyberspace it seems that just about anything goes.

Worse than that, even the press is being duped. According to the *American Journalism Review* ("The Real Computer" by Carl M. Cannon, May 2001), the mainstream press is beginning to publish stories with unchecked factoids that its staff found on the Internet that it accepted as fact. When journalists rely on unchecked information for source material and republish it in their own pieces, the erroneous information gets spread as fact. Cannon predicts that these problems are only going to get worse unless Internet users (and journalists) become more careful.

In this age of Internet nomads and mass acceptance of online information on the World Wide Web, what if new dangers emerge not from a lack of competence by database publishers or searchers but from a malevolent competence? Dangers like deliberate deception, deliberate misinformation, and half-truths that can be used to divert a seeker from the real information being sought. How many ways can people find to use new technologies to support lies, deception, misdirection, fraud, spin control, propaganda, and all other forms of misinformation? Do any protections exist for online searchers?

Internet nomads often lack the background and training to evaluate or criticize basic information sources. Since many of these nomads are knowledge workers or university students, making wise decisions on sources and searching is clearly not a matter of intelligence. Even experts can find themselves gulled by smarter experts working behind the scenes. Well-trained and suspicious information professionals constitute one level of protection. But how available are they, and for whom? Even legal protections may not hold. In most cases, Web-based data comes free to searchers. No contract, no liability? You get what you pay for? Is there any liability involved and for whom?

The entire subject of the validity of data on the Web is beginning to spawn a new industry. There are advertising-sponsored Web sites that debunk online myths and legends, magazines and newsletters that evaluate Web material—and even this book! The subject of deception on the World Wide Web extends into a variety of disciplines and aspects of daily life. We've chosen just some of them. We share tips for avoiding scams, phony charities, hoaxes, and identity theft. We tell you how to evaluate a Web site for authority and how the search engines got you to that site in the first place. We list Web sites of government offices to contact for remedies when you've been defrauded on the Internet. Most of all, we hope that this book provides a perspective on where the misleading and deceptive information comes from and how to avoid using it inappropriately.

Better Type That Again!

Web hoaxes, counterfeit sites, and other spurious information on the Internet can give even the most discriminating of searchers a hard time. In November 2000, Nancy Yanofsky, President of ProChoice Resource Center, a national nonprofit organization that provides information about reproductive rights, health, and activism, logged on to her ProChoice Resource Center Web site. She inadvertently typed prochoiceresource.*com* instead of .org as the top-level domain in the URL. She instantly found herself (and anyone else who made that error) at Abortionismurder.com, a Web site that graphically depicts mutilated fetuses and equates supporters of a woman's right to choose with the eugenicistic Nazis. Her organization promptly made a federal case out of it—literally—and sought relief, including a permanent injunction forbidding the use of its name, by filing suit in New York. The suit was based in part on the 1999 Anticybersquatting Consumer Protection Act, that among other things prohibits "cybersquatting," the unauthorized use of another's domain name with a different top-level domain, exactly what abortionismurder.com did when it used "prochoiceresource.com." Abortionismurder.com immediately capitulated; it redirected the prochoiceresource.com domain name to the ProChoice Resource Web site, transferred the domain registration and consented to a permanent injunction. Although cybersquatting is against the law, the law works only if invoked, which can be a long and expensive process. That said, we can assume that cybersquatting, along with other forms of unreliable and potentially harmful Internet content, will be with us for a long time.

E-Commerce Fraud on the Internet

The Consumer Sentinel network of agencies gathering data on e-commerce fraud reports that in 2001 there were 204,000 complaints, compared to 138,900 reported in 2000. This 47 percent increase demonstrates the growing nature of the problem. The FBI announced in May 2001 that 62 people had been arrested or have pleaded guilty to charges that they defrauded tens of thousands of consumers out of $117 million using Internet scams as varied as bogus sales offers and fraudulent investments. The *Associated Press* reported that over 56,000 consumers were victimized by online fraud schemes uncovered via the code-named "Operation Cyber Loss," conducted by the FBI and law enforcement agencies throughout the U.S. In that case alone, 39 people were indicted.

In February 2002, Scambusters notified subscribers about the Internal Revenue Service (IRS) Audit Scam. It warned that "taxpayers receive a fraudulent e-mail saying that they are under audit. (The e-mail uses the term 'IRS e-audit' in the subject line.) The taxpayer is instructed to fill out a questionnaire, which supposedly must be completed within 48 hours to avoid penalties and interest. The taxpayer is asked for his/her social security number, bank account numbers and other confidential information.

"However, the IRS does NOT notify taxpayers about pending audits via e-mail. Nor do they conduct 'e-audits.' And, the IRS certainly does NOT ask for this kind of confidential, personal information. In other words, this e-mail is NOT from the IRS."

"The old adage that you can't believe everything you read also holds true for what you read on the Internet" stated Tom Pickard, deputy director of the FBI, on May 23, 2001. That is particularly true of the Nigerian letter and its imitators that have defrauded thousands of consumers, as we tell you in Chapter 6.

Web Sites Playing Doctor

Do you really trust the medical information you find on the Web? How can you evaluate which sites are giving you valid impartial information on a subject and which ones have a hidden agenda to get you to buy a particular pharmaceutical or treatment? We will tell you about a site that recommends (after analyzing the results of an online quiz) that a 5-year-old boy suffering from low libido take Viagra. We will also tell you of a site that recommends, as a preferred life-style, that one choose to be anorexic/bulemic, a dangerous condition that can lead to death.

With estimates that vary from as few as 20,000 pages to as many as 2 million, cyberspace is filled with e-health sites. The results of a study commissioned by the California Health Care Foundation (a healthcare philanthropy) and conducted by RAND indicate that almost 100 million Americans go online to find health-related information and that 70 percent of them said that what they found influenced their treatment decisions. According to the foundation, the study found that answers to important health questions are often incomplete, and although the accuracy of much of the information was fairly high, many of the sites contained contradictory information.

Some of the claims of efficacy for treatments have not been proven, and some may even be dangerous, such as the one that suggests a self-administered intravenous treatment with 35 percent hydrogen peroxide solution. Many of these sites do not present balanced views of the issues, choosing instead to promote their agendas to a sometimes gullible readership. We have just begun to explore the ramifications of this freedom of speech on the Internet as it applies to health and medicine.

Stealing Your Identity

The Internet has made identity theft easier for the thieves. This crime has become so prevalent that early in 2002 the Federal Trade Commission (FTC) unveiled a model identity theft affidavit that will streamline the process by which victims can alert firms where a new account was opened in his/her name rather than require the victim to report each incident separately. The FTC reported that in 2001, 42 percent of the 204,000 complaints entered into a consumer fraud tracking database were related to identity theft. It was also in 2001 that lawmakers in various states began making progress in the drive to protect consumers from identity theft. Arizona has prohibited merchants from printing complete credit card numbers on receipts, a common way thieves have of assuming the identity of card holders and incurring debt. Washington state and Idaho have enacted laws toughening penalties for identity theft, while California did so as early as 1997.

The U.S. Supreme Court ruled unanimously in January 2000 to restrict the ability of state motor vehicle departments to sell or disclose personal, identifying information without an individual's consent (the Driver's Privacy Protection Act). Although the law does not ban the sale or disclosure of personal information, it does require the disclosure to be with an individual's consent. But how many of us bother to check the opt-out box on the renewals that would deny consent? Not 18 million Texans, since the state of Texas will still sell its motor vehicle database with the addresses, driver's license numbers, and birth dates of every one of the 18 million Texans with a driver's license (who didn't opt out) for just $1,600 (*Houston Chronicle*, March 11, 2001). Since much of this information is out of date or inaccurate due to human error, misinformation can be disseminated about consumers without them ever knowing it.

In the 2000 Senatorial election in Minnesota, Senator Mark Dayton's campaign bought a list of names and addresses for all 224,000 deer hunters licensed by the state and paid less than $15,000 for it. It seems the campaign focused on many issues that related to the outdoors, and he used that list effectively to target people likely to spend time outdoors. It helped him squeak through a victory in a close election. Apparently only a few hundred people have taken the state up on its offer to remove their names from the licensing list. In Minnesota, personal information from driver's license and motor vehicle records is now opt-in, meaning these people's names and addresses don't get included in the files unless they ask to be included—in writing. Fewer than 1,000 have chosen to remain on that list.

On April 30, 2001, federal Judge Ellen Segal Huvelle upheld the government's interpretation of a 1999 financial privacy law that restricts sales of personal financial information. As of July 1, 2001, credit bureaus and other major data firms were no longer allowed to sell personal information without consumer consent—opt-in rather than opt-out will be the rule. That information included names, addresses, phone numbers, and Social Security numbers. This ruling has the potential to change the landscape of marketing information available to telemarketers, spammers, and others. In this suit brought by the Federal Trade Commission, the Federal Reserve, and four other government agencies, they prevailed against TransUnion, Equifax, and Acxiom, the three major credit records agencies, as well as LexisNexis and First Data Solutions. You can be sure this will be appealed by the credit industry organizations. Until then, to paraphrase Scott McNealy of Sun Microsystems, "Privacy on the Internet? There is none. Get over it."

"Charity Creates a Multitude of Sins"

Oscar Wilde's statement introduces us to a really sleazy activity on the Web: charity scams. Charities that solicit contributions often have elaborate and impressive Web sites that give detailed information on where they spend your money. However, there are some sites that have been used by phony charities, and these can be as elaborate and impressive as the legitimate ones. We give you advice on where to check their validity and how to report those that aren't legitimate. What clues can you use to distinguish among them? There are numerous sites from legitimate organizations and agencies to help donors through evaluations. Before you give, look at some of the sites we suggest. Please don't stop contributing to honest charities via the Web—just check to make sure you aren't donating your money to scam artists.

Information in the Corporate Universe

How can they mislead you? Let me count the ways. A company can post nonexistent job openings on its Web site in order to fool competitors into thinking it is expanding into a certain area. It can use these phony job openings to solicit resumes from employees of competitor firms to see who may be unhappily employed. Uses of this information can be to find snoops or to interview these "candidates" in order to solicit information about what that employer is working on. That's just for starters. A company can release earnings information to the public in a press release and a few weeks later file dramatically different numbers to the SEC in an official document. Who's going to check the figures?

Do you really believe everything posted on a company's Web site? In early 2002 the Securities and Exchange Commission (SEC) posted a phony investment Web site to show investors how easy it is to get scammed, and got 150,000 hits in one week alone. The SEC chairman, Harvey Pitt, suggested that the agency should use the exact same tactics as the crooks in order to demonstrate the danger to a gullible public. The SEC published a fake press release touting an initial public offering. The fictitious company, McWhortle Enterprises, has an SEC-created Web site with offers of 300 percent investment returns in three months and phony testimonials from unnamed executives. People interested in investing in McWhortle investment were given a phone number to call, but before they spent any money they were informed of the scam. The SEC officials taking the calls then offered advice to the callers on how to research potential investments and avoid real scams.

There are some dramatic examples of stock manipulation and other illegal activities that have used the Web to make a quick buck, which you can read about in Chapter 3.

Why Do I Get the Results I Get?

Ask Jeeves, a search engine company, allows "branded response" ads at the top of editorial answers. Now, you can run a search on something to do with autos and an ad for Honda may appear with the results list. Gator, a piece of software working in combination with another program called OfferCompanion, can enable electronic "coupons" to appear on your computer screen as you search the Internet. As described by Tyler Hamilton in the *Toronto Star* (August 20, 2001), if you are reading an article on Forbes.com about sport utility vehicles, an ad for a Ford Explorer may appear on your screen. Forbes.com, which might have General Motors or Daimler-Chrysler as a major sponsor, can't do anything to prevent it. In fact, the article says, "Gator will often tailor its banner advertisements to completely cover the other Web site's advertisements." Spooky? Just the beginning.

Search engine technology has become so sophisticated as to enable site owners to stack the deck in favor of certain results without the customer knowing. They mislead not by the presence of certain information, but rather the lack of it. They don't tell you which companies paid for placement of their products, or other benefits. Major sponsors of a site may have their products and services rise to the top of the relevant results because the engine has been programmed to do this, not because the results are more relevant. In

EContent (May 2001), Greg Notess described how Inktomi takes money from sponsors of Web sites for programs that allow that site to rise to the top of a large results set. The Search/Submit option lets Web site owners pay by the page to have individual Web pages on their sites included in the Inktomi index. This practically guarantees that the site will appear close to the top of the results listing. The Index Connect option gives larger sites control over how Inktomi indexes their sites, what metadata are used, and how frequently the information is updated. They are public about this process, but most customers of a search engine aren't going to know which sites paid for placement and which did not.

In July 2001, Commercial Alert formally complained to the Federal Trade Commission (FTC) about deceptive advertising with paid placement and other result-ranking methods. It asked in a letter that the FTC investigate seven popular search engines: AltaVista, AOL Time Warner's Netscape, Microsoft's MSN search, Direct Hit Technologies, iWon Inc, LookSmart, and Terra Lycos. The letter says "This complaint concerns the practices of paid placement and paid inclusion without clear and conspicuous disclosure that the ads are, in fact, ads." These practices mislead and misdirect information seekers by the invisible quality of the information that has been programmed into the process.

Don't Check Your Common Sense at the Door

Connect to a Web site created by Elizabeth Kirk of Johns Hopkins University, "Information and Its Counterfeits: Propaganda, Misinformation, and Disinformation." While she defines misinformation as always unintentional in nature, and we define it as always with intent to misinform, it is nevertheless definitely useful to take the exercise on evaluating the information she presents. It can be found at http://milton.mse.jhu.edu/research/education/counterfeit.html.

Examples abound for every one of the topics in the book. Each time we spoke with friends about aspects of the subject, they gave us more Web sites that posed problems or presented data in a misleading fashion. This book is not intended to be all-inclusive. There are many more sites than those mentioned here that intend to mislead or misrepresent data in ways to advance a specific (and many times unstated) agenda. What we do set out to accomplish here is to alert readers to these red flags on the Internet. All of this information may not be on the Web as you read this, but it was at one time. The Wayback Machine introduced by Brewster Kahle in October 2001 (www.archive.org) has captured these pages if they are not still viewable at the URL we cite.

The chapters in this book were commissioned specifically for this book; they also appear in briefer article format as the series in *Searcher* in 2000–2001 entitled "Dangerous Data Ahead." They have been well received by the readership of that journal, and the expanded and updated work is what we present here.

Welcome to the chase.

Anne P. Mintz
May 2002

CHAPTER 1

Web Hoaxes, Counterfeit Sites, and Other Spurious Information on the Internet

Paul S. Piper

LipBalm Anonymous (www.kevdo.com/lipbalm) is an intriguing site. It's a twelve-step program for lip balm addicts, an idea so absurd that it is obviously false … or is it? There are people who use lip balm quite frequently until it has become a habit. There are also people who believe that lip balm producers might have few qualms about covertly adding habit-forming ingredients, such as those that might dry the lips, to substances as innocuous as lip balm. Does it matter if it is a clinical addiction or not? This site does an excellent job of mixing credible information into a mix of probable paranoia and fantasy. When Kevin Crossman, the site's author, was contacted about the veracity of his site, his written response was that he resented the accusation that his site was categorized as misinformation. "Lip balm addiction is a REAL thing. LOTS of people take our site seriously." There you have it, straight from the creator's mouth. Is it legitimate? A hoax? A spoof? How do you know? Read on.

A Rough Taxonomy

The categories these sites fall into are counterfeit, malicious, product, fictitious, parodies/spoofs/entertainment, hacks, and disinformation. Another source of disinformation on the Web is mistakes. Anyone, from the most senior editor of the most prestigious news organization to a student putting up a class project, can make honest mistakes involving everything from typos to accidental omissions. Due to the accidental nature of these errors, they will not be dealt with here.

1

A true counterfeit site is one that attempts to pass itself off as an authentic site much as a counterfeit $20 bill attempts to enter the economy as currency. The sites here mimic the look and feel of the original or attempt to, in the case of the www.gatt.org site. Some organizations have as part of their agenda the hosting of Web sites that intentionally misguide information seekers and, within their free speech rights to host information on the Net, disseminate information that is often discriminatory or factually misleading. These sites are categorized as malicious. Product sites are legitimate commercial (.com) sites that slant their information toward selling a product. The information on these sites, though not false, is often misleading and needs to be taken for what it is—an advertisement. These sites include medical and business sites, areas where misinformation can have dangerous consequences. Fictitious sites are those that represent something completely fabricated, such as a city that does not exist. Parody/spoof sites are counterfeit sites that use humor to poke fun at an original site, product, or organization. Even though their intention may be political, they typically are not malicious, and their "misinformation" is fairly obvious. And hacked sites are sites that have been modified by hackers for any number of reasons.

While misinformation is typically understood to mean "wrong" information, a lot of Web content details issues of opinion rather than fact. Information that we might consider overly biased or wrong may prove useful to someone arguing against that agenda. For example, a person who is against capital punishment might benefit greatly from knowing how death penalty advocates think. Since many of the parody and spoof sites on the Web are political, they often contain antithetical information that might prove useful given the proper context. There aren't absolutes.

These categories are not airtight and often overlap. The martin lutherking.org site, while in the counterfeit category, might be considered a malicious site; the Mankato, Minnesota, site is a spoof and also a counterfeit site. Add to this mix an enormous array of opinions, polemics, prophecies, and pundits, and it all adds up to a great convoluted complex of misinformation that needs to be deciphered. What these sites all have in common is that they pass off information that is questionable or misleading, to varying degrees, and they often do it using the illusion of legitimacy.

Counterfeit Web Sites

Counterfeit sites are the most troublesome of hoax Internet sites. The Martin Luther King site just mentioned exemplifies a site pretending to be something it is not, a Trojan horse so to speak. Counterfeit sites disguise themselves as legitimate sites for the purpose of disseminating misinformation. They are not always attempts at humor or spoof, and even when humorous, they are often misconstrued. The intentions of counterfeit sites are as varied as the sites themselves but can be roughly divided into several categories: political, for fun, or instructional.

The martinlutherking.org site is a particularly troubling example of deceptive data, while pretending to be, on the surface, an "official" Dr. Martin Luther King, Jr., site. The home page as of March 2002 depicts a photograph of King with an unflattering quote from *Newsweek* 1998, and links titled "Truth About King," "Jews and Civil Rights," "Historical Writings," "Death of the Dream," "The King Holiday," and "Suggested Books." Underlying these areas, however, are other links to sites that are of questionable relationship to Dr. King. These include instances of his supposed plagiarism, to David Duke online, and to a speech by Jesse Helms that supposedly connects King to the Communist party. One that is particularly disturbing gives a description of Martin Luther King, the night before he was shot, partying with three white women, one of whom (it claims) he beat up. The counterfeit Martin Luther King site seems specifically targeted toward student research. (Prior to March 2001, this site was less obvious in its slant, featuring a home page with a family photo, although the underlying links and pages were similar in content. The original page is still available for viewing in the Google Archives. Search the URL "martinlutherking.org" and choose the archive option.) A number of alerts appeared on library and educational LISTSERVs and warned teachers and educators of the existence of the site and the identity of the sponsor.

Two top page clues belie the true intention of this site. The e-mail link displays a link to vincent.breeding@stormfront.org. The home page for Stormfront, the site's sponsor, claims to be a resource for White nationalists, "those courageous white men and women fighting to preserve their white western culture." The link to the Web design by Candidus Productions brings up a page that states, "Welcome to the Candidus Productions Web site! We provide various Web applications for pro-White people online." But most visitors do not normally click e-mail and Web design links. Even the underlying pages, although obviously advocating White power (the recommended books include *My Awakening* by David Duke), can easily fool less sophisticated Web users because the information is presented in a "factual" manner, cites "government documents," and the design is polished and appears sympathetic to King.

One of the first counterfeit sites to draw attention was the www.makah.org (no longer extant) site that appeared during the controversy over the Makah Tribe's harvest of gray whales. The Makah's official tribal page is www.makah.com.

The Makahs, a Washington coastal tribe, had won federal appeals to harvest a few gray whales in an attempt to resurrect tribal tradition. They immediately came under attack by environmental and animal rights organizations. One of these protest groups created a Web site that mimicked the authentic tribal site. Behind its look-alike home page, however, the counterfeit site contained anti-whaling information and called the Makahs murderers. The Makah whaling issue attracted national press, and the counterfeit site began getting many hits from surfers, who assumed that .org was the real domain for the tribe.

Once behind the site, there was no attempt to disguise the bias of the information, and the third-person personal pronouns and verbal attacks clued the reader immediately to the site's agenda. However, on the Web, getting someone to the message is a primary achievement. The fake Makah site is now gone, the official site still exists, and the Makahs still harvest gray whales. Elaine Cubbins of the University of Arizona Library has created an insightful and thorough guide to evaluating Native American Web sites (see www.u.arizona. edu/~ecubbins/webcrit.html). She notes that potential for tribal misrepresentation arises when an individual tribal member or faction within the tribe creates a site and claims it is representative, or when a site is counterfeited. Dawn Jackson, a spokeswoman for the Native American Communications Council (NACC), which seeks to be a watchdog for disinformation on this subject, stated (*Newsbytes*, February 3, 1995), "The anonymity of online services allows for unscrupulous individuals to present disinformation on Native cultures and beliefs to serve their own personal agenda."

The spate of anti-World Trade Organization (WTO) protests in Seattle, in November 1999, launched the creation of another highly sophisticated, and extensive, counterfeit Web site that claims to be the home page of the WTO (www.gatt.org). (The official WTO site is www.wto.org.) While this site features underlying anti-WTO information and uses the names of popular radical celebrities (Andrei Codrescu, the Romanian author and commentator on National Public Radio, is listed as the fiscal manager of the Media Fund), these are largely inside jokes. It is a detailed and sophisticated site.

In a press release by the WTO (www.wto.org/english/news_e/pres99_e/pr151_e.htm), Director General Mike Moore stated that counterfeit Web sites created confusion for the public looking for legitimate information. And he is obviously right. According to the *New York Times* (January 7, 2001), a trade group in Salzburg, Austria, the Center for International Legal Studies, thought the page was the official WTO site and requested Mike Moore, via e-mail, to address their conference. The site's sponsors were only too happy to oblige, sending a Dr. Bichlbauer as their representative to the conference. His presentation, which claimed among other things that Americans would be better off auctioning their votes in the presidential election to the highest bidder, offended many attendees. The fracas continued, with the phony Dr. Bichlbauer supposedly hit in the face with a pie and, upon returning to the states, hospitalized due to a "biological agent" that was present in the pie. Dr. Bichlbauer's death was announced via e-mail several days later, eliciting the first recognition from the legal center that the entire thing had been a hoax. It doesn't end here, however, as a representative for the site's organizers claims that an invitation to a textile conference in Finland will lead to the successor of Dr. Bichlbauer attending.

The Ed Report (www.edreport.com) is a bogus government report that was created by two creative writers, William Gillespie and Nick Montfort. The site is deliberately blasé enough to be mistaken for bureaucratic, and is broken into segments that sound legit: Letter from the National Security Council, Charter of the Ed Commission, Summary of Findings, Latest Press Release. Named after James Ed, a fictitious 28-year veteran of the National Security Agency, the authors were inspired to create this site after the mass attention given to the Starr Report that, according to CNN, triggered the heaviest Internet traffic until that date. (The Starr Report of September 1999 detailed alleged misdeeds by President Clinton.) The Ed Commission was supposedly chartered to investigate the recruitment of civilian contractors for use in short-term roles during covert operations. The text of the actual report is subtle but hilarious. It is difficult to tell this site is a hoax until one clicks on Latest Press Release, which mentions that it won an award for New Media Writing. One of the judges, Shelley Jackson, comments that the Ed Report is "a cunning piece of mimicry that manages to maintain an almost chinkless front of offi-cialese while telling a funny, surreal, even touching story. Purporting to be a report on an ill-fated attempt by the CIA to employ civilians (including Bruce Springsteen) with a gift for ancient languages as code-talkers on a secret narcotics mission and complete with docu-mentary trimmings, it patches into the dynamics of rumor and urban myth to run its operation in the gray area between fact and fiction— a project perfectly suited to the Web, where gray areas abound."

Checking to see who registered a site (e.g., using register.com) is one way to determine validity, but even this approach can be tricky. For example, makah.org is registered to the Makah Nation in Vancouver, Canada, while makah.com is registered to the Makah Tribal Council, Neah Bay, Washington. Only further checking reveals that the tribe headquarters *is* located in Neah Bay, Washington, and the Canadian address is a front. The martinlutherking. org site is registered to Stormfront; the gatt.org site is registered to

Prince & Associates Inc., Washington, DC, with an administrative contact of jonathan@KILLYOURTV.COM. An educated guess gives this one away.

Suspicious Web Sites

Collections of photographs of lynchings, and other collections of material that some people call "hate sites," are too numerous and extensive to include here. Some of them are notorious for misinformation because they are couched in quasi-academic discourse, and are subtle or dishonest about their intentions. Others speak with seeming authority claiming that certain historically proven events did not take place at all. The Institute for Historical Review (http://ihr. org) is one example of that kind of site. A self-proclaimed nonideological, nonreligious, and nonpolitical organization, this site propagates one of the most deceitful and brutal myths around—that the mid-20th century European Holocaust didn't occur. While the site touts the number of Ph.D.s it has on its staff, claims it maintains high standards in the pursuit of exactitude in history, and is "sincere, balanced, objective, and devoid of polemics," a skeptic may question this. Certainly the statements made on this site, and others linked to it, such as "Auschwitz Myths and Facts" and the "Problem of the Gas Chambers," run counter to most of the historical literature and contain (at least) subtle anti-Semitism.

Then there's Kennewick Man. In 1996, two students discovered the remains of a 9,300-year-old skeleton on the shores of the Columbia River in Kennewick, Washington. The remains were thought by some scientists to be Caucasoid, a term referring to peoples who originally inhabited Europe, North Africa, and the Near East. The Native Americans of Washington State, however, using a law from 1990 protecting Indian graves found on federal land, claimed the skeleton as an ancestor and demanded it be handed over to them for Native American burial. A federal government agency involved agreed, and placed the remains in safe storage until the mandatory 30-day waiting period had passed. Within days, eight anthropologists, including some from the Smithsonian Institution, filed a lawsuit against the federal agency on the grounds that the tribes had not proven "cultural affiliation." It took almost five years before this case went to trial in June 2001. These are the facts about the skeleton. The Web sites, however, are not always so straightforward.

There are several sites devoted to this issue, but the one called *The Kennewick Man News* site, registered to New Nation News in Berkeley, California, (www.newnation.org/NNN-kennewick-man.html) seems to have an agenda of White power. While the controversial discussions over Kennewick Man's racial origins are legitimate, this site does not have the balance one would expect. In March 2001, a search for "Kennewick man" on HotBot and Google retrieved this site within the first ten hits. This site is deceptive in that it includes a number of press releases that question the skeleton's origin, which makes it seem like the staff writers for the various local newspapers are agreeing with the site's premise, which denies the aboriginal roots of the Kennewick Man. However, the site goes far over that line and claims that Europeans were the true first settlers in North America and have true rights to the land, not Native American tribes. Aside from the "Confederacy News" link on the first page, there are a number of other tip-offs as to where the true heart of this site lies. For example, it posts the "results" of a survey question: "What is the best solution for racial problems?" The top six responses are as follows:

- Break the USA into White, Hispanic, Black, Asian, and Other Sections: 9 percent.

- Create a biological weapon that targets some races: 9 percent.

- Return to separate but equal solution of the 1950s South: 10 percent.

- Build an organization eventually able to ethnically cleanse the USA: 15 percent.

- Create a Caucasian Homeland in part of the U.S. and secede: 16 percent.

- Abolish all laws forcing integration and minority preferences: 18 percent.

It doesn't take a weatherman to know which way this wind blows.

News

A reputed Associated Press report stated that an anti-hunting group (the Anti Hunting Happy Association) had outfitted more than 400 deer in Ohio with orange hunter's vests in an attempt to make the hunters think that whatever was wearing the vest was a human and thus not shoot to kill. The story implicated sporting goods storeowner Guy Lockey, who offered a reward for each vested deer brought in. Even though hunting season had already ended, Guy Lockey didn't exist, and it is virtually impossible to live-trap deer and put vests on them, the story made a Fox News Network report on January 7, 2002, and was picked up by ESPN.com and the Wall Street Journal Online, and various local newspapers. In fact, it wasn't a real Associated Press report at all, something that these news organizations could have verified. This was a harmless spoof, but it shows how gullible even news professionals can be when they aren't using critical evaluation skills.

While some may treat the news with certain degrees of skepticism, we as a nation depend on a free press to give us a dose of daily facts. We rely on their filters and verification processes to weed out the dubious (or at least label it as such) and blatantly false. That is why an Internet hoax that is picked up and disseminated as fact by reputable news sources should do more than raise an eyebrow. All media are vulnerable to unverified facts, something Internet users need to keep in mind when they evaluate news reports.

Disinformation

Disinformation, according to the Oxford English Dictionary (OED), came into use in 1954 and means "the dissemination of deliberately false information, especially when supplied by a government or its agent to a foreign power or the media, with the intention of influencing the policies or opinions of those who receive it." In this context, it is a subset of misinformation.

According to *Reuters* (January 5, 1997), the Police Chief of Dubai, Dhahi Khalfan Tamim, stated to the *Khaleej Times* that Israel had launched a disinformation campaign on the Internet. He further claimed that Israel was falsely attempting to portray itself as a peace-loving nation. Obviously, this official perceived the Web as not only having the capability to disseminate disinformation, but to do so effectively.

Just as the war in Vietnam was the first television war, and the war in the Persian Gulf in 1991 was the first live war, the NATO war with Serbia over Kosovo was the first Internet war. James Napoli, in a paper at Book Expo America (BEA) 2000 entitled *Waging War Digitally: The Case of Kosovo*, stated that the "Internet, like the so-called legacy media, was used by warring parties in traditional ways to propel a barrage of propaganda to win the global public to their perspective."

The *Washington Post* (January 25, 2000) detailed the propaganda war Russia had been fighting in Chechnya and how the Web was one of the primary media for dissemination. From false field reports to exaggerated data, information that supported a particular point of view was hosted on an array of Web sites belonging to the various players. Chechen fighters, often isolated from traditional news media, used a Web site as their platform to communicate with the outside world. When they claimed that documents posted on that site were secret Russian documents, the Russians retorted that the documents had been altered from the originals or forged. NATO put its spin on events,

Serbia responded with theirs, and private sites sympathetic to the Serbs, NATO, or the Albanian Kosovars appeared all over the world.

The efforts to sabotage the use of Internet communication accelerated into the creation of a group of Serbian hackers called "Black Hand" who sought to destroy Albanian and Croatian Web sites. Croatian hackers retaliated and brought down the server that hosted the pages of the Serbian National University Library (*Press Now*, October 5, 1999). Online attacks from presumed Serbian saboteurs also corrupted the NATO site, and pro-Serb Russian hackers were suspected in the temporary shut down of the White House site, attacks on NATO's servers, and the U.S. Navy's servers. NATO's Webmaster, Baul Magis, claimed there would be no in-kind retaliation (*MSNBC*, April 1, 1999, April 6, 1999).

According to the Israeli government, a number of Israeli Web sites voicing their government's perspective on the conflict with the Palestinians in the fall of 2000 were jammed with fake traffic by Islamic groups abroad, causing them to crash. The sites targeted were the Prime Minister's Office, the Foreign Ministry, and several army sites, with some of these down for as long as two days. In a separate attack, the Web site of the Knesset, Israel's Parliament, was hacked and files were tampered with and modified. This war continues. On the day that Ariel Sharon took office as Prime Minister in Israel, "hackers, in a growing cyberwar, sent visitors seeking the Hamas Web site to a pornography site" (*Wall Street Journal*, March 7, 2001). It is not clear who is responsible for any of these malicious hacks.

September 11, 2001

The aftermath of the September 11th attacks on the World Trade Center and the Pentagon has spawned enough real dangers without Internet hoaxes adding to the chaos, but unfortunately the hoaxes and misleading sites were up and running quickly. The predominant form these took were e-mail hoaxes, which are easy to create, bulk-mailed, and in times of crisis and extreme sorrow or shock, can dupe even the critically minded. Among the first of these were charity scams. (For more on this subject, read Chapter 5: Brother Have You Got A Dime? Charity Scams on the Web.)

Charity scams follow any disaster and prey on innocent, grieving people. They are as insidious in intention as the attacks themselves. They began within 24 hours, according to the Coalition Against Unsolicited Commercial Email (www.cauce.org/pressreleases) and SpamCon Foundation (http://law.spamcon.org). The fraudulent e-mail messages claimed to be part of a relief or survivor fund, and asked for donations to help those in need.

To avoid these scams, the recommendations for potential donors are as follows:

- Go directly to the Web site of the organization you want to donate to.

- If you don't know the organization or the person who solicited you, stay away from it.

- Keep in mind that, generally, no legitimate relief organization solicits for donations through bulk e-mail.

- If you do click on any link to make a donation, examine the URL shown in the browser to make sure you are still where you think you are.

Perhaps second to the scams in maliciousness are e-mail messages that capitalized on the post-traumatic panic and sought to stir up more of it. The most notable of these was the "Halloween Attack" e-mail, which basically stated that a friend of a friend had been dating a man from Afghanistan who left her shortly before the attacks. Being a loving terrorist, however, he sent her a letter warning her not to take commercial airliners on September 11th, and to stay out of malls on Halloween. The FBI investigated the e-mail and concluded that the information was "not credible."

Other e-mail hoaxes involved allegedly phony disaster predictions, most notably via astrology, numerology, and a fake Nostradamus prediction. This particular one was easily debunked within a day of its posting as it was dated over 100 years after he had lived. There will always be susceptible people who will believe these hoaxes, but the rest of us should suspect the commonly nebulous language of predictions and post-event verification, i.e., "See, I said something big would happen this fall."

A number of fake photographs hit the Internet immediately after the disaster as well. One popular one shows "the devil's face" in the smoke of the towers' collapse. Another, supposedly shot from the observation deck at the top of the World Trade Center, shows a plane flying into the second tower. Clearly bogus, since the observation deck didn't open each day until after the time of the attacks. Can everybody say Photoshop?

There are three excellent resources for tracking hoaxes and misinformation following the 9/11 attacks: The Committee for the Scientific Investigation of the Paranormal CSICOP (www.csicop.org/hoaxwatch), The Central Iowa Skeptics (www.dangerousideas.net/infowatch.asp), and SNOPES (www.snopes2.com). Their information is credible, well researched, and timely.

Subject-Specific Misinformation

While many degrees of misinformation exist on the Web, from deliberate to accidental, serious to comic, and obvious to subtle, the consequences are perhaps nowhere as severe as in the areas of health and business. Erroneous health information can quite simply lead to serious injury and even death. Bad business information can result in financial ruin. Those subjects are addressed at length in full chapters in this book.

Science and Health Information

Health information is perhaps among the most problematic of all information on the Web. Teenagers and the elderly are most susceptible to misinformation in this area, and more seniors are getting online, capitalizing on what they see as a plethora of health information, particularly with regard to drugs, disease symptoms, cures, alternatives, and so forth. The Web site *Senior Focus Radio* runs an article (as of February 2002) claiming that a "recent" survey of seniors indicated "their biggest concern about cancer information on the Internet was misinformation" (www.seniorfocusradio.com/cancerinformation. html). An example of such misinformation is a site that claims at the top of its page: "There is no cure for the common cold. There is a very simple CURE for cancer" (www.ioa.com/~dragonfly/news/kelley. html). A number of sites like this can be retrieved by anyone searching "cancer and cure" or "cure for cancer" on an Internet search engine. And although some highly respectable and authoritative medical Web sites have emerged, medical misinformation is more accessible today than it has ever been.

The AIDS Myth Site (www.virusmyth.com/aids/index.htm), registered to the Institute for Investigative Medicine, Netherlands, is an example of information that represents an extreme minority view but is not necessarily malicious. Citing a number of prominent scientists, including Kary Mullis, Nobel Prize winner for Chemistry, the site claims that there is no proof that the HIV virus causes AIDS, that AIDS is not sexually transmitted, and that people die because they are poisoned to death by anti-viral drugs. In addition, the site claims that its views are victimized by censorship.

The Group for the Scientific Reappraisal of the HIV-AIDS Hypothesis, the organization apparently behind much of the site, came into existence as a group of signatories to an open letter to the scientific community (dated June 6, 1991) submitted to *Nature*, *Science*, *The Lancet*, and *The New England Journal of Medicine*. All refused to publish it. In 1996, the group finally got a letter published in *Science*.

The site is over 500 pages long and represents a mammoth effort to argue their claims. Because of its "authority," a site like this could represent a source of dubious and potentially destructive information, or it could represent a rare doorway into another legitimate but unpopular perspective. This type of source could be dangerous to inexperienced researchers who do not compare this information to the mainstream medical literature or who do not understand that the information presented represents a minority view of the subject. This is an excellent example of how there is no easy "right" answer, and it is important to research all sides of an issue before one makes a decision.

The Global Warming Information Page (www.globalwarming.org) is an anti-global warming site that is not upfront about its position. One of the more deceptive practices is the statement near the top of the page: "Need Information for a research project? Check out our *Student Research Page* [hyperlinked] to help you quickly find the information you need." Many students will read no further and go directly to this area of the site. Here they will encounter information, including a handy "Synopsis of the Issue" that denies global warming is occurring. Global warming is obviously a complex issue, and the jury is still out, but this site is definitely a case of research entrapment.

Some unusual health-related hypotheses have been spread on the Internet. Antiperspirants cause breast cancer. Cooking in aluminum pans causes Alzheimer's disease. Costa Rican bananas carry flesh-eating bacteria. These and similar unusual scientific hypotheses can be checked at reliable public health sites, such as The Centers for Disease Control and Prevention (CDC) (www.cdc.gov), Quackwatch (www.quackwatch.com), or the sites listed at the end of this chapter. While you may think these are quackery, remember that Galileo was imprisoned for life for refusing to renounce the theory that the Earth and planets orbit the sun.

Business

The volatility of markets can undermine anyone's faith in the rationality of our economy, and nowhere is volatility more obvious than on the Internet.

In April of 1999, a counterfeit Web site of Bloomberg.com, a news service, touted a U.S. $1.35 billion acquisition of PairGain Technologies of California by ECI Telecom of Israel. The ruse sent PairGain shares soaring 31 percent on April 7, but the stock fell back to Earth after the story proved false. The frenzy started when a financial discussion page on Yahoo! included a link to the fraudulent Web site. For further information see *WiredNews* (www.wired.com/news/business/0,1367,19094,00.html). More on that in Chapter 3.

It used to be that a dissatisfied customer would yell at the clerk through an "Exchanges" window, but the Web has amped up that scenario considerably. In 1997, millions of Internet users received what was apparently unsolicited e-mail from Samsung Electronics, and thousands of recipients responded with angry e-mails of their own, protesting what they thought was corporate spamming. Those who protested received a follow-up e-mail, apparently from Samsung's legal department accusing them of illegal acts and suspected Internet terrorism. In response to this threatening e-mail, Samsung received up to 10,000 angry e-mails a day. The company estimated that damage control for the incident extended into millions of dollars. As you might have guessed, neither of the offending messages had originated with Samsung Electronics. They were apparently the output of one upset customer (*Management Review*, Jul/Aug 1998).

The majority of attacks on corporate Web sites is by disgruntled employees or customers or the politically motivated. Tommy Hilfiger, McDonald's, and other corporations have been victims of politically oriented Web attacks aimed at costing them business. And in the case of the infamous K-Mart Sucks page (www.concentric.net/~rodf/mart.htm) put up by Rod Fournier, K-Mart's original Web designer, K-Mart recognized that the content was either true or opinion, but threatened him legally for his use of the K-Mart logo. He changed the logo and his page to the Mart Sucks. You can read his side of the story at the site.

To counteract the rash of business and investment misinformation on the Internet the Securities and Exchange Commission (SEC) has set up what it calls a "Cyberforce" to surf the Internet for suspicious sites and postings, particularly those pointed out by investor complaints. By mid-2001, the SEC had received and responded to over 100,000 complaints and questions. The SEC page (www.sec.gov/investor/pubs/cyberfraud.htm) has sound information on avoiding a number of Internet scams. More on that in Chapter 6.

Fictitious Sites

While all the above sites employ some degree of fiction, the sites categorized as fictitious are not primarily humorous in intent and are not true parodies.

The Ruritania (a fictitious country) home page (www.homepages.udayton.edu/~ahern/rurindx.htm) is an ambitious project hosted by the Political Science department of the University of Dayton and used in various classes. The site is a composite of various simulations and games developed by social scientists over the past 20+ years. Ruritania is a medium-sized country of approximately 4 million people located in Scandinavia between Sweden and Norway, and the site details its history, demographics, political system, and culture. The

URL and references to simulation will give this site away immediately to sophisticated researchers, but junior high school students might not be so fortunate as to know how to evaluate them. Actually, Ruritania was a mythical kingdom with a Central American feel created by Anthony Hope in his *Prisoner of Zenda* and *Rupert of Hentzau* novels. During the process of publishing this book, this page was taken down. You can still see it by visiting www.archive.org and submitting the URL above. This service works for many URLs that are no longer extant.

The New Hartford, Minnesota, home page (www.lme.mnsu.edu/ newhartford/newhtfd.html), unlike its twin sister Mankato, Minnesota (what is it about Minnesota?), is not obviously a fake site. The biggest clue is in the URL that points to an academic server. Since one usually has faith in the veracity of an academic site (.edu), it becomes a subtle clue for some users that the domain is not governmental (.gov). Missing this clue, however, one would need to consult an atlas to ascertain it is a fictitious town.

Parodies and Spoofs

While sites that seriously counterfeit a legitimate organization's home page are relatively rare, there are a huge number of sites that parody or spoof persons, companies, and organizations. The difference between parody (a satirical imitation) and spoof (a light parody) is slight and a matter of degree, so I lump these two categories together. Because the satire is fairly obvious, there should be little occasion to mistake its content for truth. Many times you can figure this out by the name. Parody sites are often political and typically employ humor to get their message across. They can often be extremely useful to researchers looking for antithetical or alternative information. Unfortunately, people often seem more gullible with Web information and check their common sense at the door.

These sites can cause particular problems when underlying pages that are retrieved by a search engine appear as discrete bits of information divorced from the site as a whole. Many stories exist about "news" from The Onion (www.theonion.com) being used and cited in academic research. The probable cause, aside from sloppy work, is the appearance of an Onion story in a list of hits without reference to its home site.

A good directory of these sites has been compiled by the Open Directory Project (http://dmoz.org/Recreation/Humor/Computer/ Internet/Parodies).

The White House, as one might suspect, is a convenient target. Several sites have counterfeited it: www.whitehouse.com (a porn site), www.whitehouse.org (a scandalous site), and www.whitehouse.net (a comic look at White House antics). These sites also capitalize on domain name appropriation. The whitehouse.net site features viewer's feedback, much of it serious. One woman thought it disrespectful to paint the White House pink. The real White House home page is, of course, www.whitehouse.gov.

A number of fake George W. Bush sites have arisen and gotten some publicity. One extant site, the George W. Bush Campaign Headquarters (www.bushcampaignhq.com), was a spoof that admitted in its top-of-the-page introduction "For those of you who are new, a word of caution: this is not the real, official George W. Bush Election Committee's site." Another counterfeit site (www.gwbush. com) was attacked by Bush as malicious. His campaign filed a complaint with the Federal Election Commission (FEC), which delivered a cease-and-desist order demanding the parody material be killed. "It is filled with libelous and untrue statements whose aim is to damage Governor Bush in his effort 'for President' in the upcoming election," a copy of the FEC complaint reads. The parody site received 6,451,466 hits during the first 25 days of May 1999, thanks in part to the story's front-page treatment by the *New York Times* online edition. Meanwhile, the real George W. Bush Web site received only about 30,000 hits that May, according to Bush spokeswoman Mindy Tucker (*ABCNEWS* online). The authentic George Bush site is www. georgewbush.com.

Nor were Al Gore (www.algore-2000.org was taken down after the election) or Steve Forbes (www.cais.net/aschnedr/forbes.htm) immune. And, while a bit off the subject, check out the design of the Bill Gates for President page (www.billgates2000.net/intro.html). Domain grabbing and squatting have accounted for enormous traffic to a number of counterfeit sites.

Another popular parody site is the Mankato, Minnesota, page (lme.mankato.msus.edu/mankato/mankato.html), a site that depicts Mankato, Minnesota, as a tropical paradise and is described in detail by LaJean Humphries (*Searcher*, May 2000). Don Descy, who teaches instructional media and technology courses, including Web evaluation, at Mankato State University, created the Mankato site. One would be hard-pressed to see how this site could fool anyone, yet the reaction, printed on the site, by Maureen Gustafson, President/ CEO of the Mankato Area Chamber & Convention Bureau is damning. She writes, "For some time, your project on the Internet has troubled us. Though you claim it was done in the name of education many are laughing at our community rather than with it. Our office has received numerous inquiries on the fictitious information and it is very embarrassing to have to explain it as nothing more than a prank." She has apparently told Don that people do show up in Mankato expecting palm trees. The real Mankato page is www.ci.mankato. mn.us.

Products succumb to parodies quite regularly. Adbusters (www.adbusters.org/spoofads), an advertising literacy organization, has created a number of one-page spoofs on products including Absolut Vodka, Obsession Cologne, and Prozac.

Hatchoo (www.hatchoo.com/parody/index.html), a parody of Yahoo, has a brief directory of other spoof and parody sites, including "Smart Cars," "Benneton," "Mercedes Renz," and Sinatra prints (and other life) on Mars.

We've all read about cloned sheep and frogs. We now assume science has progressed so far and fast that much of what's happening behind the closed doors of labs we haven't even read about yet. So how about male pregnancy? www.malepregnancy.com is an extremely creative and intriguing site that features Mr. Lee, the first pregnant male. This is now possible we read. In-vitro fertilization (IVF) techniques were used to induce an ectopic pregnancy by implanting an embryo and placenta into the abdominal cavity just under the peritoneum. Through a rigorous infusion of hormones, the male body is stabilized to nourish the fetus. Birth is through caesarian section. The site is the creation of two artists involved in social critique, Virgil Wong and Lee Mingwei.

With entirely different intentions, the University of Santa Anita (fictitious) AIDS FACTS page (http://147.129.1.10/library/research/ AIDSFACTS.htm) was created by John Henderson of the Ithaca College Library for the purpose of Web evaluation. It lists a number of bogus AIDS "facts" attributed to, and even citing, organizations like the CDC and Johns Hopkins. Although these facts seem false to most of us ("New evidence from John Hopkins: Married women can reduce their risk from AIDS by 73.8 percent if they do not share their toothbrushes with their husbands"). There is a disclaimer at the bottom of the page ("The 'facts' on this page are intended to be outrageous and obviously bogus, because I don't want someone stumbling onto the site to mistake them for true facts."), but more naive users, or users who know nothing about AIDS/HIV and who don't bother reading thoroughly, may take these jokes as fact. It is the parody of seriousness that qualifies this as deceptive.

Clones-R-Us (www.d-b.net/dti), hosted by Dream Technologies International, claims to be the first and largest reproductive cloning provider. "We maintain fully owned labs in Costa Rica, Liberia, and Vanuatu, as well as an extensive roster of qualified surrogate birthing candidates." While elaborate, the site states in the "About Us" section, "As you've *hopefully* realized, this site is a spoof site, which simulates one possible ramification from advances in cloning science. It is hoped that this site will stimulate thought on the pros and cons of reproductive cloning—and hopefully also foster some discussion." For some great laughs, check out the price list.

The infamous article "Feline Reactions to Bearded Men," (the product of a site, www.improb.com, which also publishes the partially online journal *The Annals of Improbable Research*) is a great parody of an academic research article. A similar example is the equally infamous "report" on California's Velcro Crop (http://home. inreach.com/kumbach/velcro.html). Obviously, a traditionally formatted Web article that was not so over-the-top could easily be perceived as credible. Then again, some people may actually think that velcro is an agricultural product and not synthetic and may try to use the data with less than fulfilling results.

The employees of FunnyCrap.com (www.funnycrap.com/fake) actually create fake Web sites for a living, or they do it while they're supposed to be working. Their current list includes: God's Home page, Da Mafia's Home page, Boris Yeltsin's Super Fansite, and the Chris Cam (a spoof of Webcams).

Entertainment

Even the entertainment industry has been experiencing a rash of Internet misinformation, largely involving counterfeit stories, scripts, plot exposés, and show endings. It's hard to see most of these as anything but practical jokes, but they are troubling to the producers who often produce red herrings and alternate endings for shows they feel will generate hoaxes. The fan infatuation with a show like *The X-Files* fuels counterfeits. A search on Google for *X-Files* plots delivered 4,820 hits. Hoaxes are not the only problem, and the *X-Files* producers have witnessed entire authentic scripts of future episodes turn up on the Internet while the segment was still under production.

Rick Berman, producer of the eighth and ninth *Star Trek* films put an interesting spin on Internet plot and script hoaxes when he claimed them beneficial since there will be eight bogus scripts for every real one and fans can't tell which is authentic (*Los Angeles Times*, Mar 16, 1998).

News Groups—LISTSERV and UseNet

As a matter of course, one should seek a second opinion to any information found on UseNet groups, chat groups, or LISTSERVs. This is perhaps less true for moderated lists, but still the danger of misinformation is prevalent. Several common techniques that have been used in the past to trick readers are impersonation of a person or status (how hard is it after all to add Ph.D. or MD after your name on a UseNet posting?) and the planned leak, usually regarding business or health information.

A truly dangerous deception on the Web, particularly for children, is that of the sexual predator who pretends to be a child himself. This predator typically strikes up an online friendship with the victim, then arranges a meeting. For the first six months of their AOL chatroom romance, Katie Tarbox thought her cyber-soulmate was just a sweet and understanding 23-year-old Californian named "Mark." He turned out to be 41-year-old Frank Kufrovich. "He cared about me," she writes in her memoir about the experience, *Katie.com*, "he listened to my feelings and he always supported me with encouragement and advice."

Hacks

There is one final category of misinformation that we should probably mention, although instances are usually ephemeral and obvious—hacks. When a Web site is hacked, the content of the site is altered. Many hacked sites are simply tagged with a slogan or statement "This site hacked by …" Hackers often want to brag and leave identity clues for other hackers. Hacked sites are usually corrected immediately, although some hacks will require the site being taken down and rebuilt, which can take a few days. There are groups that specialize in political hacks, including some that target only White power sites. An incredibly extensive archive (1996–present) of hacked sites exists at 2600.com's site (www.2600.com/hacked_pages).

Web hijacks are URL redirects to unwanted sites. A user will click on a familiar URL only to be taken to an unwanted site. Since exposure on the Web is paramount, redirecting from a well-known site can result in millions of hits before the redirect is fixed, exposing millions of people to unwanted information or ads.

One Person Gathers What Another Person Spills

Many researchers think that information on the Web is suspect and not nearly as credible as that appearing in print sources. Hoax sites don't do much to alleviate this mindset, but one person's misinformation can be another person's gold mine. Hoax sites offer a number of possibilities, some of which have already been mentioned. Many such sites offer alternative perspectives to topics that have an almost hegemonic truth. Even so-called hate sites can provide useful information in bringing to light material that is typically censored from most public discourse. Only a truly free society can allow free exchange of ideas regardless of how reprehensible they might seem.

Hoax sites offer "teaching moments," and a number of them have been created for this very reason. For example, the University of Santa Anita Aids Facts; Mankato, Minnesota; malepregnancy.com; and Clones-R-Us. The best of them make us question why we believe some things and not others, providing a self-examination of how we view the world if we are going to analyze information. I found that the Lip Balm and AIDS myth sites had this effect on me.

By learning how to deconstruct hoax sites we become empowered, and we can share this knowledge. One example of this is broadcasting who is behind a counterfeit site. Finally, some of them are absolutely hilarious. But beware, you might find yourself addicted to them for your daily giggle.

While Web literacy demands intelligent Internet use, Web literacy is not really qualitatively different than information literacy. All information has bias and has to succumb to rigorous evaluation. This was driven home to me when I worked for disaster relief and we began exploring refugee statistics. The number of refugees crossing a border was not the product of some simple count, any more than the U.S. Census statistics are. It is the product of a complex set of variables. The statistics, which look hard and fast in black and white, are really estimates but are accepted by many as truth. Even when reading an article in the *New England Journal of Medicine*, it doesn't hurt to look again later on—there may be an article in *JAMA: The Journal of the American Medical Association* the next month that refutes it.

Remember, while it is important to know what you're getting, hoaxes, parodies, and other misinformation are often of value to the right person in the right context.

Where to Go for Help

The following sites are dedicated to tracking Internet hoaxes:

About's UrbanLegends and Folklore (http://urbanlegends. about.com/library/blhoax.htm) features an extensive directory that uses these codes:

• Hoax = False, deliberately deceptive information, including pranks & jokes

• UL = Urban Legend: a popularly believed narrative, most likely false

• Rumor = Unsubstantiated information forwarded with gusto

• Junk = Flotsam and jetsam of the Net

Don't Spread That Hoax, one of the oldest and most reliable of the hoax busters, features a directory as well as links to useful authoritative resources (such as www.Thomas.gov for legislative information) for checking information. However, it is not as comprehensive as one might wish (www.nonprofit.net/hoax/default.htm).

Scambusters, a comprehensive site that has been endorsed both by Yahoo! and Forbes, among others, features an e-zine, mail group, story of the month, directory of scams, tips to avoid scams, testimonials, ways to stop spams, phony and real viruses, and much more. The site is a bit difficult to navigate but well worth the look (www.scambusters.org).

SNOPES, otherwise known as The San Fernando Valley Folklore Society's Urban Legend Pages is one of the largest collections of urban legends and hoaxes on the Internet. The hoaxes and legends are all coded with colored dots indicating true, false, undetermined, and of indeterminate origin (www.snopes2.com).

The Computer Incident Advisory Capability (CIAC) of the U.S. Department of Energy produces an updated list of hoaxes. Though not an extensive list, it specializes in hoax Internet viruses and a detailed and interesting history of hoaxes on the Internet (http:// hoaxbusters.ciac.org).

While the National Fraud Center, a consumer's center for fraud, including Internet fraud, doesn't have a list of fraud sites, it does give overviews of techniques, industries, and demographics and includes an online form for reporting suspected fraud. It has invaluable information covering the most common Internet frauds: auctions (which they currently list as the worst), business opportunities and franchises, credit card safety, online credit repair, employment services, online magazine solicitations, online travel offers, pyramid schemes and illegitimate multilevel marketing, scholarship scams, sweepstakes and prize offers, and work at home offers (www.fraud.org/welmes.htm).

Countermeasures

The spectrum of misinformation on the Net will continue to proliferate unless the Internet is strictly regulated, which seems unlikely
if not impossible, not to mention undesirable. Adopting a critical
stance toward everything you read on the Web is the best protection
you can have against misinformation.

1. Look for clues in the URL. Almost all sites have some bias
   to the information posted, and though it may be slight and
   one you agree with, it's usually there. If you encounter a
   URL with a slight deviation in the name, or there is a dot-
   org when you expected a dot-com, stay on the alert. A [~]
   "name" reflects a personal site and, as such, will represent
   personal views only.

2. On the site itself, look for comic or incendiary language,
   lack of citation or authority, lack of currency, a particular
   bias toward audience, or slant of information.

3. Search smart. Use the advanced capabilities that a number
   of search engines now provide, such as domain searching.
   And use specialized search engines and directory services
   or meta-sites with holdings selected by librarians or other
   authorities in a field.

4. Check suspicious domain names with an agency like
   register.com.

5. Use print sources for verification when needed.

6. Check underlying pages, top-level pages (if at an underlying
   page), and suspicious links to verify what you get is the real
   item.

7. Regularly visit Web sites that post hoaxes.

8. Realize that misinformation is often contextual and can
   possibly prove useful in some circumstances.

CHAPTER 2

Charlatans, Leeches, and Old Wives:
Medical Misinformation

Susan M. Detwiler

Vaccinations cause the diseases they're supposed to prevent! Drinking hydrogen peroxide will flush out your system! Milk is the best source of calcium! A 5-year-old boy suffering from low libido should take Viagra! Deep coughing at the onset of a heart attack can save your life! Anorexia and bulimia are desirable lifestyles! Ultraviolet light will protect against anthrax!

Which of the above is true? Well, that depends on which direct e-mail you believe, which Web site you go to, whether you can trust the person who said it, or if you can even *figure out* who said it!

Back in a 16th-century village, you had barbers who acted as surgeons and trained physicians ("leeches") who kept up on the latest advances in medicine, such as new "cupping" or bleeding techniques. Apothecaries compounded and sold medicines, mainly herbal concoctions. Next-door neighbors supported you in your troubles by recommending meddlesome "old wives" who told you why the physician was a fraud. Charlatans came to town with noxious nostrums to cure what ailed you. As recently as the 19th century American West, the latter still circulated, earning the name of snake oil salesmen.

They're all still here. Except instead of a few hundred people, the Internet's global village now numbers more than 200 million.[1] Each classic village resident still exists, but reach and resources are wider. Truth and good news move at the speed of electrons, but so do misinformation and tales of misfortune. Medical horror stories spread like viruses. Where bribery could be spied out through a hole in the wall, we now have to track down layers of who contributes to whom. Even reputable sites offer conflicting information. And the potential for harm is multiplied by the very speed and reach that promises so much good.

This is especially true as more people connect to the Internet precisely because they seek health information. According to the Pew Internet & American Life Project,[2] 52 million American adults have used the Web to get health information, of which 91 percent of these have looked for material relating to a specific physical illness. We gather everything we can get our hands on, and we're particularly vulnerable to misinformation. When we're sick, we often become like children, grasping at anything that will make the hurt go away.

Consider the notion that a sustained, rhythmic coughing can keep you alive during a heart attack, presuming you can make it to the hospital fairly soon. This marvelous news comes to you by way of Rochester General Hospital and Mended Hearts, a heart attack victims' support group. Or so the e-mail in your inbox says. This is great news! Uncle Larry should hear of it along with Mrs. Jones, your old teacher. And all your friends on the electronic list. After all, this could save someone's life. Not really. The truth is, Rochester General Hospital never said it; Mended Hearts, which published the item in a newsletter, has retracted it. The procedure, which is occasionally used for specific types of heart attacks in emergency situations, is only done under professional supervision. In fact, the *Washington Post* (February 15, 2000) carried an article in which a physician at Brigham and Women's Hospital in Boston said the best thing to do in the event of a heart attack is to take an aspirin (to dissolve blood clots) and call 9-1-1.

Something like this is fairly easy to check at one of the many urban legends sites. If it were merely a harmless urban legend circulating through e-mail, one could laugh it away. But it doesn't stop there. As of this writing, this miraculous life-saving news is still circulating, still being posted in innumerable list archives and on hundreds of ostensible healthcare sites—all the way from the International Medical and Dental Therapy Hypnosis Association[3] to MedicsIndex,[4] a service of the Middle East Health Network. Registered in the United Kingdom and Jordan, MedicsIndex aims to create a single electronic database of health practitioners in the Middle East and Gulf Region. MedicsIndex still cites Rochester General Hospital and Mended Hearts as the authority for this misadvice. The error even appears on the PaulingTherapy site,[5] created by distributors of Linus Pauling's Heart Disease video. The version on the PaulingTherapy site ends with the line: "*Note: Aspirin has also been touted as a life saver during a heart attack. Who are we to question national advertising and the findings of the United States government? We will point out that bleeding during and after cardiovascular surgery is a serious problem that is excarbated [sic] by taking aspirin.*" Does it seem to you that the note implies skepticism over the aspirin advice while approving the coughing?

Please—Don't Help!

E-mail messages are easy to ignore. The delete key is always available. But what happens when victims of emotional illness try to support that illness in others?

Eating disorders are a serious problem among today's young women. The National Institutes of Mental Health estimates that eating disorders affect more than 5 million Americans each year, and an estimated 1,000 women die each year from anorexia. Many young women continue to believe themselves to be overweight, despite being 5 feet, 7 inches tall and weighing 90 pounds. Anorexia nervosa and other potentially fatal eating disorders are constantly being fought by the medical and psychiatric professions.

Yet on the Internet, we find Web pages and chat rooms that support this as a lifestyle choice. Far from acknowledging that these are illnesses needing treatment, these sites have names like "Anorexic and Proud" and "Anorexic Nation." Web-based diaries contain messages like this:

> if i [sic] eat under 600 cals for about a week then suddenly eat 900 cals for a few days, will i gain all the weight back …

Since it is easy to mount personal Web pages and diaries on large consumer servers like Yahoo! and Lycos, these companies became havens for the "Pro Ana" messages. As a result, they were targeted by public relations and mail campaigns asking them to remove these potentially harmful sites from their servers. In August 2001, Yahoo! was persuaded to remove from its server Web sites that promote anorexia and bulimia. Those who click on these sites get messages of *"whoops, we can't find your page."*

Unfortunately, personal Web sites proliferate like rabbits, and many go further underground onto less well known servers. A month after these sites were pulled, it is still easy to find the food diaries of young girls who mix complaints about algebra with proud proclamations that their total daily caloric intake is 500.[6] Fighting this war is a never-ending series of battles.

Who Says and Why?

This is innocence run amok. The good people of our village genuinely want to believe they're helping others, and so they forward any e-mail that looks harmless and might help. The pro-anorexia sites are run by young women who genuinely believe their own stories. Less innocent are one-sided facts and figures circulated by well-respected institutions.

Hospitals and educational institutions freely give health advice and rightly so. But where does this advice come from? And who's behind the facts? It's not always easy to tell. Even legitimate organizations sometimes fall short of full disclosure. A large, well-respected hospital in Indiana posts on its welcome page an internal link to the "got milk" quiz. Presumably, this fun little nutrition quiz has been checked for factual information by the Webmaster. Nowhere on the site does it offer the source for the quiz or its answers. But one tip-off, the phrase "Got Milk?" might indicate it came from a promotional dairy campaign. Links to photos of adults and children with "milk mustaches"—a well-known marketing image of the dairy industry—provides more evidence.

A search using the questions from the quiz yielded identical quizzes on at least three other sites: a community healthcare consortium in New York, a commercial dairy, and the Texas Agricultural Extension Service Urban Extension Program. None of them gave a source for the quiz or its answers, but the extension service had a link for more information to www.whymilk.com. From Whymilk.com, it's a quick link to the www.familyfoodzone.com and www.nutritionexplorations.com Web sites. Here, the National Dairy Council proudly proclaims "This Web site is developed by the National Dairy Council® as a public service to nutrition educators, parents, and children."

Whymilk.com doesn't list its sponsor on the Web site, but a "whois" lookup at Network Solutions shows that this is one of the domains managed by the same public relations firm managing the official Web site of Dairy Management, Inc (DMI). DMI is a joint effort of the Dairy Board and the United Dairy Industry Association, and it manages the programs of the Dairy Board, the National Dairy Council, and the American Dairy Association.[7] DMI and its counterparts make good use of the Internet in getting out their point of view. They own a number of Web sites, all geared to promoting dairy products: butterisbest.com, dairyinfo.com, dairynutrition.com, extraordinarydairy.com, ilovecheese.com, milkinfo.com, and nationaldairycouncil.org.

Who funds the programs of DMI? Well, through the Dairy Production Stabilization Act of 1983, Congress mandated a 15-cent-per-hundredweight assessment on all milk produced in the contiguous 48 states and marketed commercially by dairy farmers. The purpose was "to increase human consumption of milk and dairy products and reduce milk surpluses."[8] So the general population's absolute conviction that milk is good for you is partly the product of a business decision on the part of Congress. It was bailing out the dairy industry by creating a marketing board to reduce surpluses.

How extensive is the influence of DMI and its counterparts? Going to the American Dietetic Association Web site, we find that DMI and the National Dairy Council (NDC) each contributed more than $10,000 to the Association in fiscal year 2000, and the NDC Vice President for Nutrition and Health has been on the American Dietetic Association Foundation's Board of Directors for at least two years. A journal article found on the American Dietetic Association Web site entitled "Effects of increased consumption of fluid milk on energy and nutrient intake, body weight, and cardiovascular risk factors in healthy older adults"[9] was supported by a grant from the International Dairy Foods Association.

Now let's make one thing clear. We are not against milk! Is milk, in and of itself, evil? Of course not. Is a trade association promoting its members' products evil? Again, of course not. But it behooves the public to know the source and any potential biases of any medical information or health advice. The Indiana hospital and the New York healthcare consortium do no one a service by promoting a trade association's point of view without disclosing the source.

In fact, looking at the answers to the quiz, the health-minded Web surfer might easily be misled. One True-False question posits "Lots of different foods contain calcium." The answer on the quiz is "FALSE. About 75 percent of the calcium in the food supply comes from milk and milk products. ..." Well, that still means that 25 percent of the calcium in the food supply comes from other sources. In fact, the USDA Food Pyramid says the average person only needs two to three servings of dairy a day, should opt for low-fat or fat-free versions, and can substitute soy-based beverages with added calcium as an option.[10] Worse yet, the final True-False question is "I can get the calcium I need from a supplement." Astonishingly, the quiz answers FALSE, not based on the argument that you can't get the calcium, but because calcium supplements don't provide vitamin D. Since there are several calcium supplements that do provide vitamin D, and because there are other ways of getting vitamin D (including sunlight and full-spectrum vitamins), this seems extremely misleading.

Is the American Dietetic Association tainted by its association with the dairy industry? Probably not. In fact, it does a nice job of relating information on vegetarian and vegan diets. But users should always ask for full public disclosure. Give us the tools to be informed consumers and we salute you, but when we don't know where information comes from, or when it seems to come from someone other than the true provider, that ignorance can blind us to the possibility of bias.

Medem, a network of seven medical societies led by the American Medical Association, does a nice job of disclosing its supporters. Each page carries a list of sponsoring organizations. While pediatricians may not be thrilled that the infant formula producer, Nestlé, sponsors the pages about breastfeeding and infant nutrition, at least the sponsorship is not hidden. The link to Nestlé stops at a page that declares that the browser is leaving the Medem site and offers the option of deciding not to follow the link to Nestlé.[11] In terms of our global village, we like to know who's paying whom, so we can decide if we want to buy whatever product sponsors push our way. Kudos to those who don't hide their sources of income.

Ouch!

Which brings us to the next problem with healthcare information via electronic media. "On the Internet, no one knows you're a dog." The *New Yorker* cartoon caption summed up the comments of a high-tech dog explaining Net anonymity to his off-line colleague while corresponding online. When you go to your village physician, you know whom you're dealing with. You can see the diploma on the wall. You know people whom this person has treated. You can see if the place looks clean and if the doctor seems intelligent. You may be misled, but there are at least clues. Not so on the Internet. Anyone can claim to be anything. And even if you're dealing with a legitimate degreed doctor, how do you know if he or she is licensed in your state?

At least one Web site purports to diagnose an illness based on the answers to a series of questions. At the innocuously named "Library of the National Medical Society" (which on some pages also calls itself the American Medical Society), you lay down a $9.95 fee for access to its so-called library. Much of the information in this library is a set of links to sites full of free medical information, no-cost Web sites that you could seek out on your own. For example, you can link to the National Library of Medicine, The Merck Manual Home Edition (listed here as a *Manual of Medicine*), University of Iowa Family Practice Handbook, or RxList (listed as *Drug Index)*. Other links connect to individual online textbooks published by other companies, such as eMedicine and the Internet Dermatology Society. Note that with the exception of the National Library of Medicine and the Iowa Handbook, none of these links are identified as not being part of their "Library."

Mixed in with this potentially good set of links are one- or two-word links to treatises of dubious quality published by the "Library's" parent, CCS Publishing. By way of background, CCS Publishing is located in Laguna Hills, California, and publishes inexpensive, pocket-sized books that practitioners can use for quick look-ups. They've put these pocket books online in .pdf format. Checking through one of them, *Pediatrics*, we find the author is Paul D. Chan, MD. Dr. Chan also authored other books in the series—*Internal Medicine*, *Gynecology & Obstetrics (2002 edition!)* [originally found in 2000], and *Outpatient and Primary Care Medicine*. None of these give references for the information in them; if you want references, you're directed to contact the publisher. The books are generally around 200 pages.

What about their journals? Yes, the Library of the National Medical Society also publishes journals. Its Web site proclaims the current edition to be the current month. Under the heading *Continuing Medical Education*, the "December edition" of the *Osteoporosis* article was identical to the October edition.

Keep in mind that the following is supposed to come from a reputable medical journal as you read this first paragraph of the *Osteoporosis* article in *Continuing Medical Education*:

> If you were to take a biopsy of normal vertebral bone, you'll notice that there are a lot of trabeculae in all directions. Bone is very nicely designed to withstand the biomechanical forces that we subject it to....

And a later paragraph:

> In order to understand how we get to this point, pathophysiologically, and how the interventions that we have in hand, that we can write prescriptions for that work, I need to remind you of the basic bone biology. I think the real take-home message is that bone is not static. That we don't grown to our adult height and then that's it for bone; it's an inert scaffold that we carry around with us....[sic]

A look at the references for this chapter shows none dated later than 1995. Authored by Barbara Wood, MD, there is no information about Dr. Wood's credentials. Searching through all 50 states at SearchPointe.com,[12] we found a single Barbara Wood with an active license. This is likely not the author, as her specialty is Psychiatry.

And yet, the worst is yet to come. Remember that 5-year-old boy mentioned in the very first paragraph of this chapter? The one suffering from low libido and told to take Viagra? This is the place that gave the advice. One of the links provided by the Library of the National Medical Society is to *Online Diagnosis*: "Accurate online medical diagnosis of symptoms, illnesses, diseases, and psychiatric disorders." Linking here brings you to a list of more than 500 symptoms. The instructions say "Click on your symptom, then enter additional symptoms to receive diagnosis." The possibilities start with Abdominal Fluid and end with Yellow Skin. In between they offer Anal Bleeding, Jaw

Pain, Halitosis, Obsessive Thoughts, Vasculitis, Hypotension, and, of course, Sexual Dysfunction.

The Sexual Dysfunction page that takes the patient history has a box for "Describe symptoms," followed by "How many days have the symptoms been present?," "How old is the patient?," a few additional queries, and "Male Patient"—Yes/No, or "Female Patient"—Yes/No.

When tested, it didn't seem to matter what you entered under symptoms, days present, or age. You could say you're a 2-year-old with an itchy nose. According to the source code for the page, only the last question has any bearing on where you're linked next. If you click Female Patient—Yes, you're offered four options: "Low sexual desire," "Inability to achieve orgasm," "Painful intercourse," or "Vaginal muscle spasm during intercourse." If you click Male Patient—you're offered three options: "Decreased desire for sex—low libido," "Difficulty maintaining erection—erectile dysfunction," or "Difficulty with ejaculation—ejaculatory dysfunction." Click on that second option, and you read: "Morning erections present" or "Morning erections absent." Clicking on that first option (still remembering that we've identified ourselves as two years old), we're told to test with a Nocturnal Tumescence Ring. If no Nocturnal Erections are detected, treatment is recommended: Oral Viagra, surgically implanted prosthesis, or a vacuum tumescence device.

But what about a less ridiculous test? After all, how many 2-year-olds suffer from erectile dysfunction? So we tried for another online diagnosis. This time, bleeding gums. Once again, it made no difference what we answered, until the question, "Does the patient take aspirin?" If the answer is "No," it asks about splenomegaly or systemic rash. If the answer is again "No," the system queries for an abnormal dental exam or normal dental exam. With a normal dental exam, it says to check vitamin C levels. Diagnoses are "Injury with toothbrush, early scurvy, or phenytoin use." Hmm ... those latter two are pretty serious. Maybe the diagnostics should have considered our answer to the question of symptom duration—two days.

Who are the doctors diagnosing online? We're not sure. The four names followed by MDs have no credentials attached. One name is fairly common and shows up on the American Board of Medical Specialties Web site and CD-ROM. We don't know whether any of those listings identify this author. None of the other three show up, and none have a match in California, where CCS originates.

Legality is another question. Even if they are certified physicians, they most certainly are not licensed to practice medicine in every state of the union. There are no disclaimers on the site saying that this is just a tool to assist other physicians. There are no statements telling consumers to check with their own physicians.

If there is a doctor actually interacting with the patient to make the diagnosis, then the credentials of that doctor are critical information. If a patient is just interacting with software that has been created with the assistance of doctors, the algorithm being used should also be cited and referenced.

Even scarier is the number of links to the Library, that is, the number of other sites citing this one. According to a link search on Google, about 540 pages link to www.ccspublishing.com. More than 630 link specifically to www.medical-library.org, including even misguided libraries that publish lists of "notable sites for medical research."

Are these folks charlatans? Well, maybe. Classically, charlatans are voluble, making loud claims about their own skill or knowledge. Here, the claims to skill and knowledge are implied, rather than touted, in the mere fact that they purport to diagnose every manner of illness. Quack, perhaps? Well, again, we don't know their actual credentials. But they are definitely related to one of those classic village personages. They are certainly treading a fine line, and may be practicing medicine without a license by diagnosing across state lines.

The best thing to do when confronted with something like this is to run the other way. Find other sources that do give you the appropriate disclaimers and direct you to your own physician for accurate diagnoses. If you can't track down the source of the information, you have no idea of its quality. Dr. Wood and Dr. Chan may be excellent physicians, but you are given no way to check. The information is outdated, with an outright lie as to the date of the Continuing Medical Education journal articles. Sources are withheld or so old as to be laughable. The grammar is pitiful. Run away. Fast.

For One Thin Dime, One-Tenth of a Dollar

Next in our village gallery are the true mountebanks—folks who sell their own nostrums to cure what ails you. There are many false preventatives and cures out there. Especially in the wake of terrorist attacks on the United States, Web sites have sprung up that prey on our fears of bioterrorism. The fact that there is no proof that ultraviolet light will kill or destroy airborne anthrax and most any airborne bacteria, spore, mold, or organism that may harm human health does not keep the unscrupulous from taking the money of those they can dupe into believing the hype. On January 2, 2002, the U.S. government said it had warned more than 70 sites selling products that they claimed would protect against biowarfare agents to cease and desist from making the false claims. Either they missed one, or a new one has sprung up, because such a claim was accessed on May 30, 2002.[13]

But even before these attacks, mountebanks were preying on the gullible. Often, the sites are tied into promotions for books and videos about conspiracies among the medical establishment, which, of course, strives to keep these cures from the general public. Titles of these videos are designed to shock: *Emerging AIDS & Ebola: Nature, Accident, or Intentional?* and *The Nazi-American Biomedical/ Biowarfare Connection*[14] are just two examples. The site that carried these boasted more than 107,000 visitors from October 19, 1999 to October 18, 2000. Whether most of the 107,000 believed the tales is questionable, but it's likely that many followed links from similar sites in an effort to find out "THE TRUTH."

While most people will see through these rants, there is a subtle insidiousness to cures that use everyday household items. Take, for instance, the seemingly harmless hydrogen peroxide (H_2O_2), which is ubiquitous. Most households have a bottle of a 3 percent solution of H_2O_2 tucked away somewhere. It's the substance that made "bleached blondes" a household phrase and is well-known for its use in cleaning cuts and abrasions. But despite its innocuous place in our homes, the Occupational Safety & Health Administration (OSHA) has a health guideline for hydrogen peroxide that warns how it can irritate the eyes, mucous membranes, and skin, and that inhalation may cause extreme respiratory irritation. In large enough doses, systemic poisoning may occur, resulting in vomiting, diarrhea, tremors, convulsions, pulmonary edema, or shock. During *in vitro* human tests, hydrogen peroxide has caused DNA damage. Acute exposure may cause mild bronchitis or pulmonary edema and corneal ulceration.[15]

Clearly, anything more than a 3–5 percent solution of this substance is a chemical to be reckoned with; even at low levels, one should think twice about ingesting it, much less contemplate an intravenous solution. Yet intravenous hydrogen peroxide therapy is precisely what is recommended by a number of Web sites. At Ozone Services,[16] H_2O_2 therapy is described:

> Hydrogen peroxide is infused into the circulatory system through a vein in the arm...in the blood it encounters two enzymes: catalase and CytochromeC ...In this way the benefits of hydrogen peroxide are made available to all cells...the effect of singlet oxygen in the human body is two-fold. It kills, or severely inhibits the growth of, anaerobic organisms (bacteria and viruses which use carbon dioxide for fuel and leave oxygen as a by-product)...anaerobic bacteria are pathogens, the organisms which cause disease. All viruses are anaerobic.

These identical words appear in a paper by Ron Kennedy, MD, at MedicalLibrary.net.[17] Both sites offer lists of physicians who conduct this therapy. True to form, another site claims there is a conspiracy to keep knowledge of H_2O_2 therapy out of the hands of the public, so the pharmaceutical companies and physicians can reap the benefit of trillions of dollars of drug sales.[18] Most disturbing is that these sites that promote oxygenation therapy make it sound as if the nasty adverse effects are merely proof that the therapy is working.

> One woman experienced sudden severe nose bleeding with the elimination of two large blood clots from her right nostril. She can now breath through the nostril for the first time in years! Another person had bleeding from the mouth when he spit up huge amounts of mucous. Another had rectal bleeding as his hemorrhoids reduced. These are natural cleansing processes, and they will be of short duration as you continue the program...There are hundreds of published articles against the use of hydrogen peroxide as a therapeutic agent because this cleansing process was misinterpreted as being 'BAD'. It is the necessary price for recovery of your precious health. Don't be misled by a "Healing Crisis"!! Rather, be GRATEFUL FOR IT![19]

Yet if you look more closely on the Web, you can find the facts about H_2O_2 therapy. One of the main proponents of H_2O_2 IV therapy is Kurt Donsbach, a chiropractor originally licensed in Montana, who then used a forged document to obtain a license to practice naturopathy in Oregon. Donsbach is now in Rosarita Beach, Baja Mexico, using "Bio-Oxidative Therapy" with a claimed remission rate of 70 percent in more than 300 patients who have "tried everything else" and been told their cases were hopeless.[20] What the proponents of bio-oxidative therapy don't tell you is that Donsbach is not a doctor. At one time he pleaded guilty to practicing medicine without a license in California, and since then has left a trail of misrepresentations and illegal medicinal claims. His Hospital Santa Monica uses hydrogen peroxide intravenously, orally, in ear drops, a nasal spray, a tooth gel, a pain gel, breath drops, and enemas, for the purpose of "aging rejuvenation, allergies, arthritis, cancer, cardiovascular, cataracts, immune stimulation, and multiple sclerosis."[21] In 1988, the U.S. Postal Service issued a cease-and-desist order to Donsbach, to stop him from claiming that hydrogen peroxide is fit for human consumption.[22]

In 1989, the Food and Drug Administration (FDA) issued a press release that industrial strength hydrogen peroxide, illegally promoted to treat AIDS and cancer, had caused at least one death in Texas and several more serious injuries. Although the 35 percent solutions were sold to be diluted and used in "Hyper-Oxygenation Therapy," there was no proof that either the product or the therapy had any medicinal value. To quote the FDA press release, "Buyers are being cheated and subjected to significant risks and family members are being injured."[23]

In addition to any questions one might have about the appropriateness of a 35 percent hydrogen peroxide therapy delivered intravenously, there are also hazards associated with self-administration of intravenous solutions, such as possible infection (even hydrogen peroxide can be nonsterile), injecting air boluses (which can be fatal) as well as damage to veins, not to mention the hazards associated with any other chemical contaminants.

These sites get an impressively high number of hits. Unlike our little village of olden days where the mountebank gets run out of town once he's unmasked, the sites keep springing up in our global village. Anyone with a computer and a telephone line can create a professional looking Web site, and anyone who questions the validity of the information can hear from proponents all over the world. From January 1999 to October 2000, the site carrying the Kennedy paper received over 3 million hits. And on America Online (AOL), the subject of H_2O_2 infusion therapy has been a topic of discussion on message boards, with only those who confirm its positive effects answering queries. Even Dr. Weil at DrWeil.com has been questioned about its efficacy. Fortunately, Dr. Weil's measured response is a good antidote to the hype:

"One of the reasons people take antioxidant vitamins and minerals is to prevent the oxidative damage caused by chemicals such as hydrogen peroxide and ozone. You can't have it both ways here—hydrogen peroxide and ozone can't both promote healing and be so toxic...save it for the next time you have a yen to go blond."[24]

Doctor? Who Needs a Doctor?

Speaking of message boards, it's time to make a stop at the village well, as townsfolk stop and chat about their concerns. Today, our village well consists of the communities, message boards, and chat rooms on several highly frequented networks. In a one-month period, AOL garners almost 80 million unique visitors. About: The Human Internet has more than 20 million, and iVillage.com almost 8 million.[25] What these three networks offer are communities wherein people chat about their lives and concerns. Just like at the well, bad information can be as prevalent as good.

According to a study at Johns Hopkins School of Public Health, vaccines are one of the reasons behind the dramatic 50 percent increase in Americans' life expectancies over the course of the 20th century.[26] You wouldn't know it if you relied on Internet chat rooms for your information. An AOL message board search for "vaccination OR immunization OR vaccines" resulted in 1158 hits in just one month. Here's a sampling of the messages: "the unofficial policy of the World Health Organization and...'Save the Children's Fund' and...[other vaccine promoting] organizations is one of murder and genocide...," "just get in touch with a certified Homeopath and stop going to doctors," "I guess the drug companies wanted a big increase in U.S. sales of the hepatitis B vaccine, because all of a sudden the CDC started hyping the disease as a huge health threat." The messages on iVillage ran in a similar vein, with messages that link to sites like *Biological Manipulation of Human Populations*, using quotes from the *1955* Surgeon General that "No batch of vaccine can be proved safe before it is given to children"[27] and to the personal homepage of a D. K. Yuryev, proudly proclaiming that his paper was rejected by *Nature, Lancet, International Immunology,* and the *New York Academy of Science*, and therefore he is publishing it on the Web. In the introduction, he states that "I'm afraid, this article too obviously implies an idea that vaccinology and AIDS campaign are governed by idiots...."[28] The sites promoted and quoted by the anti-vaccine crowd are highly inbred, with each having lists of links to similar sites that link to each other.

Following the trails begun with these messages, the health searcher is led to articles like *Vaccines: The Truth Revealed.*[29] Here we are told that the government has a computer database containing several thousand names of disabled and dead babies who were alive just prior to receiving vaccines. In actuality, there *is* a Vaccine Adverse Event Reporting System (VAERS), operated by the Centers for Disease Control and Prevention (CDC) in conjunction with the Food & Drug Administration (FDA).[30] Approximately 10,000–12,000 VAERS reports are filed annually, with about 15 percent classified as serious, i.e., seizure, high fever, life-threatening illness, or death. Any adverse event that occurs after a vaccination may be reportable, whether or not the event is related to the actual vaccine. More than ten million vaccinations are given each year. Doing the math, this means that less than .1 percent (that's *point one percent*) of all vaccinations result in a VAERS report, and less than .02 percent (*point oh two percent)* are classified as serious.

One of the sadder aspects of these popular message boards is that the very same systems that allow bad information to go unchallenged in their communities, also make available excellent, mediated information. On the About.com system, a board-certified pediatrician is the "Guide" to Pediatrics. At pediatrics.about.com, a well-written balanced view of vaccine safety is available, with links to resources like the parent pamphlets required to be given to vaccine recipients, the VAERS, and the FDA.[31] All the information in the article is sourced. It's just like in our representative village. The people at the well turn to each other for support, with the highly vocal anti-establishment responding. Meanwhile, those in a position to offer facts are ignored.

Speaking Out of Both Sides of the Mouth

Of course, just because a person is in a position to offer legitimate facts doesn't mean she or he won't be contradicted by another expert. Even in the village, doctors would disagree. On the Web, it would be expected that different sites might have different opinions. But what about when that disagreement happens on the same reputable site?

When it comes to complementary and alternative medicine, there is often some controversy as to how useful a particular therapy is. The reputable national health information sites aren't immune to this debate. Checking for the validity of chiropractors as medical professionals on the drKoop.com site, we conducted a sitewide search. The first two of six results were editorials against chiropractors as pseudomedical practitioners. Yet included in these same results were a factual explanation of the chiropractic profession, and a Q&A that discusses the potential usefulness of chiropractic manipulation for neck or back pain. Unfortunately, this is one test you won't be able to replicate. As reputable as drKoop.com was, the organization filed for bankruptcy in December 2001, and stopped updating the site in midmonth. Yet if you look for the site, the front page will still be there, with the date automatically changing so that it looks current.

WebMD, the most popular of the health information Web sites, had a similar dichotomy. A general search for homeopathy resulted in several articles explaining the history and possible validity of homeopathic remedies, including studies published in the *British Medical Journal*. Yet the results of an identical search on the WebMD message board began with the title "Homeopathy, the Ultimate Fake."

Even mainstream Western medical therapy may be debated on the same medical site. Patients who question whether to begin hormone replacement therapy are likely to check on the major medical Web sites for help. A search for hormone replacement therapy on Intelihealth returned several consumer level articles titled *"Breast Density on Mammography Affected by HRT Regimen," "Hormone Replacement Therapy and Lobular Breast Cancer,"* and *"Hormone Replacement Therapy for Heart Disease."*

When it comes to advice, maybe our villagers would do well to heed the old saying, *buyer beware.*

You'll Need a Prescription for That

Speaking of *buyer beware*, let's step away from the village, for a moment, and ride into the city of London. Early in the history of the British Royal College of Physicians, its members asked Her Majesty Queen Elizabeth to command that "arsenic, sublimate, and opium should be sold to only those persons willing to give their names, and that no apothecary should sell or prescribe medicine without a physician's prescription."[32] This battle is still being fought, only now the scale is multiplied a thousandfold. Most of us with any kind of activity on the Web have become used to receiving e-mails promising anonymous prescriptions to lifestyle drugs. Maybe Viagra for erectile dysfunction; perhaps Propecia for hair loss.

Ostensibly, these sites have physicians just waiting to "approve" you for purchase of the drug. Of course, every one that I've checked requires you to acknowledge that you're not taking any medications that might react with the drug in question and promise to have a physical examination prior to consuming the pharmaceutical.[33] In fact, the agreement in at least one of these has the prospective buyer agreeing "I further certify and affirm that I am aware of and know of the potentially lethal side effects of Propecia, if I have ingested or taken other medications that are contraindicated with use of Propecia. I certify truthfully that I have not been taking any such medications." Nowhere on the site, however, do they list these contraindicated medications! In the Frequently Asked Questions, the only contraindications are women, children, and anyone allergic to any of the ingredients. Again, nowhere on the site do they list the ingredients. What about the question of whether the "prescribing physician" is properly licensed? To get around that question, the buyer must certify, "I AGREE THAT ALL ON-LINE MEDICAL CONSULTATIONS, DIAGNOSES, AND TREATMENTS (INCLUDING PRESCRIPTIONS FOR THE TREATMENT OF HAIR LOSS) WILL BE DEEMED TO HAVE OCCURRED IN THE STATE WHERE THE PHYSICIAN IS PHYSICALLY LOCATED AND LICENSED TO PRACTICE MEDICINE."[34]

There is some hope that these sites will feel the brush of the law. While buyer agreements may work in most states, Pennsylvania has barred two of these companies from selling any prescriptions at all to citizens of Pennsylvania. As of November 2, 2000, both sites must prominently post that these services are not available to residents of Pennsylvania, and if you've previously purchased from them, the consultation fee may be refunded until March 2001.[35] These kinds of sites are under constant investigation by the FDA. Unfortunately, there is no reason to believe that they will stop or even slow down. A month after receiving an e-mail invitation to purchase Viagra, I checked and found the site no longer there, but in the interim I received several additional invitations. As long as there are towns-people vain enough to circumvent the law in order to grow hair, or are unsure enough of their own virility to bypass a physical in favor of quick access to miracle cures, the unscrupulous apothecaries will continue to have their way.

If you think you're immune by virtue of never, ever going to a Web site under your own name, you're not. Published hard copy alumni directories have become fodder for the scam mill. Shortly after my *alma mater* published a directory, I received an e-mail with the subject line: Albany Alumni. It was spam, selling something called "Crystal Vision," with the "most powerful antioxidants for macular health as well as nutrients that promote healthy functioning eyes." There was an illegible signature, over the tagline "Your Alumni Friend." Of course the return address was a nonsense word. Oh yes … if I ordered imme-diately, I would receive a free bottle of echinacea.

One Last Villager

So all the village members are still here. The charlatans who sell their own nostrums, the physicians ("leeches") who provide the truth, the apothecaries who fill prescriptions (both legitimate ones and those who are not), and the "old wives" who sit at the well and mind your business for you. And, there's one more role to be played. Frankly, there are also village idiots in enough numbers to make the scams worthwhile.

When Does Breaking Health News Become Permanent Information?

In order to evaluate the speed with which new information is placed on medical Web sites, The Detwiler Group undertook to test selected sites for information about a newly approved drug and an FDA warning about an existing pharmaceutical. According to research published by The Detwiler Group, the timeliness and dissemination of medical and pharmaceutical information leaves some room for improvement.

Initial tests began October 2, 2000 and concluded January 3, 2001. Over the course of three months, a total of eleven sites were periodically searched for mentions of either the new drug or the FDA warning.

The results were disheartening. On April 24, 2000, the Novartis drug Exelon (rivastigmine tartrate) was approved by the FDA for use in mild to moderate cases of Alzheimer's disease or dementia. On June 21, 2000, Novartis announced that the drug was on pharmacy shelves. As of January 3, 2001, almost nine months later, LaurusHealth, *HealthAnswers*, and WebMD did not have the drug listed in their drug databases, although *HealthAnswers* did mention it in a patient education article on Alzheimer's. The *Alzheimer's Disease Education and Referral Center* fact sheet on Alzheimer's disease was dated 1995, and a search of the site noted Exelon as pending approval. None of the sites that listed Exelon in their databases had patient education articles that included the drug.

On November 6, 2000, the FDA issued a warning about phenylpropanolamine (PPA), a drug commonly used as a decongestant and diet aid in over-the-counter (OTC) pharmaceuticals. The administration had determined that users of medications containing this drug had a higher risk of hemorrhagic stroke than those who did not use PPA. The FDA requested that manufacturers stop marketing drugs using PPA as an ingredient. On November 7, 2000, several drug stores voluntarily removed from their shelves OTC drugs that contained PPA. Of six Web sites tested on January 3, 2001, only Medscape linked its PPA monograph to the FDA warning. Only Intelihealth maintained a prominent warning on its Web site.

An estimated 100 million Americans use the Internet to get information about diseases and therapies, yet even the best known sites aren't fulfilling their promise. The implications are significant. Pharmaceutical manufacturers spend billions of dollars to promote their products directly to consumers, but a key avenue for finding more information is closed. Health information consumers rely on prominent health Web sites for up-to-date information on diseases and drugs, but the sites are not upholding their side of the bargain. Unless news items are incorporated into reference materials, they quickly become invisible. Relying on outsourced drug databases is an acceptable alternative but only if the uploads are frequent and the database producers actively maintain their information.

Avoiding the Charlatans

There are many ways to protect yourself from the unscrupulous and the well-meaning but misguided folks in the village. The FDA takes an active role particularly in the areas of unlawful drug sales. As of October 2000, the FDA had issued 80 warning letters, 18 seizures, and 11 recall actions, as well as setting in motion seven arrests on criminal charges related to the Internet and two pharmacy convictions.[36]

The oldest system for validating healthcare Web sites, Health on the Net (HON), went live in 1996 with a system for identifying healthcare sites that adhere to specific standards. HON is a Swiss nonprofit foundation begun through the workings of a 1995 consortium on telemedicine. While a HON certificate does not guarantee high quality information, a site with a HON certificate must adhere to certain basic ethical standards in presenting information. There are eight principles,[37] which cover such items as sourcing the information, ensuring that readers know the information is only an adjunct to a doctor/patient relationship, providing clear disclosure of sponsorship or funding, and availability of direct contact with the Web providers. If a site has received a HON certificate, it may display that symbol on its Web site. Each certificate is assigned a number and linked back to the HON site. If you run your cursor over the certificate, you see a HON certificate number associated with the link, evidence that the certificate is still valid. Since a site must apply to receive the HON certificate, lack of a certificate is not an automatic disqualification. However, a valid certificate is a good indication of a site that adheres to at least certain minimal standards.

In 1997, the Internet Healthcare Coalition (IHC) was formed, dedicated to the promotion of high quality healthcare information on the Internet. The coalition includes organizations such as the Association of Cancer Online Resources, PharmInfo, PanAmerican Health Organization, Medscape, Intelihealth, and other publishers and providers of health information. Much of IHC's efforts are directed toward creating a common code of ethics for health information on the Internet, and in May 2000, it released a nine-page International Code of Ethics for healthcare sites and services on the Internet.[38] This code is much more detailed than the HON code but doesn't provide for a certificate or indication of a site's adherence to it. Unfortunately, it leaves the researcher out in the cold, relying on his or her own efforts to determine if a site lives up to a high ethical standard.

In November 1999, the Health Internet Ethics (Hi-Ethics) organization was formed, from some of the largest, most widely used health resources on the Internet. Founding members include drKoop.com, InteliHealth, LaurusHealth.com, and AOL. In May 2000, Hi-Ethics released a set of 14 ethical principles[39] for the health Internet that cover many of the same principles as IHC and HON but focus more on issues relating to commercial sites. Privacy figures prominently in its concerns, as does full disclosure of sources of funding and sources of data. Hi-Ethics members gave themselves until November 2000 to comply with the code; as of December 2000, Hi-Ethics had signed an agreement with TRUSTe, the leading online privacy seal program, to develop an E-Health Seal for sites that adhere to the Hi-Ethics principles.

With three somewhat competing organizations developing similar codes of ethics, the IHC spearheaded a joint commission among them. In October 2000, the three organizations announced that they will work together to ensure that the e-health codes share a common terminology that the public can understand.

Meanwhile, however, barring the HON seal, there isn't a lot that can tell users at a glance whether a site is good or not. So what should an Internet health information seeker do? The answer isn't much different from what you should do if confronted with information in some other medium.[40] THINK!

1. Know what you're looking for.

Even though it's difficult to stay calm and focused when you're considering the health of yourself or a loved one, remember that you can't find what you're looking for unless you know what it is. The old cliche, "If you don't know where you're going, any road will get you there," is as true here as when behind the wheel. Before sitting down at the computer, consider what it is you seek. Background information on a disease? Accepted therapies? Clinical trials of potential cures? Physicians or hospitals that treat the disorder? If you know what you want, you're less likely to follow link after link, wasting time and getting nowhere. If the link you find doesn't focus on what you seek, go back to the search results and start again.

2. Start in the right place.

Starting in the right place may mean using a good search engine or starting with a known, high-quality, medical Web site. If you use a general search engine, be aware of how it ranks the results. HotBot (www.hotbot.com) is a popularity contest. Top links are those that receive the most hits. Probably good for finding information about Britney Spears; not so good for medical information. Google (www.google.com) is much better. By ranking sites according to how many other sites link to them, the top sites are generally those with a higher credibility. It's not foolproof, but for diseases or disorders that are not extremely rare, the top sites returned by Google are usually good places to start. For more obscure items, AltaVista (www.altavista.com) may be useful as it has an extremely broad base of sites in its inventory. However, AltaVista changes its ranking method periodically, so it becomes very important to follow the remaining guidelines scrupulously for evaluating results.

Professional associations of medical professionals who research or treat the specific disorder are excellent places to begin. Most of these associations maintain public resources on their sites, including actual information about the disease or links to organizations that will have more information. To find these associations, you can use a general search engine, but make sure you put in just the disorder and/or the treating physician type, and the word "association." Don't put in "cure" or "treatment" or "therapy," or you leave yourself open to the charlatans who baste their sites liberally with the word cure.

Starting with known quality medical Web sites is also a good idea, but the public generally isn't aware of them. You can start with the Health on the Net, Internet Healthcare Coalition, or Hi-Ethics sites, to find links to their members. However, many other excellent sites have not bothered to register with any of these despite their essential agreement with the principles of ethics. To find sites reviewed by professionals, you might start with these: MEDLINEPlus (www.medlineplus.gov) or Healthfinder (www.healthfinder.gov) from the U.S. Department of Health & Human Services; Healthweb (http://healthweb.org), with a set of pages that include links to sites reviewed by medical librarians and professionals and arranged by topic; and the Hardin metadirectory (www.lib.uiowa.edu/hardin/md) that maintains lists of places to find more lists of topic-specific resources.

Sites designed for medical professionals are also good places to start, as many of them maintain consumer-level information as well. A few of the many good professional sites that allow nonprofessionals to get good information include Medem (www.medem.com) and Virtual Hospital (www.vh.org). For cancer-specific questions, two excellent places to start are the University of Texas MD Anderson Cancer Care Center (www.mdanderson.org) and Oncolink (http://oncolink.upenn.edu) from University of Pennsylvania Cancer Center.

3. *Maintain a healthy skepticism.*

In beginning journalism, students are taught that the lead paragraph of an article should cover Who, What, When, Where, Why, and How. Evaluating information on the Web requires the same 5Ws and H. Who wrote the piece? That is, is this a medical professional? Does the site give you credentials? Are those credentials valid? Look them up! What is the source of the data? If there are no footnotes or references, be skeptical. Even if there are references, subject them to the same scrutiny. When was this piece written? When was it last updated? If there's no date on the piece, how do you know it's still current? No matter how good the credentials of the site, outdated information is still outdated information. The Alzheimer's Disease Education and Referral Center (ADEAR) (www.alzheimers.org) does very good work. However, its fact sheet on Alzheimer's is dated 1995. Several new advances in Alzheimer research have been made since then.

Where did the site get its funding? If the site seems bent on selling you the latest cure for the disorder, it's a fairly good bet that the sole purpose of the site is to sell its products. Run the other way. If the site just happens to have advertising, or prominently displays sponsorship by a commercial entity, it's probably a better choice. The key is to read the advertising or funding policy, if the site makes it available.

Why was the piece written? The best bet is if the piece is solely intended to be informative, as part of a professional medical site (commercial or association). If the piece is written for the purpose of selling a product, again, run away. More subtle agendas may push a certain point of view—for example, the People for the Ethical Treatment of Animals (PETA) site might only publish information about the negative findings about milk rather than a balanced view. If that's the case, it's important to learn about the site's agenda and balance it with alternative views—maybe by touching on the National Dairy Council site, as well.

How did you find the information? This is a point many overlook. If you find this site through a series of links from other sites, remember that it retains the bias of every site prior to the one you're on. Just like in AIDS, where the professionals warn that you don't sleep with just one person, but with every person that one has slept with before, the site you're on is a product of the biases of every site that led you here. To get a different point of view, you have to go back to your original search results, and start another trail.

4. Give it the smell test.

If the site promises miraculous cures or claims to cure different diseases with the same substance, it's probably a hoax. If it sells drugs without a doctor's visit, it's probably skirting the law. If it doesn't give you a way to verify the information, or if the most recent references are more than 5 years old, be wary. If it's a personal Web site, it's likely to have a personal agenda. If you found it through an e-mail, check one of the urban legends Web sites, like Urban Legends (http://urbanlegends.about.com) or Urban Legends Reference Page (www.snopes2.com). In other words, if it smells fishy, it probably is.

5. When in doubt—ask a professional.

Most medical librarians and professionals find out about new sites through networking with each other or reading their professional journals. It is their job to keep up with the best resources out there and they immerse themselves in the subjects. Many hospital libraries have consumer help desks; if not, they're happy to point you in the right direction to conduct your own research. If you're not sure about the information you've found, ask your doctor.

There are many ways to protect yourself from the charlatans, but it all comes down to the same guidelines as for everything else. Be smart. Don't turn off your brain. THINK!

Checklist for Ordering Medicines Online

Carol Ebbinghouse

The list below covers the basics for ordering just about anything online, but many of the issues are unique to ordering medications (prescription or OTC) on the Internet.

1. Do you want this information (what drugs you order) on the Internet for all to see? Be especially wary of unfamiliar names with no privacy or security provisions in their "terms and conditions" file. Look for TRUSTe or other privacy certification and carefully read the terms and conditions. Remember that certification by TRUSTe just means that the company discloses its policies on divulging your personal information—not that the policies are exemplary. Companies that sell your personal and transactional information to anyone with money can still get certified, as long as they clearly spell out in their terms and conditions what they do with your information.

2. Check the FDA's Web site (www.fda.gov/oc/buyonline) for the latest tips and warnings on buying drugs online and see the warning letters to overseas companies caught selling illegal medicines, etc., to Americans.

3. Visit the National Association of Boards of Pharmacy's Verified Internet Pharmacy Practice Sites program at www.nabp.net/vipps/intro.asp. The VIPPS seal of approval requires that a site is properly licensed and has licensed pharmacists online to answer questions.

4. The Web site should indicate the address, phone number, fax number, and e-mail address for contacting sponsors. Be wary of addresses that are just Post Office boxes. Never deal with an online pharmacy based overseas. The drugs may not be pure, or genuine, and they may never arrive if they're intercepted and confiscated by Customs.

5. The Web site should indicate the state where the online pharmacy is located and the states in which it is licensed to deliver prescriptions. Be sure the state you live in is on that list, or don't use the service.

6. Good Web sites should provide a description of the drug, the required FDA information on side effects, contraindications, etc., and include hyperlinks to the manufacturer's site.

7. Look for a licensed online pharmacist to answer your questions by e-mail.

8. Reputable e-pharmacies require a faxed copy of your prescription or a phone call from your physicians.

9. Always be sure that the site will accept your insurance. This is usually done on the order form. If there is a problem with insurance, the staff at the Web site should call you.

10. Before you complete your order, check the shipping charges. These may wipe out any savings on the prescription. In addition, you may find that by having the delivery made to one of your local pharmacies, you can avoid shipping charges altogether.

11. Users should be able to review transaction information (information, products and services listed, prices, total, and shipping and handling expenses) prior to execution of the sale. And after execution, users should receive purchase information as well as a shipping tracking number if appropriate. Response times for fulfillment should be clearly stated.

12. Be sure the site uses secure technology with encryption for financial transactions.

13. If you are defrauded, go to www.fda.gov/oc/buyonline to report the incident.

References

1. InfoTech Trends, Data Analysis Group.
2. *The online health care revolution: How the Web helps Americans take better care of themselves.* The Pew Internet & American Life Project. www.pewinternet.org released November 26, 2000.
3. The International Medical and Dental Therapy Hypnosis Association. www.infinityinst.com
4. MedicsIndex. www.medicsindex.org
5. PaulingTherapy. www.paulingtherapy.com
6. http://anasbitch.diaryland.com. Accessed September 7, 2001.
7. USDA Report to Congress on the Dairy Promotion Programs—2000. www.ams.usda.gov/dairy/prb_intro.htm
8. National Dairy Promotion and Research Program, USDA Web site. www.ams.usda.gov/dairy/ndb.htm
9. Barr, S. I., et al., "Effects of increased consumption of fluid milk on energy and nutrient intake, body weight, and cardiovascular risk factors in healthy older adults," *Journal of the American Dietetic Association*, 2000, 100:810–817.
10. *Using the Dietary Guidelines for Americans.* Accessed at www.usda.gov/cnpp/Pubs/DG2000/Index.htm March 26, 2002.
11. Carrns, A., "Doctors' Web Site Gets Sponsorship from Nestlé," *Wall Street Journal*, October 27, 2000.
12. SearchPointe. www.searchpointe.com
13. www.ddchem.com/sun_aire.htm accessed May 30, 2002.
14. *Tetrahedron Incorporated.* www.tetrahedron.org accessed on March 26, 2002.
15. Occupational Safety & Health Administration, U.S. Department of Labor, *Technical Links>Health Guidelines>Hydrogen Peroxide.* www.osha-slc.gov/SLTC/healthguidelines/hydrogenperoxide/index.html#recognition accessed March 26, 2002.
16. Ozone Services. www.o3zone.com accessed March 26, 2002.
17. Kennedy, R., *Intravenous Hydrogen Peroxide Therapy.* www.medical-library.net/sites/_iv_hydrogen_peroxide_therapy. html accessed March 26, 2002.
18. *Ozone...does it work?* www.cat007.com/o2.htm accessed March 26, 2002.
19. *Oxygen Therapy H2O2 – Hydrogen Peroxide Therapy.* H2O2HydrogenPeroxide.com. http://h2o2hydrogenperoxide.com/alt.html accessed March 26, 2002.
20. *OxyFile #9.* Oxygen and Ozone Therapies. www.oxytherapy.com/oxyfiles/oxy00009.html accessed March 26, 2002.
21. Barrett, S., *The Unhealthy Alliance.* American Council on Science and Health Special Report, © 1988. www.hcrc.org/contrib/acsh/booklets/unhlthy.html accessed March 26, 2002.
22. *Hydrogen Peroxide (H2O2) Unconventional Cancer Therapies.* BC Cancer Agency. http://bccancer.bc.ca/uct/hydrogenperoxide-h202.shtml accessed March 26, 2002.
23. *Industrial Strength Hydrogen Peroxide.* Release provided by the Food and Drug Administration. www.fda.gov/bbs/topics/NEWS/NEW00122.html accessed September 7, 2001.

24. *Hydrogen Peroxide, Ozone, and Oxygen Therapy.* Ask Dr. Weil.
www.pathfinder.com/drweil/archiveqa/0,2283,91,00.html accessed March 26,
2002.

25. *Media Metrix Top 50 US Web & Digital Media Properties for September
2000.* Media Metrix. www.mediametrix.com accessed September 7, 2001.

26. *American Life Span Jumped Dramatically in 20th Century.* Reuters Health.
December 5, 2000.

27. *Biological Manipulation of Human Populations* © Leading Edge International
Research Group. www.trufax.org/menu/bio.html accessed March 26, 2002.

28. D. K. Yuryev's homepage. *Toward Understanding of Vaccines.*
www/prc/ru/~yur77/toward.htm

29. *Vaccines: The Truth Revealed.* www.odomnet.com/vaccines/
introduc.htm accessed September 7, 2001.

30. *Vaccine Adverse Event Reporting System* Center for Biologics Evaluation and
Research. www.fda.gov/cber/vaers/what.htm accessed March 26, 2002.

31. Ianelli, V., MD. *Understanding Vaccine Safety.* About: The Human Network.
http://pediatrics.about.com/library/blvaccine_safety.htm accessed March 26,
2002.

32. Lord Moran, "On Credulity," *The Lancet.* January 23, 1954.

33. Order Viagra Online. www.1-orders-prescriptions-online.com accessed
September 7, 2001. CyberHealthServices. www.cyberhealthservices.com
accessed September 7, 2001.

34. Kwikmed.com. http://kwikmed.com/cgi-bin/pg.cgi?affid=121960&pg=prope-
cia-order.html accessed March 26, 2002.

35. *Online Prescription Drug Business Barred in Penn.* PR Newswire via COM-
TEX via Hoover's.

36. Knowledge@wharton. *The FDA Hunts Snake-Oil Salesmen Through
Cyberspace.* CNET news.com, October 30, 2000. http://news.cnet.com/news/
0-1005-200-3295367.html accessed March 26, 2002.

37. Health on the Net Code. www.hon.ch/HONcode/Conduct.html accessed
March 26, 2002.

38. Internet Healthcare Coalition. www.ihealthcoalition.org/ethics/code0524.pdf
accessed March 26, 2002.

39. Hi-Ethics. www.hiethics.com/Principles/index.asp accessed March 26, 2002.

40. Based on *Avoiding the Charlatans.* © 2000–2001 Susan Detwiler.
Unpublished presentation to St. Luke's Episcopal Hospital. December 14,
2000.Written by Carol Ebbinghouse.

CHAPTER 3

It's a Dangerous World Out There:
Misinformation in the Corporate Universe

Helene Kassler

On August 25, 2000, 6-year-old wire service Internet Wire distributed a press release announcing a triple whammy of negative news for fiber optic manufacturer Emulex. The CEO was resigning, it was under investigation by the Securities and Exchange Commission (SEC), and the firm was revising its latest earnings report to reflect a loss instead of a profit. Picked up by Bloomberg, CNBC, and then Dow Jones Newswires, the story swiftly hit the Internet-based investor message boards, where it was replicated and redistributed. In a matter of hours, Emulex lost more than $2 billion in market value, with many trades coming from individual investors responding to the dramatic news.

The problem was, none of this so-called news story was true. Mark Jakob, a college student and former employee of Internet Wire (who had resigned one week earlier) was accused as the perpetrator. He was in a financial hole as a "short seller" for betting that the Emulex stock price would go down, i.e., selling borrowed shares with the expectation of repurchasing them later at a lower price. Instead, the stock price rose and the 23-year-old owed $97,000. To recover his loss, he formed a plan based on inside knowledge of Internet Wire's daily workings to drive down the price of Emulex. After the price drop, he repurchased the 3,000 shares he had sold short. He made almost $250,000 from these transactions.

Using phrases distinctive for Internet Wire clients, Jakob submitted, during the overnight shift, the bogus press release, which Internet Wire then distributed without verification. Bloomberg, CNBC, and Dow Jones Newswires picked up the story and passed it along as well that

Friday morning, again without confirmation. And so the deceptive seeds were sown.

The story made it to the Yahoo! Finance site within 15 minutes. In a matter of hours, the stock lost 60 percent of its value. When Emulex executives discovered the hoax, they contacted NASDAQ, which halted trading. However, NASDAQ let that morning's trades stand—to the consternation of many small-time and day traders quick on the trigger finger to sell. Within a week, the FBI arrested the former employee—tracking him down through the Internet protocol numbers on the computer used at his community college and a hotel room he had rented in Las Vegas. As reported by the Associated Press (August 31, 2000, "Man Charged for Fake Emulex Release"), U.S. Attorney Alejandro Mayorkas wryly commented, "We in law enforcement know how to use the Internet, too."

When the dust settled, CBS.MarketWatch.com dropped Internet Wire as a news source. And a law firm filed a class action lawsuit against Internet Wire and Bloomberg in New York on behalf of Emulex investors, accusing the news services of "recklessly disseminating materially false and misleading information." (As of March 2002, the suit had been dismissed twice in court but was still on appeal.) Jakob's actions had cost investors nearly $110 million. In July of 2001, he settled with the SEC on stock manipulation charges, agreeing to turn over $241,000 he made trading Emulex stock, $97,000 (the amount of trading losses he avoided), $15,000 in interest, and a penalty of $102,642. The total amount will be held on behalf of defrauded investors, and turned over to them should they succeed in their class action lawsuit against Jakob. On August 6, 2001, Mark Jakob was sentenced to 44 months in prison.

History shows that not all stock manipulation pushes prices in the upward direction. In fact, it appears easier to push prices downward with negative buzz.

While the aforementioned events stunned the investing community, this was not a new, isolated, or Web-specific incident. As James K. Glassman noted in the *Wall Street Journal* (August 30, 2000, "Stock Hoax Should Affirm Faith in Markets"), "Hoaxing for fun and profit, of course, predates the Internet. In 1989 alone there were phony tales planted about Sybase, Northwest Airlines, and Pan Am. But with the new wild, wild Web, two things have changed: The ability to defraud convincingly has been democratized, and the effects of a fraud are instant." Moreover, the rate of fraud has dramatically accelerated. The Security and Exchange Commission's (SEC) Office of Internet Enforcement fields hundreds of complaints per day. As of March 2001, the SEC had taken more than 200 Internet-related enforcement actions involving more than 750 individuals and organizations—nearly half of which took place in the prior 14 months.

A Long History of Deception

Using misleading or erroneous information with disastrous effects in the world of finance and industry isn't new. It has a long and healthy history. Corporate deception probably dates back centuries, but new technologies, including the Internet, enable rapid-fire dissemination of information—whether true or false. Moreover, these new technologies cast a very wide net and allow swift repetition of information *plus* misinformation.

On New Year's Eve 1999, the dawn of a new millennium, it is estimated that a billion people worldwide tuned in to watch the global festivities on television. In the U.S., 8.6 million watched the CBS broadcasts with Dan Rather overlooking Times Square. Highly visible was the CBS logo, its all-seeing eye looking out from a building behind Mr. Rather. Few viewers realized at the time that they were witnessing CBS erasing the competition with deceptive technology. For where the CBS logo appeared on television, in the real bricks and mortar world, an NBC peacock lit up the night on the Astrovision screen. CBS had digitally erased the competition—electronically superimposing its own virtual logo over the physical "real" display of the NBC peacock. In response to questions concerning deception, Andrew Heyward, CBS News president, was quoted by *Reuters* (January 13, 2000, "NBC's Virtual War with CBS") as saying "I think reasonable people can disagree as to whether it is an appropriate use of video technology. ... This is part of the evolution of graphics. They get more and more sophisticated ... it does raise new issues." Also according to *Reuters* that day, Rather admitted that the TV trickery was "a mistake" in an interview with the *New York Times*. "At the very least we should have pointed out to viewers that we were doing it," he said. "I did not grasp the possible ethical implications of this, and that was wrong on my part."

Reality itself seems to stand on very shaky ground these days. It's a slippery slope growing ever steeper, ever slicker. And how odd, that at a time when "reality" television shows are all the rage, reality becomes even more difficult to identify. Perhaps our inability to discern truth on the Internet or on TV explains some of the appeal of such "false" reality shows.

As the Emulex example shows, today's technologies offer the corporate world, and individuals with a stake in the corporate world, more ways in which to deceive.

But corporations consist of individuals, individuals who make corporate decisions. In addition, stockholders, current employees, former employees, and customers all have access to a massive electronic soapbox, access available whether the information they spread is true or false. Technologies, including the Web, e-mail, electronic message boards, and online discussion groups allow individuals to disseminate lies and truths to millions of people in quick succession. And every repetition of the communication, whether in its original form or in variations, confirms the claims for those who may see the report multiple times. It is usually people who deceive and not the technologies. Technologies just make deception swifter, more effective, and more invisible.

The Wicked Web They Weave

Emulex joined an increasingly long and frightening list of companies struck by phony news stories all too quickly disseminated on the Internet. In March of 2000, Lucent Technologies' stock took a one-day hit of 3.6 percent—a $7.1 billion loss in market capitalization—in response to a phony news release warning of lower earnings for the firm's second quarter. A Houston day-trader was arrested and charged with securities fraud a week later. The SEC accused him of posting the fake press release more than 20 times on a Yahoo! message board. Also of note, his aliases were quite similar to pseudonyms of knowledgeable posters who had accurately posted pessimistic estimates on Lucent in early 2000 (just prior to Lucent's January 6, 2000 press release with earnings warnings). One example: he posted under the alias "kahuna_and_the_brain," while the earlier well-informed poster went under the handle "brain_and_the_kahuna." The perpetrator was convicted in March 2001 of securities fraud and "reached a settlement" with the SEC in August of 2001. He was slated for sentencing in September 2001. However, sentencing was delayed until March of 2002, as federal courthouses were closed due to the terrorist attacks on the World Trade Center and Pentagon on September 11, 2001; he could receive 10 years in prison and be fined $1 million.

If you think this kind of stock manipulation is limited to experienced stock professionals, think again. It's child's play in this age when the young know the technologies better than their elders. Think back to the fall of 2000, when the SEC first charged a minor with stock manipulation. A 15-year-old New Jersey youth was charged with using message boards to hype penny stocks he was trading through his father's custodial accounts—all at the age of 14. He bought inexpensive stocks costing just a few dollars per share and then hyped them through e-mail, relying heavily on Yahoo! investor message boards. His profits on each trade ranged from more than $11,000 to nearly $74,000. Within 24 hours he would sell his shares at a profit, sometimes placing limit orders to sell stocks at anticipated peak prices when the markets closed—while he was in school.

The teenager settled with the SEC, without admitting or denying the commission's finding. He agreed to repay $285,000 ($272,826 in profits plus $12,174 in interest) to settle SEC charges of stock manipulation.

Cautionary quotes appeared across the country. According to the *Los Angeles Times* (September 21, 2000, "15-Year-Old Fined in Manipulation of Stock Prices"), the SEC enforcement director Richard H. Walker noted: "The Internet has become a staple of young people from grade school on, and this case shows that you can't hide your identity on message boards whether you're 50 or 20 or 10." And in the *Record/Northern New Jersey* (September 22, 2000), Mark Herr, New Jersey's director of consumer affairs, was quoted as saying, "An Internet chat room has all the reliability and all the validity of a gossip column, if that much."

In its press release on September 20, 2000, "SEC Brings Fraud Charges in Internet Manipulation Scheme," the SEC offered its own warning. Ronald C. Long, Administrator of the Philadelphia District Office cautioned: "I implore investors to be highly skeptical of any advice they receive from the Internet. People should do thorough research before making investment decisions and verify all information before acting on it."

More often, however, the originator of the rumors is never caught—despite the magnitude of the aftermath. On Thursday, November 2, 2000, rumors began swirling around electronic chat rooms and investor bulletin boards that Larry Ellison, the well-known co-founder, chairman, and CEO of Oracle had either resigned, fallen ill, or passed away. Larry, (then the second richest person in the world according to *Forbes Magazine*) was fine. Nevertheless, within a matter of hours, the rumors had spread around the world and were mentioned by CNBC. Oracle stock, the most heavily traded NASDAQ stock that day, lost almost 30 percent of its value at one point. At days' end, Oracle shares fell $1.81 or 6 percent, finishing the trading sessions at $29.56. The original rumormonger was never identified and no charges were ever filed.

Battling Elusive Rumors:
Meet John Doe; Sue John Doe

Companies are fighting back along two lines, according to Howard Mintz in the *San Jose Mercury News* (November 28, 1999, "'Cybersmear' Lawsuits Raise Privacy Concerns"). On the first front, some firms are suing—trying to uncover the face and name behind the anonymous poster. Roughly 70 such lawsuits were filed between 1998 and 2000. This list includes a top-of-the-line roster of major companies such as high-tech powerhouses Sun Microsystems, E*TRADE, Raytheon, and even low-tech soft-weave specialist, Fruit of the Loom. The "anti-cybersmear" campaigns are out to uncover people posting critical comments or financially harmful information. The first line of attack has been to subpoena investor bulletin board hosts, particularly Yahoo! and AOL, to uncover the identity of anonymous posters.

San Diego-based Titan Corporation is one company fighting back. Its stock was hit hard by allegedly bogus messages posted at Yahoo! from May through August 2000, according to the *Los Angeles Times* (August 31, 2000, "Titan Subpoenas Yahoo! to Give Names of Anonymous Users"). The attack included false reports of low earnings and of fraudulent accounting. In addition, a phony analyst report questioning the firm's business practices was distributed to institutional investors. Despite meeting earning estimates, the company's stock plummeted, with its market capitalization falling from $2.6 billion in June to $1.3 billion in August 2000. Titan subpoenaed Yahoo! for the anonymous posters' identities and filed suit for damages in late August. Further, the company obtained a court order preventing individuals and investment firms from destroying paper or electronic records of stock trades. Titan's CEO, Gene Ray, alleges that the posters were short sellers who bet that the stock price would go down. (See Countering a Cybersmear of Your Company in Chapter 11.)

Other companies are trying to insure that their employees do not disclose trade secrets or insider information. In one such "unmasking" lawsuit, Alza Corporation sought to identify employees it suspected of revealing inside information concerning the company's upcoming acquisition by Abbott Labs. Defense giant Raytheon similarly went on the defense against forum posters in 1999. It identified the chatters' identities through a subpoena to Yahoo! although some of the "inside information" turned out to be either incorrect or already public knowledge. Four of the employees left the company. Raytheon requested an injunction against future revelations of company secrets, compensatory damages, and legal expenses but ultimately dropped the lawsuit. In fact, several of the lawsuits were dropped once the posters were identified.

The situation pits freedom of speech advocates against companies fearing disclosure of trade secrets and inside information. The debate over online privacy in this arena shapes up as a question over whether the discussion boards are a conference call or a park soapbox, each eligible for quite different rights of privacy.

On another battlefront, companies are sending their own employees or hiring consultants to battle cybersmears. In *The Industry Standard* (June 26, 2000, "Getting the Dirt"), Mubarak Dahir reported on a variety of techniques companies use to gather information on competitors using the Internet. One firm mentioned in the article, NetCurrents, monitors the Internet for clients. According to NetCurrents' Vice President of Sales, Rebecca Callahan, her firm has been asked, and has walked away from, companies requesting help in spreading rumors, hyping stocks, or harassing publicly critical individuals. Moreover, the SEC now targets those who perpetrate "cybersmears." These investors are usually short sellers who bet—with a stacked deck of rumor e-mails—that the share price will drop when the negative talk has its desired effect.

Sometimes It Is the Technology

Sometimes, though, it's not an individual or company that sets out to deceive—it really is a technological flaw. Take, for example, the $18,000 finding of damages against E*TRADE for a glitch in its computer trading system. The system erroneously declined an order for Ronald Clark of San Mateo, California, due to insufficient funds. An arbitration panel from the National Association of Securities Dealers (which runs the NASDAQ stock exchange) ruled in favor of Clark and ordered E*TRADE to pay Clark the expected profits had the proper purchase taken place. Trading delays and outages at Ameritrade have led that firm to pay customers several million dollars. Customers have filed class lawsuits against E*TRADE, Ameritrade, and Schwab for technology-related problems at the online trading companies.

On July 31, 2000, a software upgrade at the Internet banking service of Barclays PLC hit a glitch: Some users could see other customers' accounts. Barclays closed its service for several hours and reinstalled the old software until the flaw was corrected.

Few companies are immune from the dangers of new technology. French Bull SA, the French hardware and software company (which sells security software) was caught up in a profound irony. Sensitive customer data was publicly revealed on a data-processing server. While files were supposed to be confidential and password-protected, that protection was no longer in evidence. Security analysts at Kitetoa discovered the gaffe and notified the company. On August 31, 2000, Bull announced the glitch and that it didn't know how long the glitch had occurred. Was the exposed information valuable to competitors, clients, or hackers? According to Bull, none of the unshielded data on clients such as France Telecom, Barclays, the British Royal Air Force, the Italian Army, and Aérospatiale's missile division was sensitive. You be the judge. Data inadvertently posted included customer names, contact information, server type, location, configuration, and the cost of equipment.

When it's the technology, it can be quite frightening. In the spring of 2000, Cox Communications (a cable television company that had started offering local phone service) accidentally provided Pacific Bell with the unlisted address and phone numbers for more than 11,000 customers, which the phone company then included in 1.3 million copies of the San Diego white pages. Dozens of police officers with unlisted numbers were included in the phone books. Cox placed the blame on "incompatible software." The state public utilities commission ordered both companies to retrieve 400,000 copies of the directories already distributed.

In a technology-based example with an ironic twist, California semiconductor maker LSI Logic ran into problems with its new supply chain management system. The system held up the shipping of $10 million in merchandise by one day, pushing the posting into the next fiscal quarter. The company had missed revenue expectations by $20 million for the 2nd quarter 2000, with the computer slip contributing $10 million, or half the shortfall. Investors hit the stock hard after the shortfall announcement, battering the stock down 30 percent the next day. In fact, Leonard Lee wrote a "Glitches of the Week" column for several years for the IT-focused news service *Newsbytes*. The column offered a sidesplitting and scary look at "the latest in the weird, bizarre, and unfortunate when it comes to technology." A few more choice examples: Kaiser Permanente accidentally e-mailed information (some including sensitive medical details) to the wrong patients (858 of them) as a result of human and technical snafus. In Minnesota, 8,000 students erroneously failed the high school standardized math test because the answer key was out of order for some of the tests. The scoring error at National Computer Systems Inc. wasn't discovered for six months. A favorite snafu involved 500,000 instant multimillionaire awards, thanks to Smith Barney, back in 1997. Each individual account erroneously received more than $19 million. But it was only a "virtual windfall." The money could only be "viewed" longingly over the Internet.

Pump and Dump—the Internet Way

More than 23 companies and individuals were charged with microcap stock manipulation by the SEC in March 2001, the fifth cyberfraud crackdown by that agency since 1998. The sweep involved numerous "pump and dump" schemes in which the perpetrators hyped small cap stocks (typically companies with very little published available information) through various Internet channels. By purchasing the stock, unwitting investors created high demand and "pumped" up the stock price. The perpetrators sold their shares at the top, the hype stopped and the share price dropped precipitously, with the victims facing severe financial losses. In the latest sweep documented in that case, the perpetrators pumped up the market capitalization of the stocks by more than $300 million and raised $2.5 million in proceeds for themselves. Hype was spread by spam e-mails, electronic newsletters, Web sites, hyperlinks, message boards, and other Internet media. This type of fraud has a long history—but it is marvelously facilitated by the instant and mass communication offered by the wild Web.

In the SEC press release issued at the time of the sweep, the organization's Director of Enforcement, Richard H. Walker, reported "What used to require a network of professional promoters and brokers, banks of telephones, and months to accomplish can now be done in minutes by a single person using the Internet and a home computer. Thinly traded microcap stocks are particularly susceptible to online manipulations. That's why we have made this area one of our highest enforcement priorities. Ultimately, however, the best way for investors to protect themselves against all forms of Internet fraud, including pump and dump schemes, is to do their homework and to be highly skeptical of information they receive from strangers on Internet Web sites, message boards, and chat rooms."

Even in times of national crisis, criminals carry on. In the wake of the October 2001 anthrax attacks, Spectrum Brands, a New York firm attempted an Internet-built pump and dump stock scheme based on a $125 anthrax-killing ultraviolet device. Licensed by Spectrum Brands from another company, the appliance kills live anthrax—not the spores being disseminated through the mail at the time. Spectrum Brands, allegedly knowing that fact, nevertheless claimed that the device "combated terrorism." In November 2001, the firm sent unsolicited spam e-mail to consumers and posted claims on its Web site that the hand-held device wipes out surface germs in seconds—including anthrax. They also predicted a tenfold increase in the Spectrum Brands stock price. No surprise, the stock price did jump dramatically to a high of $15 in November, but dropped back again after a Bloomberg news story questioned the product's efficacy. In December 2001, the SEC filed stock manipulation charges against four Spectrum Brands insiders who sold their shares at artificially high prices in November. In February of 2002, the stock was back trading at 11 cents per share.

As demonstrated by the Emulex case, perpetrators are not only facing stiff fines but are receiving prison time as well. A case that began in 1999 involved small cap hype by two men in their early twenties who used computer labs at UCLA to pump a penny stock. The pair bought thousands of shares of stock in a commercial printer, boosted its price by posting hundreds of phony tips on Internet message boards, and then made a $350,000 profit when they sold their shares. The stock swindlers were prosecuted by the SEC and the California U.S. Attorney's office; the two pleaded guilty to securities fraud charges and agreed to pay more than $213,000 in restitution. Although their crimes were in electronic space, they will be spending real time in a hard prison cell. Sentences of 10 months for one and 15 months for the other perpetrator were handed down in January 2001.

How do the hustlers view their targets? In yet another pump and dump scheme prosecuted by the SEC, several men in their early twenties (law school students) were the swindlers. As evidence against the con men, the SEC used a defrauding blueprint the lead perpetrator had posted on a Web site which stated: "buy a bunch of this garbage stock," "tell your idiot subscribers about how great the stock is, and, like sheep, they will run out and buy it," "dump the shares you bought a few hours ago to all of these suckers," "watch the stock steadily tank for the next month," and "laugh all the way to the bank."

And Sometimes It Is the Company

While many of the recent headline-grabbing stock manipulation stories center on individuals out for personal gain, unscrupulous companies and corporate executives are certainly not above using the Internet to pump up a firm's stock value. Back in 1996 and 1997, in the toddler days of the Web, the SEC uncovered a complex web of deception spun by Charles Huttoe, the former chairman of Systems of Excellence, Inc. (with the memorable stock symbol SEXI).

Huttoe gave 250,000 shares of his company to Theodore R. Melcher, Jr., publisher of the "SGA Goldstar Whisper Stocks" newsletter, a subscription stock tip newsletter distributed over the Internet and in other formats. Melcher then touted the stocks to his subscribers and also on Internet-based investor-oriented bulletin boards over a period of three years. The scam resulted in more than 10,000 SEXI-hyping Internet messages and illegal gains of more than $10 million for those involved. Huttoe was sentenced on one count of securities fraud and one count of money laundering in a plea agreement, fined $10,000, and sentenced to a 46-month prison term. Melcher, who pleaded guilty to "conspiracy to commit securities fraud," was sentenced to federal prison for 12 months and fined $20,000. SEXI's auditor also pleaded guilty to one count of conspiracy to commit securities fraud and bank fraud but died prior to sentencing. All told, six individuals pleaded guilty to conspiracy to commit securities fraud and other charges. So far, the SEC has recovered approximately $11 million from the SEXI case, which will be returned to defrauded investors.

The final upshot of this SEXI deal? The SEC revoked the registration of the SEXI stock on May 30, 2000. According to the "SEC's LITIGATION RELEASE NO. 16632 / July 20, 2000" this action will "prevent further parties from acquiring the now defunct company and using its securities for use in future manipulations."

Other Tricks of the Trade

Some people like a more direct approach to digital era theft. On August 23, 2000, three men were arrested in London for trying to rob the British online bank London's Egg PLC. The British men, who applied for fraudulent loans and credit cards, were caught after six months of cooperation between the bank and police. And how were they caught? Electronically, of course. Egg installed tracking software that helped identify the hopeful thieves. *Computerworld* reported (August 23, 2001, "Police Arrest E-Bank Robbery Suspects") this was the first instance of an attempted online theft at Egg and "the first publicized instance for the Internet banking industry." In that article, Bret Sigillo, regional director of information security at New York-based Predictive Systems, Inc., noted "It's usually not in a bank's best interest to notify the public that something like this has happened." It does tend to make potential patrons feel insecure. In a *Reuters* story ("Police Nab Three for Net Bank Heist," August 23, 2000), National Crime Squad spokeswoman Judi Prue sounded an alarm concerning this new development of organized crime moving onto the Net. "This obviously is a very new area criminals are getting into, and expanding into, so it's something in which we have really got to keep one step ahead of them." In the same Reuters story, the police claimed Egg lost thousands of pounds; Egg officials, however stated: "We confirm Egg's security remains unbreached and customers' money is secure." Would the thieves have received virtual money?

The fortunate thing is that the criminals are being caught in fairly rapid time, hoisted with a slew of their own Internet Protocol (IP) petards.

In April 1999, a then-employee at PairGain Technologies, Inc., of Tustin, California, used an amalgam of technologies to pump up the value of his stock holdings in PairGain. He was caught within two weeks. The 25-year-old man had created a dummy Web page to mimic Bloomberg.com that announced that PairGain was to be acquired by an Israeli company for more than $1 billion. He then sent e-mail to stock discussion sites with a link to the bogus page. PairGain stock shot up more than 30 percent before dropping when the Net hoax was revealed. The perpetrator tried mightily to cover his tracks by using free services including Web hosting from Angelfire.com and e-mail from Hotmail.com (leaving no money trail to a real person).

Nevertheless, he was caught when his employer's IP address was identified at the Angelfire and Hotmail services. In addition, PairGain cooperated with the U.S. attorney's office, identifying the employee who had accessed these sites at specific times. He pleaded guilty on securities fraud charges, was ordered to pay $92,000 in restitution, and was restricted in his ability to do business over the Internet.

And in our litigious age, Michael Bloomberg filed a lawsuit against the anonymous Web page publisher even before the criminal was identified. Poor Michael Bloomberg seems to be a favorite target of miscreants. Bloomberg was targeted yet again in August of 2000. This time, three individuals from Kazakhstan attempted to extort $200,000 from Mr. Bloomberg for their promised silence concerning alleged security problems at his Web site. Bloomberg cooperated with police, and the three were arrested in London.

In another widely publicized cyber-extortion story, a computer hacker overcame the electronic security measures of online music retailer CD Universe, in December 1999, and stole 300,000 customers' credit card numbers from the firm's databases. The hacker then demanded $100,000 in exchange for not publicizing the credit card numbers. When the company refused the extortion attempt, the hacker posted 25,000 of the stolen numbers on the Web. The company notified the FBI and the site was shut down. And the culprit? He goes by the name of Maxim and describes himself as a 19-year-old from Russia.

Mr. Bloomberg and CD Universe officials might rest easier with new insurance offerings now available that will cover up to $100 million in lost revenues and information assets as a result of Internet and e-commerce security breaches. Such insurance is typically offered by firms specializing in network security and can include coverage for extortion, according to Ann Harrison in *Computerworld* (July 12, 2000, "Counterpane offers Internet Security Insurance"). And several insurance companies now offer insurance specifically for online banks to cover losses as a result of denial of service attacks, site defacements, viruses, and privacy violations.

But why go to all that subterfuge with dummy sites and anonymous e-mail accounts when you can just hack into a company's Web site and post whatever news you like? Aastrom Biosciences, a biotechnology company, faced just that reality on the morning of February 17, 2000. Hackers broke into the site and posted a phony news release that the firm was merging with Geron Corporation, another biotechnology firm. Both stocks went soaring before the fraud was exposed and trading for the stock suspended on NASDAQ, as requested by Aastrom. In addition, the electronic intruder modified the company's second quarter earnings press release posted at the Aastrom site to reflect the pending merger.

Web site defacement became a widely popular activity in 2000 and 2001 with few organizations escaping the wrath of comic and serious hackers. Numerous government sites were attacked, including the FBI, the President's official online home page, the official U.S. Senate site, and NASA. No one appears to be immune. Quite embarrassingly, the Internet security firm RSA was attacked and defaced. Cybernanny, the software designed to guard children against undesirable content, and SaferInternet.org, a European Commission-sponsored Web site that encourages a safer Internet, had their own sites hacked and defaced as well. Cybernanny's defacement was particularly glaring for its obscene content. Trust what you see at a news site? Don't bet the bank on it. The AP News site was also defaced in March of 2001, although the news service claims that editorial "operations" were not affected. Nor does being a global company protect against such hacks, since McDonald's and Burger King sites in England have been defaced. While McDonald's site received a humorous treatment from "fluffy bunny," the Burger King UK site was defaced with a mock-up of its arch-rival's site—McDonald's UK.

Web Sleight of Hand

The Internet also allows far more purposeful misdirection. In the *Wall Street Journal* (October 13, 1999, "A Secret Cat-and-Mouse Game Online"), Michael Moss finally documented what had been rumored for years: Companies redirect competitors to alternative specialized Web pages devoid of useful competitive information. By identifying the user's originating domain name, companies can choose who sees the real site and who sees the dummy. When visitors from four likely rivals visited Eframes.com in 1999, they were sent to a Web page claiming "Coming in time for Christmas." Variations on this game abound. The same *Wall Street Journal* story reported that Oracle Corporation and rival Siebel Systems were tangled in a spy versus spy spat. Siebel was trying to hire Oracle employees. So when the Siebel Web site recognized visitors from the Oracle domain, it shunted them directly to the Siebel's jobs page. These games keep escalating. One of Cisco's rivals directed viewers to an outdated Cisco Web page to promote the superiority of its own products. Cisco turned around and grabbed redirected viewers coming in that way and sent them to its latest site.

General Net Confusion

Even domain names add to the general Net confusion. In the *Wall Street Journal* (October 25, 1999, "Name Game Winners"), Rodney Ho identified a handful of Web site domains that don't lead where you would anticipate. For example, one would anticipate Procter & Gamble to have scooped up all product-related domain names early on in the wild race for domain registrations. Guess again. Cascade.com does not belong to Procter & Gamble but is owned and run by Cascade Wholesale Hardware, Inc., which registered the domain name back in 1994. Similarly, PeterPan.com does not impart knowledge about peanut butter, but promotes PPI Entertainment, dedicated to lifestyle products such as workout tapes.

Many people might also remember the early days of the search engine AltaVista. After developing the search service, Digital Equipment Corporation (DEC) licensed the rights to the AltaVista name from a San Jose, California, man. However, DEC neglected to secure the rights to the domain name as well. So, for several years and despite much legal wrangling, visitors at www.altavista.com who thought they could search the Web for relevant information were instead entreated to purchase software to develop multimedia postcards for the Web. The actual search engine could only be found at www.altavista.digital.com. Only after Compaq acquired DEC did Compaq pony up what was reported to be the largest sum for a domain name until that time—$3.35 million for the altavista.com crown jewel.

More Net confusion should arise with the introduction of the seven new top-level domains approved by the Internet Corporation for Assigned Names and Numbers (ICANN), the independent regulatory body that now manages the Internet's domain name system. Good, memorable, mostly short names are growing increasingly scarce, especially in the desirable dot-com top-level domain (location, location, and location). So, ICANN has opened up seven new top-level domains: *.aero, .biz, .coop, .info, .museum, .name*, and *.pro*. However, each new top-level domain introduction increases the number of domain name lawsuits between trademark holders and cybersquatters.

On June 21, 2000, Nike's Web site was pagejacked and redirected to a phony site critical of Nike hosted on servers in Scotland. The redirection was accomplished through bogus e-mail sent to the domain registrar, Network Solutions, Inc. (NSI), without the required password according to Nike. A three-way slugfest ensued. The Scottish company blamed Nike for being inattentive to the security of its domain but failed in its attempt to bill Nike for overloading its servers. Nike laid responsibility at the feet of NSI for making changes based on faked e-mail. NSI claims it is just a conduit for registrations. This is truly a case for King Solomon the Wise, or at least the writers of *Mission: Impossible.*

No Escape from a Dirty Web of Deception

Pornographers, often at the leading edge of technologies, have also added their own page to Web-based dirty tricks. The Federal Trade Commission (FTC) successfully began prosecuting an international smut ring in 1999 (and expanded the scope in 2000) which habitually redirected innocent Web surfers to, and then captured them at, hardcore pornographic sites. After copying 25 million assorted Web pages (including such innocent sites as the *Harvard Law Review* and the Japanese Friendship Garden), the Portuguese and Australian defendants inserted codes into the imposter sites that automatically redirected consumers to their own adult-oriented sites. Once there, the "exit" and "back" buttons of viewers' browsers were incapacitated—forcing them to stay at the hard core Web sites. What was the logic of this scam? The culprits charged premium online advertising rates for kidnapped viewers who were forced to watch page after page of sexually explicit materials and high-priced ads.

Will the Real Price Please Stand Up?

One of the most notorious stories of commercial technological wizardry revolved around Amazon's "trial" of varying prices for DVDs in September of 2000. Some people accused Amazon of "dynamic pricing," which is setting the price levels for the DVDs based on income levels or past purchases. The original Wunderkind of the dot-coms had to defend itself vigorously, with Jeff Bezos telling a press conference that Amazon did not engage in dynamic pricing. Instead, Amazon claimed it was trying to find proper price points by randomly changing DVD prices. Ultimately, Amazon refunded nearly 7,000 customers an average $3 apiece. Does $21,000 redeem a reputation?

And how did Amazon get caught? Customers compared DVD prices in online discussion groups and discovered the discrepancies. It seems that technology can reveal how technology is used to beguile. And the same technology that can promulgate error can find truth and administer justice.

The Dangers When Business Becomes Personal

The situation grows even murkier when the business and personal dangers of the new electronic world intermingle. Take, for example, the frightening story of NASA employee Jay Dyson, as documented by Adam Penenberg in *Forbes* (February 21, 2000, "A Private Little

Cyberwar). One of the network security team at NASA, Dyson attempted, on his own, to identify hackers who had pierced NASA's network. Dyson's online postings in search of the hackers commenced a multiyear "cyberwar" with devastating effects on Dyson's personal life. The hackers successfully vandalized Dyson's personal and business Web pages, attacked the networks of his ISPs, accessed his wife's online account at work (and threatened her), and had his personal and home business telephones shut off. Ultimately, the cyberbattle led to a divorce from his wife. One of the hackers was caught; one still remains at large. During the fray, Dyson began arming himself with real guns.

In another tale of the personal mixing it up with business, we need look no further than the EDGAR database from the Securities and Exchange Commission. In particular, prior to 1997, the 13D and 13G forms (required of individuals holding more than 5 percent of the voting shares in a public company) included an entry for the individual's Social Security Number to distinguish John Doe 1 from John Doe 2. A Social Security Number, as most people know, is the master key, the crown jewel, the Rosetta stone so to speak, for success in identity theft. Thus, the social security numbers of Bill Gates and Paul Allen, of Microsoft fame, were posted for all to see at the EDGAR site as of 1999, as reported by Ann Harrison in *Computerworld* (September 24, 2000, "SEC Database Exposes Social Security Numbers"). The SEC no longer requires this information and allows shareholders to request that the information be withdrawn from public viewing. However, as of 9/13/2001, Paul Allen's number was still available for public viewing in one such document, a year after the *Computerworld* report's publication.

Rewriting Boundaries Electronically

What happens when a corporate entity rewrites national boundaries with a simple upload of a Web page? CNN found out. In response to protests by the American-Arab Anti-Discrimination Committee in March 2000, CNN's online weather map began describing Jerusalem not as part of Israel but as an international city, a city without a country. Only after the American Jewish Congress (AJC) objected to this designation, did CNN change the identification. In his protest letter to CNN, AJC Executive Director Phil Baum noted dismay that the "network should have separated Jerusalem from Israel and to have made the astounding and politically biased news judgment that Jerusalem is now an international city."

On August 3, 2000, CNN returned Jerusalem's identification as part of Israel but added an asterisk with the following explanation: "The status of Jerusalem, the seat of Israeli government, is the most contentious issue in the Israeli-Palestinian peace talks. Palestinian and Arab leaders consider part of Jerusalem the capital of the prospective Palestinian state." More protests flew. The AJC and the American-Arab Anti-Discrimination Committee objected to the new note, each from different perspectives. In the *Jerusalem Post* (September 13, 2000, "Eye on the Media: CNN's Weather Vane"), Andrea Levin noted "In no other cases where a city's sovereignty is contested—such as Lhasa, Taipei, or Jammu—does CNN qualify the national affiliation with a political notation. (Their respective listings are Lhasa, China; Taipei, Taiwan; and Jammu, India.)." As of April, 2002, the asterisk is still there. CNN appears to be using its corporate resources to do more than just report the news.

Keeping Up with Mouse Capers

Agencies around the world are trying hard to keep up with electronic criminals and the dangers of the new technologies. The International Criminal Police Organization (Interpol) has collaborated with private companies to combat Internet crime. In an interview in *Foreign Policy* (January 1, 2001, "Meet the World's Top Cop"), Interpol's secretary general, Raymond Kendall, described the agency's cooperative efforts as two-way information exchanges between Interpol and private companies that would provide early warnings of Internet threats. In describing the benefits of the collaboration, Kendall noted, "In the future, more private companies will have access to global intelligence, without cost, to assist them in defending their Internet activities from cyberterrorism and 'hactivism.' At the same time, law enforcement agencies will be able to benefit from sophisticated technology intelligence gathered by leading Internet firms." As of October 2000, Interpol employed only a half dozen investigators to focus on cybercrime for its 178 member countries.

On this side of the pond, the SEC has proclaimed the battle against cybercrime as its leading priority. In 1998, the SEC established the Office of Internet Enforcement (OIE), at the request of Richard Walker, then newly appointed enforcement director. OIE now coordinates the Internet surveillance activities of the "Cyberforce," encompassing a group of over 200 Commission attorneys, accountants, and investigators nationwide. In conjunction with the SEC's Office of Investor Education and Assistance, OIE also manages the SEC Complaint Center, which receives hundreds of complaints per day. OIE also coordinates Internet-related "Enforcement Sweeps."

In addition to its most recent cyberfraud crackdown on pump and dump schemes in March 2001, the SEC's five Internet "sweeps" have targeted, "the touting of publicly traded companies (October 1998 and February 1999), the sale of bogus investment opportunities (May 1999), and the perpetration of 'pump-and-dump' stock schemes (September 2000)" according to a March 1, 2001, SEC press release ("SEC Charges 23 Companies and Individuals in Cases Involving Broad Spectrum of Internet Securities Fraud").

In the last week of January 2002, more than 150,000 individuals visited the pre-IPO Web site of biohazard detector-manufacturer McWhortle Enterprises (www.mcwhortle.com). Visitors were treated to lofty praises from a stock analyst and an audio interview with CEO James McWhortle. But quite a surprise was in store for visitors who clicked through the "invest now" and "ready to buy buttons." They reached a page (www.mcwhortle.com/onlinebid.htm) that screamed, **"If you responded to an investment idea like this ... *You could get scammed!"*** This was an investment lesson courtesy of the SEC and other government agencies, rather than an investment opportunity from a real company. The "instructive" page went on to explain:

> McWhortle Enterprises does not exist. It is a complete fabrication, posted by the Securities and Exchange Commission, the Federal Trade Commission, the North American Securities Administrators Association, and the National Association of Securities Dealers to alert investors to potential on-line frauds. We created this site because we've all seen an increase in the number of investment scams preying on our fears of anthrax and other bio-hazards.
>
> This site shows some of the telltale signs of on-line investment fraud. Promises of fast and high profits, with little or no risk, are classic red flags of fraud. Remember— if it sounds too good to be true, it ususally is!

Earlier that month, the SEC had initiated its unusual educational venture by quietly posting phony Web sites from various nonexisting companies, touting colossal investing opportunities. The "lesson" was put into play with the cooperation of PR Newswire (who notified Bloomberg News, Dow Jones News Service and Reuters in advance of the simulation). The SEC distributed a fake press release from "McWhortle Enterprises," publicizing the company and claiming the SEC had preapproved the IPO—which is not a practice of the SEC. While some people have criticized the SEC's instructional effort, others have praised it as an excellent way to educate the investing public in a way that makes it quite real—they were almost scammed.

As to other activities, the SEC also plans to establish an automated surveillance system (to replace human "scanners") that will constantly monitor the Internet for nearly 40 words or phrases characteristic of stock manipulation, such as "get rich quick" or "make money now." Gathered from publicly accessible portions of the Web, the material would be amassed in a database for analysis by SEC investigators. In January 2000, the SEC invited more than 100 companies to bid on operating the $1 million surveillance system but was on the receiving end of a rash of privacy-related criticism from a wide-ranging array of companies, politicians, and privacy rights organizations.

So too, the FTC formed an Internet Lab in 1999 dedicated to fighting fraud and deception on the Web. In October 2000, the FTC agreed to share information and coordinate with two British agencies, the UK Department of Trade and Industry and the UK Office of Fair Trading.

Nor will the FBI leave online crime untouched. In May of 2000, Janet Reno announced the formation of the Internet Fraud Complaint Center (IFCC) in collaboration with the National White Collar Crime Center. The IFCC (www.ifccfbi.gov) logs consumer complaints with Internet-related problems, whether the deception takes place at Web sites, in chat rooms, or via e-mail—nationally and internationally. Referrals are made to appropriate authorities for prosecution. The IFCC also aids in pursuing the criminals involved in the identified fraud schemes.

Just a year after its formation, the IFCC netted a big win in "Operation Cyber Loss." This nationwide multiagency investigation into Internet fraud resulted in criminal federal and state fraud charges being filed against 90 individuals and companies. Citizen complaints fielded by the IFCC were turned over for investigation and prosecution. On May 23, 2001, law enforcement personnel swept across the country, making arrests for such swindles as nondelivery of goods from online auctions, multilevel marketing and pyramid schemes, and investment and credit card frauds. All told, 56,000 victims reportedly had losses totaling $117 million.

Reflecting the magnitude of the problem, Operation Cyber Loss was a coordinated effort of a remarkably wide array of federal, state, and local law enforcement organizations including the FBI, Department of Justice, U.S. Postal Inspectors Service, the Internal Revenue Service, the Securities and Exchange Commission, U.S. Customs Service, and 15 local law enforcement agencies from east to west coast. It also included the cooperation of eBay, Yahoo!, Microsoft, Motley Fool, and Pay Pal (an online payment system), an important cooperation considering that the majority of the complaints over the prior year involved auction sites.

Prime Pickings for Bonnie and Clyde

On the same day Operation Cyber Loss publicized its nationwide crackdown, the U.S. House Subcommittee on Commerce, Trade, and Consumer Protection was hosting hearings entitled "Online Fraud and Crime: Are Consumers Safe?" In his testimony to that subcommittee, Bruce Swartz, deputy assistant attorney general (Department of Justice, Washington, DC) noted that "Internet fraud, in all of its forms, is one of the fastest growing and most pervasive forms of white-collar crime." Billy Tauzin (R-La.), Chairman of the subcommittee, was quoted as observing, "The Internet gives miscreants special capabilities. ... Bonnie and Clyde would have loved this environment," according to Patrick Thibodeau in *Computerworld* (May 23, 2001).

Are there dangers ahead? Certainly. However, there are also tremendous benefits from newly introduced technologies and those that lie ahead. As recently as the mid-1990s, online searchers had to pay top dollar for each wire story, did not have access to the same corporate information at the same time as Wall Street analysts, and had to pay large sums for clipping services for news alerts. Today there's a plethora of alerting service choices—many for free. In addition, the SEC's fair disclosure ruling assures individual investors access to far more company information than ever before, including conference calls with company executives that are invaluable information-rich resources. And we are just beginning to experience the benefits of the wireless world.

At times, the new technologies have clearly enriched our lives. At other times it seems they steal precious time, broadcast personal data, and generate misinformation. It is clear, however, that as individuals, we need to heighten our suspicion to resist the temptations of Web-based scam artists and to develop stronger radar to see through deceptive technologies. The examples relayed here demonstrate that the Internet should be approached with far greater skepticism than many of us undoubtedly used in the early days of the Web revolution. In this new networked frontier without borders, thankfully, our modern-day Eliot Ness counterparts have joined forces worldwide and developed collective global muscle to battle today's electronic Bonnies and Clydes.

Where to Go for Help

The examples provided here illustrate how technologies can be used to deceive, whether in the hands of an adult, a youth, or a corporation, and whether a phony Web site, junk e-mail, or purposely deceptive information spread in electronic discussion groups. Remember the old adage not to believe everything you read? Add the Internet to that warning as well. So what is one to do?

Diligence. Research. Verify, verify, verify. Check with other trusted electronic or print resources. Check with knowledgeable people in your organization or industry. Check with the SEC. Check directly with the company in question.

The SEC offers an excellent collection of advice pages at its center on the Internet and Online Trading (www.sec.gov/investor/online.shtml). The site offers advice on frauds involving pump and dump, pre-IPO offerings, and micro-cap stocks. One page in particular, "Internet Fraud: How to Avoid Internet Investment Scams" (www.sec.gov/investor/pubs/cyberfraud.htm), advises a very healthy dose of skepticism. Several recommendations include:

- Don't assume that people online are who they claim they are.

- Ask online promoters whether, and how much, they've been paid to tout the opportunity.

- Find out where the company is incorporated. Then call that state's secretary of state and ask if the company is incorporated there. If so, obtain its current annual report on file.

- Search in the SEC's EDGAR database (www.sec.gov/cgi-bin/srch-edgar) of corporate filings (for companies with more than 500 investors and more than $10 million in total assets).

- Ask your state securities regulator or the SEC if complaints have been filed about the company, its managers, or the promoter.

- Explore the resources at your public library, where you might find information about lawsuits, liens, credit reports, payment analyses, investment reports, and more.

- Before investing, gather written financial documents, such as prospectuses, annual reports, offering circulars, and financial statements. Compare printed documentation with what you have seen online.

- Beware if you are told that no written information is available.

- Consult a dependable financial advisor, broker, or lawyer concerning investments you learn about online.

Put on a detective's cap. Look up the registration of the domain name at WHOIS (http://networksolutions.com/cgi-bin/whois/whois). Get in touch with the technical or administrative contact. Use WHOIS again (in the search by name) to see what other sites those contacts have registered. What are those sites like? Is there a style of bias in the sites? When examining a site, look at the actual URL. Does the main domain name look correct? If you can't tell the sponsor of the site, start deleting segments of the URL until you arrive at the home page and can identify the owner.

Countermeasures

If you can't locate full contact information, including name, address, and phone number, start investigating. Sadly, many companies don't always put that information on the front page. But a complete absence of this information should worry you. Check to see that the site is "owned" by a reputable organization or a knowledgeable person. Search for other articles or sites authored by the named individual. Search for other references to the organization. Check the validity and sponsorship of those sites as well. Remember to use your common sense. In the case of the Nike pagejacking, it was highly unlikely that the firm would purposely post self-critical information.

For electronic discussion groups and message boards:

- Identify a pattern of posts by the individuals whose postings you find so interesting.

- See if there is a search function that allows you to collect, follow, or search for all their postings.

- Look for their full name and contact information and be on your guard if they are completely anonymous.

- Beware of sites that are always hyping or always panning a particular company or product.

- Look to see if any of their predictions come true, if they are on target or off-the-wall.

- Again, verify comments with other trustworthy sources, whether they are print, electronic, or personal sources.

In the *Los Angeles Times* (August 26, 2000, "No Quick Fix Seen for Eliminating False News Releases, Security Experts Say"), Walter Hamilton offered investor-oriented warnings, just after the Emulex scandal. In the sidebar, the newspaper offered several suggestions for identifying phony press releases:

- Watch out for poorly written press releases.

- Keep watch for stories issued from new PR firms.

- Be suspicious of news issued on Fridays, typically minor news days.

- Be skeptical of press releases inserted into messages at stock chat rooms.

- Also, don't act hastily on single news reports, either for business purposes or for investments.

- Follow research advice offered by reliable organizations such as that found at the SEC's center on the Internet and Online Trading (www.sec.gov/investor/online.shtml).

After the Emulex, PairGain, and Lucent phony news stock scandals, many commentators observed that investors who really knew each company, and who had done their research, did not join the big sell-off. They no doubt performed more research to verify the information and assess what it meant for the future. Again, verification and research pay off.

CHAPTER 4

Internet Users at Risk:
The Identity/Privacy Target Zone

Stephen E. Arnold

"Security on the Internet. There is none. Get over it." This is a statement attributed to Scott McNealy, President of Sun Microsystems, and about a dozen other high-profile technology executives. The pithy statement echoes one-line gags from Groucho Marx. But privacy and security in a public network is no joking matter.

Anyone who uses the Internet without stringent privacy measures enters an "Internet Target Zone." This chapter will discuss how fraud and deception can occur. Without such knowledge, users and builders of the Net cannot protect themselves or even know the extent of their risks. Sometimes we will describe software or procedures that may seem unfriendly to some users but essential and benign to others. For example, monitoring methods help companies avoid liability for actions of individual employees on the Net, but the employees may regard the oversight as Big Brother management excess. One man's meat is another man's poison.

As the Internet swells beyond 200 million users worldwide, concerns about protecting privacy may be ballooning even faster. There is growing evidence that the general public has begun to sense just how tenuous its right to privacy has become. A *Business Week*/Harris poll found that 57 percent of Americans believe that "the government should pass laws now for how personal information can be collected and used on the Internet."

Neither the telephone, the motion pictures, the radio, or broadcast television engendered the fast-changing, specter-like security challenges of the Internet. Enter the zone depicted in Figure 4.1. Take your chances.

Consider electronic commerce credit transactions. Electronic commerce runs on credit card transactions. Handing over a credit card at a

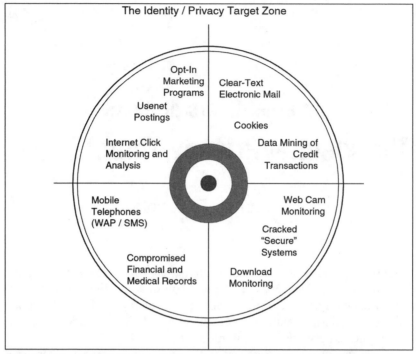

Figure 4.1   An Internet user becomes a target for wrongdoers who would like to capture information that can be used to create a false indentity, purchase products without concern for payment, and obtain information that could be used for illegal or improper activities.

restaurant causes little if any security jitters. A newbie or newcomer to the Internet encounters a fuzzier, less tangible world. In a restaurant, a customer who falls victim to credit card theft believes he can go back to the establishment, find the owner or manager, and seek satisfaction. On the Internet, the crime can be as difficult to grasp as a shadow, a digital one at that.

Almost two-thirds of Internet users who shop online more than once a week are women, according to a survey by PeopleSupport, an Internet customer service provider. About 19 percent of Internet users shop online once a week, 22 percent do so once a month, and 43 percent are infrequent Internet shoppers. Just under 16 percent have never shopped online. Over 60 percent of frequent shoppers have been online for more than five years, but 20 percent have used the Web for less than three months. Just over a third of those who shop online more than once a week would prefer to get product information by electronic mail, while 26.5 percent would like live text chat; 6 percent, self-help; and 32 percent, a toll-free number.[1]

Millions of online shoppers click "Yes, I would like to receive information about this product" buttons. Blithely indifferent to opt-in marketing schemes, these consumers are throwing gasoline on the privacy inferno.

Monitoring Action

Clicks, downloads, preferences, purchases, electronic mail, and voice messages sent via Internet telephony are all actions that can be watched, processed, and counted. A generation of children is coming of age with classrooms viewable by parents who want to keep tabs on their progeny.

In a small town near Louisville, Kentucky, hardly a hotbed of Internet innovation, Webcams have arrived (see Figure 4.2). One wonders how students will react to the radical change in classroom

Figure 4.2   A school in rural Kentucky will allow parents and other authorized "viewers" to observe classroom activities at this school for pre-high school students.

privacy. One wonders if a pedophile will use the feed to select and target victims after he or she snags a username and password.

Security has another connotation as well. The Internet revolution embraces digital video as readily as millions of electronic mail messages. Relatives, voyeurs, or worse can check up on their progeny by clicking to a Web site. Web cams, video cameras that feed their signal into an Internet server, broadcast the activities in front of the Charge-Coupled Device (CCD) lens.[2] What if a pederast compromises the system and uses it to target a victim?

Data Mining

Amazon.com is one of the Internet retailers most respected by the general public. Amazon offers customers a way to "personalize" their shopping experience. By providing information to Amazon, the customer can get access to what Amazon calls "recommendations." Using sophisticated software tools, Amazon can map a customer to a cluster, perform some mathematical calculations, and create a list of books or records that similarly interested customers have purchased. The data mining and affinity algorithms enrich a registered user's shopping experience as though a live person were quietly, unobtrusively accompanying the customer.

Amazon also offers "Purchase Circles," a summary of book purchases by corporate account. A person interested in the reading at major consulting firms can quickly compare A.T. Kearney's purchases with Booz, Allen & Hamilton's, a feature some might find mildly entertaining.

The Lingo of Security

The terminology of privacy and security (see Figure 4.3) is arcane, partly due to security's unspoken rule: "Never talk about security to untrusted individuals." The faint aroma of paranoia wafts along the corridors of security. There is more than a grain of truth in the old joke, "If I tell you, I'll have to kill you." Unfortunately, the exploding user community needs awareness of privacy, security, identity theft, and several other incendiary issues now more than ever.

Some evidence as to the lack of solid facts about how vulnerable Internet systems are to users who want something for nothing falls readily to hand. Consider Pay Pal, an online payment system that allows a person to purchase a product from an eBay seller using a credit card. Pay Pal was designed to eliminate the need for the buyer to go to a bank, buy a money order, mail or send the payment via an

Security Jargon

A short list of the terminology that fills popular and trade press writing:

Term	Definition
Affinity marketing	Once a person is placed in a cluster, mathematical algorithms can predict certain patterns or predispositions of behavior for the group. No individual action can be predicted, but in an affinity group, a certain number of individuals will adopt the predicted behavior. Affinity group marketing, therefore, allows a person in a group who bought X to be offered product Y. The marketer knows that a certain number of people will buy Y because they bought X.
Agents	Scripts that perform specific tasks and are equipped with some type of mechanism that allows the script to take different actions depending upon a situation. At this time agents cannot readily communicate with one another. However, inter-agent communication promises to create a new class of more flexible, effective automatic data collection and analysis functions.
Black or dark site	Available in the cache of some servers.
Cookie	A handle, transaction ID, or other token of agreement between cooperating programs. "I give him a packet, he gives me back a cookie." The claim check you get from a dry-cleaning shop is a perfect mundane example of a cookie. Less powerful than cgi-bin scripts programmed to perform ET functions, cookies are widely prevalent to expedite transactions or access.
Cracking	Controversy surrounds the distinction of "cracker" and "hacker" and "cracking" and "hacking." A cracker is a person who enters a site with malicious intent.
Data mining	A series of routines that look at data, make decisions about how the data relate, and then outputs reports driven by the content of large collections of information, collections too large for individuals to review as productively– for example, a year's collection of American Express credit card users' transactions.
Encryption	Encoding a clear text message into a collection of normally unreadable letters and symbols.
ET	A program sent from one computer to another, usually unbeknownst to the recipient. The program builds a collection of information and then transmits the data to its home base. ET is a play on the motion picture where an extraterrestrial creature wants to "phone home," that is, send information from one remote place to a home base.
Hacking	Exploring for personal satisfaction or from curiosity the ins and outs of software, hardware, and systems.
Identity theft	A person steals such information as another person's SSN, credit card number, and checking account information. Using these "proofs" of identity, the criminal pretends to be someone else, running up charges against the dupe's accounts.
Kerberos	A network authentication protocol that allows one computer to provide its identity to another across an insecure network through an exchange of encrypted messages. Once identity is verified, the protocol gives each computer an encryption key for a secure session.
Opt-in marketing	With permission to resell or use the address for direct marketing of other products and services.
Password	A secret string of words and numbers used to prove to an online system that a person logging on to the system is the person he or she is supposed to be.
Pervasive network	Exists wherever the Internet user wants to connect. The connection can be "live" for whatever interval the Internet user requires or desires.

Public Key Infrastructure	PKI is a system that will allow people to obtain encryption codes and permit authorized recipients to view a document changed from clear text to an unreadable format. The "key" is needed to read the message. PKI assumes a standard for "keys" that is widely used and easily available. Canada is one of the leaders in PKI and is the world's first multicertificate authority PKI.
Single Sign On	A software program that automatically replaces many passwords with a single point of entry.
Sniffer	A script that looks for words, phrases, terms, concepts, and tendencies in digital messages. Sniffers are difficult to detect, since they operate at the server level and provide few, if any, traces of their presence. Network latency may provide an indication of a sniffing process. Separate software is required to interpret what the sniffer senses.
Spider	A script designed to traverse a Web site by following links. It can be set up to copy an entire site or to save specific types of files or data.
Spoofing	Making a message or process appear to come from another source. Because systems and users "trust" known sources, spoofing allows a wrongdoer to enter the target system.
User name	The name an individual uses to identify himself or herself to an online system.
Wireless Application Protocol Short Messaging Service	The WAP allows mobile devices to receive properly encoded Web pages. The SMS allows a mobile device to send a text message entered with a keypad or stylus from a properly equipped device. Voice and text messages can be intercepted.

Figure 4.3   Security jargon.

express service, and then hope the seller would ship the product the day payment was received. Pay Pal cut out some of the process, making the seller happy to get the money faster and the buyer happy to get the purchase faster.

But for some new Pay Pal customers, setting up an account on a service like Pay Pal has become more annoying than the trip to the bank. The would-be Pay Pal user must wait for a secure Web site to download and then paint the screen. The customer-to-be fills out a long, complex, detailed form. One inevitable question is, "Will Pay Pal protect my personal information?"[3] The would-be user then must wait two or more weeks for the delivery of his or her new password by the U.S. Postal Service to a street address. Armed with the mailed notification, the would-be Pay Pal user then must log back on the site, use the code number in the mailed letter from Pay Pal, and transfer up to $500 in funds billed to a credit card. Finally the new user must wait another 7 to 12 days for the verification of his or her credit card account. Once the funds have been verified, another e-mail notifies the customer that Pay Pal is now ready for use. The elapsed time can easily extend for three weeks to a month or more. The verifications include user identity, user's physical address, and credit card validity. Trust is not something Pay Pal assumes.

Why?

More Silence, Please

Talking off the record, finance and security executives say that more than 30 percent of Web credit card transactions cause some type of problem. A large percentage of these are fraudulent. Security professionals know to keep their lips zipped. Security is a problem best discussed by insiders regardless of what side of the law each is on.

Network security is a serious business. A search of LexisNexis or Northern Light returns precious little information about security breaches at financial services firms, stock brokers, defense contractors, insurance companies, and Fortune 500 companies. Incidents occur, but the understanding is that security concern is a deal breaker. Network security is a complex job, and it is nearly impossible for technical professionals to keep up with the fixes, settings, and configurations necessary to keep hackers, crackers, thieves, and misguided teens at bay.

When a problem occurs, it has to be one too big to cover up. In 1999, the Los Alamos security setup lost hard drives with sensitive nuclear information. The devices turned up behind a copy machine. The hue and cry over security fell away quickly. Yet even minor security stories are bad for business.

Equally startling is the report from ZDNet concerning America Online's (AOL) privacy peccadilloes.[4] In a lawsuit naming AOL/ Netscape, the plaintiff alleged that the company's Smart Download feature, a component of some AOL installations, illegally monitors downloads of executable files with the extension ".exe" and ".zip." The law firm of Abbey, Gardy, & Squitieri filed suit in 2000 against AOL in federal court in New York, claiming that the software developed by Netscape Communications Corp. illegally monitors users' actions. AOL acquired the software when it bought Netscape in November 1998.

The Smart Download service automatically activates whenever a user downloads files from the Web. The suit claims that Smart Download captures and transmits back to Netscape uniquely identifiable information when a person visits a Web site and downloads software. The suit says, "Unbeknownst to the members of the Class, and without their authorization, defendants have been spying on their Internet activities." With this information, one could create a profile of a customer's file transfers. The music and entertainment industries are interested in getting the names and other information about people who may have downloaded copyrighted music or films.

In addition to charges of compromising the privacy of its subscribers voluntarily, AOL has also been called one of the most hacked services on the Web. The company has admitted more than once that vandals had broken into its service and gained access to an undisclosed number of member accounts.[5]

AOL, however, is far from being alone in drawing the ire of an ever more privacy conscious public.

An anonymous Internet user filed suit in May 2000 against Yahoo! charging that the company violated both state and federal law, as well as its own privacy policy, when it handed over personal information to another company that was suing the user for defamation.

Answer Think, an online consulting group, requested the information after "Aquacool_2000" posted a number of derogatory remarks about the company on a free message board maintained by Yahoo!. One of the many questions at stake is what right companies have to disclose personal information about private individuals utilizing their services. Where does free speech end and fair disclosure begin?

For those who do not know how systems work, the wireless connections and the high-speed lines that bring music and video to the computing device look like magic of a high caliber. Books foster the metaphor as well. A bestseller in 1998 told the story of the Internet under the title *Where Wizards Stay Up Late*.[6] For those who have $250 per year to spend, *Privacy Times* offers a newsletter that will curdle the blood of the most ardent Internet surf-and-be-damned soul.[7] Not surprisingly, "instant books" have been rushed through the publishing process to capitalize on a growing anxiety about security. One example is Jerome Schneider and Allison Hope Weiner's *Hiding Your Money*. The subtitle hits the fear button, "Everything you need to know about keeping your money and valuables safe from predators and greedy creditors."

"Identity-theft remains at the top of the list of privacy violations," said Evan Hendricks, who runs the watchdog *Privacy Times*. "If you use the Internet a lot, you have to cross your fingers and hope all that data you are forking over isn't used against you. It is very much the wild, wild West out there."

"Virtual" Criminals

Identity theft is an old crime given a jolt of digital Internet steroids. The Internet allows a person who steals a credit card or another's identity to avoid detection. The clever thief becomes a virtual identity, operating through a service that hides a person's electronic mail address. Anonymizer.com provides this service as do dozens of other Web sites.[8] A clever criminal uses digital sleight of hand to escape prosecution.

The Software and Information Industry Association published a white paper that tells the harrowing story of Lt. Col. Jones, the victim of a criminal using the real Lt. Col. Jones's identity to run up tens of thousands of dollars on the victim's credit card accounts. The misuse of Lt. Col. Jones's identity began in late 1999. Nearly nine months later, the suspect had not been located.

U.S. Military's Use of Social Security Numbers

The trigger point for Lt. Col. Jones's credit woes began with his Social Security Number (SSN). Other credit problems begin with people who complete personal information profiles from links on public discussion groups or who fall prey to Web crooks who create a bogus electronic commerce site.[9] The unwitting Internet user provides data, and the crook closes up shop. Once the wrongdoer has the vital information in hand, he or she can use the data to make purchases. Alternatively, the thief sells the data to a third party.

Law enforcement and financial services security professionals are confronted with increasingly clever criminals. But technology is only an accelerant, not a cause. One major problem is that many organizations and companies use a person's SSN as a person's identification number. The SSN may be used by government entities, health insurance companies, colleges, and, until recently in Kentucky, as a person's driver's license number.

Old and New Crime Blend

Stolen identity nightmares afflict about 500,000 Americans annually, and account for more than $2 billion recorded in fraud losses, with the actual figure likely much larger. The duped often do not want the details of the incident widely known. Hiding the dirty laundry of security problems is preferable to the publicity surrounding the breakdown.

Consider this story of identity theft using manual and Internet technology in a synergistic manner: In April 2000, Tennessee authorities indicted James R. Jackson and Derek Cunningham on charges of buying nearly $750,000 worth of diamonds and Rolex watches using credit card numbers stolen from current and deceased top executives, including the late publisher Nackey Loeb of The Union Leader. Among victims were the chief operating officer of Coca-Cola Enterprises, the chief executive officer of Hilton Hotels, and the chairman and chief executive officer of Lehman Brothers Holdings, prosecutors said. Other victims included the estates of deceased executives, including a former chairman and chief executive officer of Wendy's International, a former administrator of Cedars-Sinai Medical Center in Los Angeles, and Loeb, who had died Jan. 8.

The indictment alleged that the perpetrators targeted prominent members of the nation's business community and obtained personal information about them. The men impersonated their victims in telephone calls to banks and credit card companies. The men changed the billing addresses on the accounts to hotels in Tennessee, Arkansas, and Mississippi. The men allegedly chose diamonds and watches viewed on the Internet Web sites of jewelry dealers and then arranged to send payments by using the stolen credit card numbers or arranging for banks to wire the money. The merchandise was shipped to hotels whose addresses Jackson had provided to the banks and credit card companies as new billing addresses. The men then made reservations at the hotels in the names of victims and notified the hotels to expect packages to be delivered to the individuals, the government alleged. One of the victim's daughters learned of the scam after people claiming to be her mother called the Bank of New Hampshire trying to access the mother's checking account. The man making the call had the SSN and birth date, but the bank would not provide the information to the caller because the caller did not have the account number.

People: The Weak Link in Security

A government employee, equipped with secure computer systems, can make a poor decision. The *Detroit News* (*Gannett News Service*) told a story of Mr. Feakes (April 2000), underscoring the weak link in many systems, i.e., a careless employee filling "routine requests." Dave Feakes lived in Fressenden, North Dakota. Feakes purchased an independent insurance brokerage. Feakes received a call from his bank wanting to know why he had applied for a hefty loan to buy a new pickup when he had just taken one out for a new utility vehicle. A short time later a South Dakota bank called asking for payment on bounced checks totaling almost $9,000. Feakes then applied for a new driver's license. The clerk told Feakes he was not Dave Feakes. The computer spit out a license with Feakes's name and SSN but another man's photograph.

After two years of work, Feakes figured out what happened. The thief got a copy of Feakes's birth certificate for $10 from the state of North Dakota. The con man used the birth certificate to convince the driver license clerk to create a duplicate driver's license. With the license, birth certificate, and SSN, the con man called Feakes's bank. Using the lost-my-wallet story, the con man asked for Feakes's checking account information. The con man used this information to open new checking accounts and make purchases.

In each of these examples, those duped had access to various online information systems. The breakdown in "security" had little to do with online systems. The failures had a great deal to do with human nature. Despite the increased vulnerabilities of certain types of online transactions, security boils down to individual behavior. The only secure computer is one that has the plug pulled and sits in the middle of a locked room. When a person can get in the room, security is compromised.

Ignorance Equates to Vulnerability

Conjure up a mental picture of a theater. The stage is dark. The house lights are down. A magician takes the stage bathed in a spotlight. The audience can see every move the magician makes clearly. With a snap of the fingers, a person levitates. A few moments later, the magician pulls hundreds of colorful silk scarves from his mouth. A few people in the audience know how the magician performed his tricks. Those who lack this knowledge shake their heads in wonderment. "Magic," a few may say.

A pervasive network exists in such wired cities as Austin, Texas, Tokyo, Japan, and Helsinki, Finland, among others. Online connections are possible from mobile telephones that tuck into a pocket or a full-scale computer that nestles in a student's canvas backpack.

With an ease that rivals the magician's sleight of hand, a person can access an online service and whiz through electronic mail, buy and sell stock, or perform a mind-boggling array of functions. A newcomer to the online system often says, "Amazing" after first sampling online services.

System administrators can be gulled as easily as the average Internet user. If the blame could be placed on the Internet user, security would be a simpler problem. The user can do everything right and still be robbed of a credit card number or worse. There are dozens of tricks a hacker can use to steal information from a server. Many of these lie solely within the control of the system administrator for an Internet Service Provider (ISP) or an organization's network administrator.

Networks, like personal computers, have to be set up. Each network operating system (NOS) has dozens, if not hundreds, of specialized settings. Harried network administrators or careless systems engineers may accept the default values when building a network.

Most users are blithely ignorant when the network they use has been compromised. Some systems can be entered improperly simply by using the command prompt and a telnet session to log into the server. Some servers offer file transfer protocol (ftp) services. These sites can be viewed by anyone with the ftp products that come with most operating systems.

A crook can use utilities like those created by Blue Squirrel Software or Soft Byte Labs' Black Widow. Black Widow, which costs about $40, can scan a Web site and present found files in an Explorer-like window. The user can retrieve just about any files associated with the site as long as other pages have a link to them. Unlinked "gems" reward the spider's user. Black Widow also features resumable downloads for those hard-to-get files. It is compatible with HTTP and HTTPS server types. Black Widow is an off-line browser, a site scanner, a site-mapping tool, and a "site ripper."

A person with more technical savvy may want to use the "rootkit" to snag system and user data. A rootkit places special entries in the root of a server. These entries are then used by the hacker to create a back door to the system. A Trojan horse "time bomb" utility can include a time-to-run function that allows a cracker to execute a hidden series of tasks or daemons without the user's knowledge. This type of attack can then come to life when the user is off work. These hidden tasks can then create or exploit vulnerabilities in a system.[10]

Criminals with a strong technical background can modify the operating system kernel itself by recompiling the operating system. Patches can be added to the operating system that provide the criminal with administrator privileges or routines installed that scour the server for data, compress it, and send it by electronic mail to the criminal. Another approach is to add a new kernel module to the operating system. The "enhancement" allows the criminal to access the system or perform one or more specific tasks designed to compromise privacy and security.[11]

Once a criminal has root or administrator privileges, the system is not secure. A list of cracker actions facilitated by these tricks includes the following:

- Rootkits. A rootkit is a group of programs (modifications of regularly used system programs) that help an intruder remain undetected after he or she has already compromised a system, for example, a modified "ls" program. Normally "ls" lists files, but a rootkit version may prevent the intruder's files from being listed when the true system administrator runs the command.

- Password poaching. The intruder obtains user names and passwords. With these key pieces of information, the cracker can enter new systems with the identity of the original user.

- Account takeover. The intruder uses the accounts of the true user for his or her own purposes, including setting up a person's electronic mail account. Bogus electronic mail accounts are frequently used to verify passwords for certain commercial sites. Thus, a criminal armed with an e-mail identity and a credit card can pyramid other scams masquerading as another person.

- Fraudulent transactions. The intruder uses the existing accounts to make fraudulent purchases. A drop address is required, gleaned from information on the server. When the delivery arrives, the cracker arranges for a third-party to "sign" for the package or if no signature is required, accept delivery.

- New account creation. Using the data found on the server or in electronic mail, the criminal creates new accounts in the name of one or more people whose information was hijacked.

Figure 4.4 provides a summary of 12 ways information can be obtained to gain access to personal details about an individual. With the right pieces of information, anyone's identity can be compromised.

One of the more interesting software tools available for monitoring a person's Internet activities is called Spector 2.1. Once installed on an individual's computer, Spector records PC and Internet activity, much like a camcorder, and lets the person who installed the software play back the recorded information. Spector records all applications loaded, all Web sites visited, all chat conversations, and all incoming and outgoing e-mail activity. One can see whatever the personal computer user sees. Spector is one of the first automatic screen recording software designed for consumers and corporations. The software automatically takes snapshots of the display screen, as often as once per second, or as infrequently as once every few minutes.[12]

An interesting service is available from Docusearch. The operation is staffed by licensed private investigators. A selection of the reports the firm offers includes locating a person using an SSN or a person's name, searching for neighbors or date of birth, and finding a current address for an associated telephone number. The firm says this about itself:

Docusearch.com offers an array of informative searches designed to help you find the information you need to know, today! No matter where you live in this world; you can now access data about people residing in the United States. This is the information age, and information is

Twelve Tactics for Stealing Personal Information

Tactic	How It Works
Dumpster dive or steal a person's mail to locate credit card numbers, bank statement, or other information.	One or more people go through discarded materials. The tactic is one of the most reliable and easily used by professional and amateur alike.
Capture personal information from an Internet user.	Ask for information as part of a qualification for accessing a site.
Place a small file on a user's computer that tracks the user's actions.	The "cookie" allows an Internet site to record a wide range of information about a user's actions. This includes sites visited, files downloaded, etc.
Intercept electronic mail.	Electronic mail can be intercepted by anyone with access to the mail server account. In an ISP or information technology department, usually two or more people will have access to the mail accounts. These individuals can copy, read, and delete any mail that resides within the system. Encrypting electronic mail is a must.[13]
Steal a laptop or notebook.	A thief grabs a computer in a notebook. Instead of taking the notebook out of the airport, the thief sits down, looks for passwords and other useful data, then discards the notebook.
Create a fake electronic commerce site, offer products at a great price, and require detailed personal information from would-be buyers.	A person creates a Web site and uses it to capture an individual's credit card information, shipping address, and other details. These data can be used by the thief or re-sold via the Internet to other individuals.
Snoop within a personal computer.	A person gains access to a home or office legally or illegally and looks for passwords or personal information on machines or networks.
Gain unauthorized access to an online system and place programs on the server to allow an unauthorized person to access the system.	Unless properly set up and protected, computers hooked to a network can be located and accessed by those with knowledge about networked computers.
Ask for the information or "social engineering."	Identify an AOL user. Call the person and ask for account information in order to verify that the system is working properly.
Walk up to a computer and look for passwords and logon instructions taped to the monitor, the desktop, or wall.	Users have difficulty remembering passwords and complicated login instructions. So they leave them around.
Create a public posting in a UseNet forum. Provide a URL or link to a Web page with a form posted asking for more information.	The person creating the link to the form can ask the duped Internet user for credit information and other data. These data can be used by the thief or sold to another party to use.
Use public information sources.	Individuals and Web sites provide SSNs, personal profiles, and background information for a fee. The person wanting information goes to a Web site or hires a person to obtain the data.

Figure 4.4   Twelve tactics for stealing personal information.

power! Controversial? Maybe, but wouldn't you sleep easier knowing a little bit more about a prospective business
partner, employee, babysitter, neighbor or significant
other? All search requests are ordered here, on our secure
server and the results are posted to a password protected
client area, where you can view them in the comfort and
privacy of your home or office. All information obtained is
held in strict confidence and no one is alerted or notified
of your search (including the Subject). Today begins a new
era in the information age. Don't be left in the dark.[14]

The company's fees range from $14 for a telephone number trace
to $249 for a corporate bank account. Customers settle their accounts
online with a credit card, by facsimile with the credit card information, or by traditional mail service.

Not surprisingly, different cultures react in ways that some
American marketers find peculiar, even perverse. The European
Union takes a dim view of the American habit of mining databases,
reselling electronic mail addresses, and generally stripping an individual of his or her privacy. Europeans are nervous about the exploits
of their criminals as well. In June 2000, a computer cracker breached
the security of an Internet Service Provider (ISP) in Great Britain and
tapped into credit card data for 24,000 users. The victims included
scientists at the top-secret Defence Evaluation and Research Agency,
senior government officials, and senior managers at British Broadcasting Corporation.

Various studies of abuses of Internet privacy point to a growing
concern about the unaccountability of enterprises operating in the
Internet ecology.[15] Internet users put less faith in the government than
in enterprises. Not surprisingly, males between the ages of 19 and 25
are most likely to exchange information over the Internet. Trusted
Web sites by mainstream Web users in the United States include
Yahoo! and established financial institutions.[16]

Mathematics and Privacy Empower
Data Mining

The difficulties faced by online advertising companies selling banner ads can be summed up in a single thought: People ignore them.
To get around this, these companies have increased their efforts to
track the public's surfing habits with "cookies," small files of code
sent from one computer to another, that can identify users and monitor their actions as they negotiate the Web.

Through data mining's recursive mathematics, software can locate and identify actions that fit together. An example would be American Express's use of Cross Z fractal technology to determine from all American Express credit card transactions on Mother's Day what related purchases fit in the cluster of buyers. Link analysis is the mathematical process of identifying probable causal relationships.

As online systems become as common as automatic cash machines and as easy to use, the likelihood of security problems, including identity-related crimes, rises. Millions of Internet users key in their name, address, home and work telephone, facsimile, electronic mail address, and credit card number with only a moment's hesitation and sometimes not even that.

Double Click, an Internet direct marketing company, acquired a company that aggregates marketing data and matches it to consumers' names, addresses, and affinity group or cluster.[17] Double Click bought Abacus, another firm specializing in data extraction and analysis. Double Click said that it would use software from the two firms to blend its data for more precise marketing. Double Click stepped over the line. The Federal Trade Commission (FTC) pounced, and the stock quickly shed value. Double Click, Engage, and AdForce, among others, quickly changed their tune in response to a privacy backlash. The tactics have changed. The mathematical algorithms still run, but these companies have changed their positioning strategy.

There are many data mining companies. Some, like Cognos, are esoteric. Others are designed for Web marketers who want to run marketing campaigns to exploit similarities or tendencies in clusters of buyers. Internet sites use products from companies like Net Perceptions. The approach is to "fuzzify" statistics. In this mathematical technique, an individual user is placed in a cluster. The tendencies of the cluster are analyzed and useful information extracted and written to a report the marketer can use for an electronic mail campaign or a Web marketing program.

The trajectory of data mining technology is moving rapidly. The opt-in marketing company, Promotions.com, makes a strong point in its advertisements about respecting the privacy of individual users, but the company uses comparatively low-power algorithms.[18] In fact, most of the popular Internet-centric tools are not much more than undergraduate statistical routines spiffed up and rerigged for the Web. The industrial-strength programs, widely used in police and government intelligence work, are making their way into the commercial marketplace.

The Federal Bureau of Investigation (FBI) uses a system called "Carnivore" that reads electronic mail, figures out the meaning, and routes the possibly useful messages from criminal suspects to FBI analysts.[19] Carnivore must be installed with the assistance of ISPs who handle mail. The system eavesdrops without the suspects knowing their message traffic has been compromised. The throughput of the system is in excess of six gigabytes (about six billion bytes or two million electronic mail messages) every 24 hours. Carnivore, in the parlance of security professionals, is a sniffer. Like other sniffers, it cannot process encrypted messages encoded with such tools as Pretty Good Privacy (PGP) or an equivalent software program.[20]

The digitization of information allows a person with the requisite knowledge to assemble a composite report on one or more people rapidly. The military and police have used products from such companies as i2 Limited (Cambridge, England) that can process telephone bills, credit card statements, field operatives' notes, and other types of data and create a visual picture of the relationships that exist among events and people. A typical visual representation of this type of system's outputs appears in Figure 4.5.

A computer user—whether by design as a Web surfer or by accident when making a mobile telephone call—leaves a well-marked trail of bright yellow digital footprints. Programs like i2 Limited's read these footprints and produce a visual picture of user actions. If a link

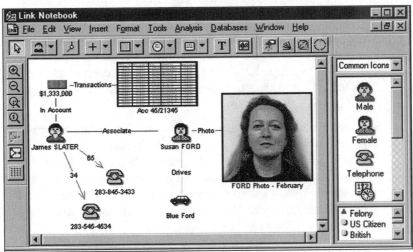

Figure 4.5   Cambridge-based i2 Limited's software can process a wide range of data sources and construct an illustrated link diagram. A click on an object in the diagram will display the source data. An Excel table and a mug shot are shown on the "Link Notebook" screen.

exists between a footprint and a picture, the image of the person will appear in the report. What types of systems leave digital footprints?

- Mobile telephones that can pinpoint one's location within three meters. Mobile telephones transmit their locations to the systems that route calls to them. These data can be and are captured for various purposes.

- Banks that surreptitiously sell your financial secrets. The new publication *iMarketing News* contains dozens of advertisements for electronic mailing lists and demographic reports from major sites that resell customer data.[21] Most of these lists are based on the customer's providing permission to the site operator to send electronic mail and use the name for marketing purposes. Resale of the data is one "marketing purpose."

- Computer technology that secretly profiles you when you go online. These are the ubiquitous "cookies."

- A healthcare system that shares medical information. Med Records Web's (www.medrecordsweb.com) site operators say, "We believe at Med Records Web, Inc., that a patient, attorney, or insurance company should not have to face hurdles when it comes to obtaining copies of medical records fast and efficiently for self or for clients." The fee? $24.99 for 200 pages or less delivered online.

- Airport scanning devices that see and "sniff" for trace gases on your person and in your luggage. International points of entry are equipped with sophisticated online systems that match passport data to other databases from such companies as CPS Systems (Australia).[22]

- Tiny surveillance cameras everywhere: workplaces, campuses, lobbies, elevators, restaurants, locker rooms. Web-centric video is revolutionizing surveillance. For a sampling of what can be accomplished with "hidden cams," take a quick click to www.guzei.com/live/camera. Be sure to load the Cyrillic character set. To buy a hidden cam outfit, consider Surveillance Solution's products.[23]

- Growing pressure to require all Americans to carry a national identification card and DNA registries for everyone that would permit tracking.

The American Bar Association offers some useful tips as shown in Figure 4.6.[24]

A Digital Bulletproof Vest: Checklist For Preventing Credit/Identity Theft

Category	Detail
Key information to guard from identity thieves	SSN Maiden names Birth date Past addresses Driver's license number
How criminals get your data	Ordering credit reports Asking in a seemingly harmless way Digging through garbage Stealing mail Snatching purses Learning it from the victim—for example, from résumés or family genealogies posted online
Prevention tips	Don't give out your SSN unless necessary (i.e., not to merchants who don't really need it) Request your credit report regularly Shred personal documents before putting them in the trash Check W-2 for extra earnings (it could indicate someone else working under your name)
Victim assistance	Privacy Rights Clearinghouse: 619-298-3396, www.privacyrights.org U.S. Public Interest Research Group: 202-546-9707, www.pirg.org/uspirg Contact www.identitytheft.org Contact the FTC at 877-438-4338 Report the problem to the FBI at www.ifcc.fbi.gov Contact the local police

Figure 4.6   A digital bulletproof vest.

Legislation or Technology?

Security legislation continues to flow from Washington, DC, the European Union, and various countries where the Internet has swept into the lives of citizens and businesses. In the United States in June 2000, the FTC issued a call for privacy legislation. There were almost two dozen privacy bills moving through Congress in an election year.

The Platform for Privacy Preferences Project, usually referred to by the acronym P3P, began in 1997 at the Massachusetts Institute of Technology, under the auspices of the World Wide Web Consortium (W3C). The P3P initiative focuses on devising software that standardizes Internet privacy policies and renders them in clear, easy-to-understand English. The partners in P3P are IBM, AT&T, Microsoft Corporation, American Express, Nokia, and the Direct Marketing Association.

P3P works by asking the Internet user to complete a form that captures privacy preferences. Each P3P compliant site will use the privacy preferences to match the user's privacy preferences with the privacy policies of each site. If the site's and the user's privacy preferences do not match, the user is given the option of overriding his or her privacy preferences and accessing the site. If the user does not want to visit a site that falls below the user's privacy threshold, the user's browser does not log on to the site. P3P does not block access to a site nor does it provide any data to a site that the user has not agreed to provide. A formal P3P specification was posted on the Internet late in 2000 (www.w3.org/TR/P3P).

The General Services Administration created the position of a computer security "czar." The person in this position will facilitate the establishment of governmentwide security policy and guidelines across the entire government and work with the Office of Management and Budget to enforce these policies and guidelines.[25]

The U.S. government federal Chief Information Officers' Council has set up a Privacy, Security, and Critical Infrastructure subcommittee. This group will explore PKI, electronic signatures, and encryption. The Department of Defense and the National Institute of Standards and Technology (NIST) have established technical working groups to address PKI and fund pilot programs. States are jumping on the bandwagon. Political in-fighting is evident between the FTC and the Software and Information Industry Association (SIIA) over the role of the U.S. government.

Many Web sites have privacy statements, but they are often difficult to find, written in legalese, and enforced sometimes loosely, sometimes not at all.

For the foreseeable future, Internet users should guard their privacy with encryption and common sense. Companies and organizations will want to buy specialized services and tools from such firms as Internet Security Systems, an enterprise with more than 21 of the top 25 U.S. financial institutions.[26] The Golden Age of Online may be on the way, but the dark clouds of privacy and security could trigger an Ice Age in a click of Internet time.

References

1. These data come from a recent study sponsored by Peoplesoft. The results were posted by Nua, an Internet consultancy, in July 2000.

2. A Charge-Coupled Device (CCD) lens is a combination of optical and digital technology. The light strikes the device, the image is converted into ones and zeroes, and can be immediately fed to a server for real-time access via the Internet to the image and sound captured by the camera.

3. Toysmart got in hot water when it advertised the sale of its customer list in the *Wall Street Journal*. The U.S. Federal Trade Commission has taken action to halt the sale of Toysmart's customer database. After Toysmart went out of business, its principal asset was the customer data. Walt Disney Co., a principal owner of Toysmart, has been tarred by the uproar over privacy concerns that exploded in a class action suit to block the sale of personal data that Toysmart allegedly said it would never divulge. Other companies that may sell customer information include Boo.com and CraftShop.com.

4. Lisa M. Bowman, *ZDNet News*, AOL/Netscape hit with privacy lawsuit, July 7, 2000.

5. *Reuters*, "AOL Says Hackers Broke into Some Member Accounts," June 16, 2000.

6. *Where Wizards Stay Up Late: The Origins of the Internet*, by Katie Hafner, Matthew Lyon. (January 1998).

7. www.privacytimes.com and the newsletter are published by Evan Hendricks.

8. www.anonymizer.com. Other companies offering software services for user anonymity include Freedom by Zero Knowledge Systems and Norton Internet Security by Symantec.

9. Any electronic mail software that supports Hypertext Markup Language (HTML) can embed an active link to another site in the text of a message. The only safeguard is to complete personal information forms on sites where the integrity of the operator is known. Providing personal data to an unknown site is risky.

10. For more information about Trojan horse programs, see www.securityfocus. com and www.2600.com, among others. A search of www.deja.com or www.remarq. com can yield useful information about these cracking techniques.

11. System administrators must be required to review security logs. Organizations without a system administrator oversight function are at risk. Windows 2000 security can be supplemented with third-party products like RSA Security's SecrID (www.rsasecurity.com). In Windows NT and 2000, the system event viewer and policy change services provide clues to cracker activity.

12. The software is available at www.child-monitor.com/spector. It costs about $50.

13. A well-known encryption system is Pretty Good Privacy (PGP). Once the user installs the software and signs up, an encryption key is issued. A privacy key looks like this: 42 57 B3 D2 39 8E 74 C3 5E 4D AC 43 25 D2 26 D4. The software is available at http://web.mit.edu/network/pgp.html.

14. The site is located at www.docusearch.com.

15. See the Cheskin Research Web site at www.cheskin.com for information about the relationship of privacy and trust in different countries.

16. *Business 2.0*, July 2000, provides a summary of trust factors in Internet space. See pages 166 *ff*.
17. Cluster analysis is the chief claim to fame for Claritas. However, Claritas cluster analyses can easily reach six figures. Lower cost services have sprouted to meet the demand for rough-and-ready clustering.
18. Opt-in means that the person completing an electronic mail or paper form checks a box that gives the recipient of the card permission to use the electronic mail address in other marketing programs.
19. On the international front, Echelon performs that same function. The U.S. National Security Agency (NSA) is participating in this program with Great Britain and Australia, among other countries.
20. Encrypted messages can be "broken" or decoded. Encrypted messages must be processed by separate subsystems. The security agencies classify the methods for breaking encrypted messages in the hopes of keeping an advantage over individuals who believe encrypted messages are secure.
21. *iMarketing News* is a publication of Mill Hollow Corporation. The editorial office is at 100 Sixth Avenue, New York, NY 10013. The firm's Web site is www. dmnews.com.
22. For information about the CPS Systems "border" products, visit www.cps.com.
23. The TSS catalog is located at http://shopping.epix.net/cgi-bin/surveillance solutions/index.html.
24. www.abanet.org/journal/oct98/10FIDSB.HTML
25. The first person to hold this position is Barry C. West. He can be reached at barry.west@gsa.gov.
26. The company's Web site is located at www.iss.net.

CHAPTER 5

Brother Have You Got a Dime?
Charity Scams on the Web

Carol Ebbinghouse

It happened fast, really fast. Within hours of the destruction of the World Trade Center in New York on September 11, 2001, there were reports of online solicitations from "representatives" of charities[1] and relief agencies. Fortunately, many savvy recipients of such solicitations by e-mail and telephone were reluctant to give their credit card information to these solicitors and complained to law enforcement authorities. With good reason, it seems. The very next day ScamBusters posted:

> Make Sure Your Help Goes Where You Intended! In the wake of yesterday's events, publishing an issue of Internet ScamBusters was the last thing on our minds. Given the info below, we hope you'll see why we felt we had no other responsible option.

> We've received reports of spammers sending out calls for assistance for emergency relief funds, and directing the recipients to contribute money to the Red Cross—through the spammers' Web sites.

> Many of these spammers are trying to steal money and credit card numbers.

> Do NOT respond to these e-mails!

> If you wish to contribute money to an organization, we recommend that you do so directly through the organization's site, or to a local chapter. ...

> ... We normally don't ask this—and please make sure you do NOT spam this issue: however, we'd like you to

consider forwarding this issue of Internet ScamBusters to
people you know who are new to the Internet, as well as
those you think would benefit from this issue. These
sorts of scams are usually directed at inexperienced
surfers.

According to *Forbes* (June 25, 2001), some $150 million was con-
tributed online to health groups in 2000. The market for this type of
solicitation is enormous. If you put up a Web site and give it a name
that sounds like a disease-related research group or relief group there
are lots of people who will donate money. And it goes without saying that not all of these groups are legitimate. *Reuters* reported
(August 17, 2000) that Internet users are being bombarded with
sympathy e-mails that are fake, promising that for each address to
which you forward a specific e-mail with a tragic tale of a child in
need, that specific charities or corporations will donate money to the
ill child. They report that "one frequent message says the American
Red Cross will donate three cents to cancer research as part of 7-
year-old cancer patient Jessica Mydek's dying wish. Another says
the Make-A-Wish Foundation will pay seven cents toward the hospital bills of 7-year-old Amy Bruce, who it says is suffering from
lung cancer caused by secondhand smoke and a large brain tumor
caused by repeated beatings. Another making the rounds says BCC
Software will donate five cents to help with 7-year-old Kalin Relek's
operation for internal bleeding after he was struck by a car. But it
seems none of these 7-year-olds exists." All three organizations
denied any connection to these e-mails, and the two charities posted
messages on their sites disclaiming these fundraising efforts. The
American Red Cross and the Make-A-Wish Foundation are commonly used for this type of Internet charity scam.

But charity scams aren't limited to disasters or reports about dying
children. They function on smaller scales, more locally focused.
Recently, I pulled two envelopes enclosing two large, empty plastic
bags from off my doorknob. The outfits that had tagged my house
each wanted a donation of household goods to be placed in the bag
and left out for pick-up on different days. Each sounded familiar as a
recognized charity. I wanted to verify that a good cause would get my
old clothes and clock radio, so I looked them up on GuideStar
(www.guidestar.org/search/index.adp) and instantly discovered that
one was a local branch of a well-established national charity. The
other I could not verify, either as a national or local group. Now perhaps that second bag came from a benevolent group. I don't know, but
I wasn't going to take any chances that I could not legitimately deduct
the value of my donation from my income for tax purposes.

It took no time at all to decide to put some items out on Tuesday for the verified charity and not Wednesday for the unverified one. This little amount of effort—two extra minutes on the Internet—let me rest easy that my donated goods would go to a good, legitimate cause, and that I could deduct my contribution after getting a receipt from them for a noncash donation. It would have been that much easier for me if the organization's Web site address appeared on either envelope or even on the plastic bags!

Many legitimate charities use the Web to make it easy for us to find them, identify with their cause, bond with their organization, make contributions, and gather information to take to our employers for matching donations. It enables them to get their message out, without time-consuming photocopying or expensive postage for mailing their Form 990s (an official form required by the Internal Revenue Service or IRS), annual reports, and other documents that potential donors request. It's an ideal distribution mechanism for these bona fide organizations.

Unfortunately, it's also an ideal distribution mechanism for organizations that are not bona fide. For potential donors using the Web, there is good information available on the Web to help determine which organization is trustworthy and which isn't. A splashy Web site with fancy Java applications is not a definitive indication that the backers are legitimate. A copy of the Form 990 filed with the IRS is definitive that they are, but even better would be the listing of information about the organization, a directory of local affiliates or branches, contact information, and a description of the mission. Without the appropriate information and documents, donors cannot make an informed decision.

Intentional misinformation abounds in the world of charities and nonprofit organizations. According to the Better Business Bureau (BBB), "The public needs to be just as cautious in reacting to the Internet appeals as they would in response to any other solicitation effort, if not more so. The BBB encourages people to go to www.give.org with all of its information on whether a charity meets their standards or not. A recently issued exposure draft of new charity standards contains provisions addressing Internet related issues. What distinguishes the BBB is the comprehensiveness of the evaluations (990 forms, plus other documents, etc.) in determing whether a particular charity meets these standards. The public can also file a complaint against a charity in connection with their Internet activity with the BBB. High tech does not necessarily mean high ethics."[2] Even if one gives the dozens of national charities the benefit of the doubt and attributes the absence of annual reports on their Web sites to oversight rather than deliberate misinformation, the attitude of the BBB reflects the high standards people should set for charities, on or off the Net. Every dollar contributed to fraudulent charities or misspent in unnecessary administrative expenditures is a dollar that fails to reach someone in dire need.

The report goes on to describe various apparent charities that through misinformation (especially in chain letters) or missing information mislead those seeking to do some good in the world. It points out that government regulation is not ready yet to go after Internet perpetrators. "The full Internet role for state government agencies is still being formed. For example, questions as to whether groups soliciting on the Internet need to register with all of the existing state charity registration offices has yet to be clearly answered. It will probably take time for these issues to be hammered out ... but please remember that registration with a state agency does not constitute approval or endorsement by the state. ... The deceitful possibilities are as limitless as the con artists' imagination and they don't even need to pack a bag when they decide to 'leave their Web address.'"

The Council of Better Business Bureaus (CBBB) Foundation has circulated a discussion document to establish accountability issues in the third revision of the CBBB Standards for Charitable Solicitations at www.give.org/srp/preface.asp. Among the other issues, the standards discussion will address "accuracy of financial reporting."

The Watchdogs

Different types of organizations are actively involved in this arena. Among them, nonprofit organizations such as the National Charities Information Bureau at www.give.org or www.ncib.org, the National Center for Charitable Statistics at www.nccs.urban.org, the Better Business Bureau Online[3] (BBB and BBBOnline), government agencies such as the IRS,[4] the Federal Trade Commission[5] (FTC), state Attorneys General offices[6] and others.[7] Some nonprofit organizations[8] specifically study the nonprofit sector and report on statistics[9] of giving. Finally, there are individuals[10] who collect information for nonprofits struggling to comply with myriad federal and state disclosure rules, nonprofit accountability standards, and evaluation criteria tools, as well as other public accountability resources.

Several organizations perform their own research on individual charities and prepare reports for consumers and businesses. In particular, the NCIB and Charitable Choices survey hundreds of charities and provide detailed information about them on the Internet. According to Charitable Choices (www.charitablechoices.org/howtouse.asp), they built this site to make it easy for you to learn a lot about a broad range of *accountable* charities. It's such a valuable resource we're including an excerpt here:

How to find charities:

> By what they do: On our home page, you can click on any of 25 categories, ranging from "Aging" to "Youth." You will get a list of charities whose work fits these categories.

> By location: Also on our home page, you can get a list of charities working nationally or internationally or a list of charities working in the DC metropolitan area.

> By using our alphabetical index.

What you will find:

> Each charity's mailing, e-mail and Web addresses, as well as its phone and fax numbers.

> A brief description of its work and the year it began.

> How much it spends on fund-raising and administrative costs. (This percentage is determined by the federal government and is based on an analysis of the reports each charity must file every year with the Internal Revenue Service.)

> Its 4-digit Combined Federal Campaign number.

> Its answers to basic questions many donors ask about charities:

>> Why do you exist?

>> What have you accomplished?

>> How do you help people in my community?

>> Why do you need my support?

>> How can I be sure you will use my money wisely and won't waste it?

Other groups post IRS Form 990s along with their own information on individual charities on the Internet for donors to search. The American Institute of Philanthropy (AIP) is a watchdog group (www.charitywatch.org) that helps donors looking for reliable information about charities by searching out complete information on charities and providing information missing from charitable organization reports. It's a definite stopping point before opening your checkbook. It maintains a *Rating Guide,* which "gives a letter grade rating and other statistics on the financial performance of about 400 major American charities ... provides information on the percentage of funds each charity spends on its charitable purpose, its cost to raise $100, whether it holds massive asset reserves, and an overall grade from 'A+' to 'F'." Before you send a donation to a specific group, you can consider how well they spend your dollars by referring to the AIP's *Charity Rating Guide.*

For less known local organizations, as well as the large ones, you might try the GuideStar site's database of over 620,000 charities. The online information on my local "Friends of the Library" included financial data, a .pdf file of the entire IRS Form 990, the employer ID number, address and contact information, programs and activities, the amount of any donation that is deductible, and explanations of the financial data and Form 990.

Other watchdog organizations follow groups claiming to donate a portion of their sales profits to charities and/or those claiming to provide training and jobs for the poor or disabled. See Figure 5.1 for additional tips.

The Independent Sector has prepared a "Donor Bill of Rights" for full and accurate information about not-for-profit organizations and "A Checklist of Accountability." That checklist recommends that nonprofit organizations be responsible to the public by disseminating and making available the current IRS form, the IRS form 1023, most recent financial audit report, annual report, governing documents, a list of board members and officers, staff roster, and their long-range plan.

Finally there are charity portals[11] and individual charity Web sites that accept donations directly to a charity. The charity portals have widely different approaches: Some are nonprofits themselves (e.g., www.netaid.org), while others are commercial (www.helping.org). The commercial portals may make their money from selling advertising banners and/or taking a percentage or flat fee for each donation sent to a charity. If the charities have to pay for the ads or make a percentage contribution, that diminishes the money available for the charity to dispense to those in need, but there is no intent to defraud or mislead involved. If for-profit concerns pay for the ads to get the credit for their corporate consciences, then the commercial charity portal would have less need to cut into the charity's revenue.

These kinds of issues have led many nonprofits to set up their own Web sites for accepting online donations directly. The field is growing:

Charitable Shopping Sites

Before you give online to a charitable shopping site make sure the site is legitimate. If you cannot locate any other information about the site on the Web, don't shop there. There are plenty of other virtual shops for a cause. A few of the more frequently mentioned sites that "contribute" a percentage of their profits to specified charities include www.igive.com, www.4charity.com, and www.greatergood.com. However, there are many, many more, such as www.afundraiser.com and www.webcharity.com.

A final caveat: Check the "terms and conditions" as well as any privacy and security policies *before* you register, contribute, or order anything from these sites. Most belong to privacy organizations, but that really just means that they disclose what they do with your personal information; it does not mean that they never disclose your data. You may find yourself getting mounds of e-mails, spams, and charitable as well as other solicitations from organizations you have never heard of. You might find yourself on some new e-newsletter mailing list dealing with a cause you abhor. Be careful. Trust no one with your personal information. If you do decide to register on a site, or contribute to some cause, or order a product for which a percentage goes to a charity, look for an opt-out option in the privacy disclosure statement to keep your information secure.

Figure 5.1   Charitable shopping sites.

The Red Cross raised $170,000 on its Web site in fiscal 1998; in FY1999 (ending July 1, 1999), donations grew to $2.5 million. However, in just the first two weeks after the World Trade Center disaster of September 11, 2001, the Red Cross raised over $200 million.

Businesses Give, Too

Businesses are especially vulnerable to solicitations by charities. Services that provide information for charitably minded businesses include the FTC,[12] the BBB,[13] and the National Fraud Information Center.[14]

Businesses should be especially wary. Follow the suggestions from the FTC.[15] The BBB[16] has a number of publications with general business guidelines on business giving along with tips on charitable giving and tax deductions for charitable contributions (in addition to publications on avoiding other schemes and scams against businesses). The BBB Guidelines for Business Giving[17] provide questions businesspeople should ask when solicited for canisters on sales counters, tickets to cultural "benefit" events, advertising in charity publications, offers of merchandise,[18] and marketing proposals that promise that the purchase of a product of ABC Corporation will generate a contribution to XYZ charity.

Using the Web to Avoid Charity Scams

Not only is the Web a mechanism for perpetrating charity scams, it can also be used to avoid them. Here are some rules to follow when evaluating charity sites on the Web and deciding where to donate, whether it's your money, your time, or your used automobile.[19]

1. Know the charity's name, purpose, or mission, how it attempts to achieve its goals, and how much of each dollar donated goes to charitable purposes. Local charities are easier to become familiar with; you can meet and volunteer with the leadership directly, and if you suspect some wrongdoing, go to local law enforcement authorities. Be wary if the charity sounds like a charity you know. Check it out (with one of the sources below) before you give.

2. Whether solicited on the phone or in person, always ask for identification.

3. Before you give, go to the following sites to locate special reports on the particular charity:

   - www.guidestar.org/index.adp to search the GuideStar database on more than 620,000 nonprofit organizations. Even small local nonprofits are listed here.

   - www.bbb.org/reports/charity.asp for BBB reports on specific charitable organizations. Extremely thorough reports, although best coverage is of national organizations.

   - www.charitywatch.org/list.html#p for AIP's Charity Rating list of organizations.

   - www.give.org/reports/index.asp provides a sample report and a searchable database of charities that have been investigated.

   - www.charitablechoices.org to locate approved charities by name or category.

   - www.give.org/links/govregs.asp for state agency information on the charity and www.give.org/links/infosource.asp for links to state and other organizations with information, in addition to www.mcf.org/mcf/links/nat_phil.htm. Many of these sites have searchable databases of registered or member organizations. These are your last/best chances for finding local organizations that you could not locate at the sites listed earlier.

4. If not already located, determine whether it is really a tax-deductible vs. a tax-exempt organization according to the IRS at apps.irs.gov/search/eosearch.html.

5. Locate the IRS Form 990 at either www.guidestar.org or www.nccs.urban.org/990.

6. Check any state agency records in your state through the BBB Wise Giving Alliance with Give.org (www.give.org/links/govregs.asp).

7. Get the charity's phone number and contact the charity by phone to make sure it exists. Request a copy of the charity's annual report that includes a list of members of the governing body, audited financial statements, description of program, along with a statement of functional expenses (to see how it allocates "overhead" among the program categories in the budget). Also ask for descriptive and financial information for all revenue-generating activities (fees for service, for-profit subsidiaries, payment from for-profit organizations to use the organization's name (such as affinity credit cards, licensing agreements, shop-for-a-cause promotions, etc.). Ask for proof that your contribution is tax deductible. Honest charities encourage your interest. If you were solicited, ask if the charity has authorized the use of its name by the solicitor (to avoid dealing with a fraudulent solicitor), and be especially careful to call if the request comes from a local public safety organization (e.g., law enforcement or firefighters). If you don't already have a copy, request the organization's IRS Form 990. It must provide this form to you at a reasonable time and place (although it may charge a reasonable fee for making copies). If it doesn't, you can go straight to: IRS Customer Service office, TE/GE Division, Customer Service, P.O. Box 2508, Cincinnati, OH 45201, or call (877) 829-5500 (toll-free). If the form is incomplete, there are other sanctions.

8. If you represent a business, ask questions specifically relevant to business solicitations at www.bbb.org/library/busgive.asp.

9. Always get a receipt for any donation, and only use a check unless you are familiar with the charity. Only after you know the charity well should you consider using a

credit card. If you use a credit card, make sure the site safely encrypts your information. Have one place where you keep all records of your donations.

When to Suspect a Scam

1. If there is high pressure to contribute or if the organization only wants cash. Always make any check out to the full name of the charity, not just the initials or the solicitor's name.

2. If you ask for literature on the organization, beware if there "isn't time" to send written material.

3. If you are told you have won money or a valuable prize but never entered a competition.

4. If an organization wants to pick up your contribution rather than use the U.S. mail (mail fraud is a federal crime).

5. If you get an invoice claiming that you have made a pledge when you have not. This is illegal.

6. If a solicitor won't tell you if he or she works for a commercial fundraiser and is being paid. If he or she is, ask for the name of the commercial fundraiser and for proof of registration with the state. Call the charity to determine whether it authorized the solicitor.

7. If a solicitor threatens you, hang up and call the local consumer fraud division of your local district attorney's office and the BBB.

How to Report a Possible Charity Scam

What do you do when you suspect wrongdoing? How do you investigate a nonprofit organization? To whom should you turn to if you suspect fraud? There are several courses of action on the state, federal, and self-help level. These are the same as you should follow when you suspect fraud in the world of bricks and mortar.

First, gather all the information you can. File complaints with the Attorney General[20] for your state,[21] the Secretary of State,[22] local (city and/or county) agencies with which charities soliciting in your state must register, the local (city or county) prosecutor or District Attorney, as well as the FTC[23] and the IRS.[24] Government agencies differ in their ability to prosecute abusive charities, ones that use misleading solicitations or misuse funds raised from the public. On occasion, a number of states will jointly prosecute a particularly abusive charity. These actions frequently result in fines and an agreement to stop conducting the abusive activities. Reports to the FTC, SEC, and the National Fraud Information Center go into a central database that local, state, and federal prosecutors can search. Report Internet fraud incidents to the National Fraud Information Center at www.fraud.org/internet/intset.htm.

The federal government decides whether an organization qualifies as tax-exempt or not, while the states are supposed to ensure that charitable organizations actually behave that way. However, the IRS has a new power. It may now impose sanctions on individuals who abuse their positions of control over charities for their personal benefit. Until recently, the IRS could only punish the organization itself.

If you suspect that the leadership in a charity has diverted or mismanaged funds, or defrauded a charity, contact both the Attorney General in your state and the IRS. These offices may go after the directors to recover any missing funds and return them to the charity. Watch out for self-dealing between directors and the charity by trustees. Also be alert to any loans from the charity to a director or officer, losses of charitable assets through speculative investments, or excessive amounts paid for salaries, benefits, travel, entertainment, legal, and other professional services. Watch for any sale of charity assets to "for profits" at a price unfair to the charity or any other illegal use of charitable funds. Of course, if you suspect criminal activity, go directly to the local prosecutor or district attorney of the local charity.

Besides government agencies, you can also file an inquiry with the BBB's Wise Giving Alliance; it may, with enough inquiries, investigate.[25] You can locate your nearest BBB office, or the office nearest the subject of your complaint, by going to www.bbb.org/bureaus/ index.asp. Their online consumer complaint form is available on the Internet.[26] The BBB maintains an Internet library of tips on scams directed at businesses[27] and provides "alerts" dealing with new types of "scams" as they are discovered.

Don't let these potential pitfalls stop you from making charitable contributions. Use the Web to inform yourself about the legitimate organizations you admire, and then make that donation. Donors and organizations alike can benefit from taking full advantage of the resources and information opportunities online. The Internet's a natural access point for those who want to feel good by doing good. Just be discriminating about the information you use, no matter the medium.

References

1. The government responded to the questionable solicitations in a special report at www.usdoj.gov/criminal/fraud/WTCPent-SpecRpt.htm, and the Better Business Bureau also alerted consumers and businesses at www.give.org/news/Sept2001.asp.

2. Comments from interview with Bennett Weiner of the Better Business Bureau, February 26, 2002.

3. See www.give.org/reports/index.asp . You can get reports on individual charities from Give.org, that merged with the BBB's Philanthropic Advisory Service (PAS).

4. See http://apps.irs.gov/search/eosearch.html for more information.

5. See www.ftc.gov/bcp/conline/pubs/tmarkg/charity.htm for more information. To file a complaint about a charity, go to https://rn.ftc.gov/dod/wsolcq$.startup? Z_ORG_CODE=PU01 or https://www.ftc.gov/ftc/complaint.htm.

6. Go to www.give.org/links/govregs.asp for a list of the agencies that regulate charities in each of the states. See the National Association of Attorneys General at www.naag.org/ag/full_ag_table.cfm and www.pueblo.gsa.gov/crh/state.htm for state and county offices. See www.caag.state.ca.us/charities/faq.htm for information on California charities.

7. The BBB and Give.org have compiled a list of many government and private agencies by state, available at www.give.org/links/govregs.asp. The NCIB has also compiled a state-by-state list of government regulators that permit examination of financial data pertaining to charities within that state or out-of-state charities that raise funds within the state.

8. For information and statistics on the nonprofit sector, see the American Association of Fund Raising Counsel at www.aafrc.org, the Independent Sector at www.independentsector.org, the National Center for Charitable Statistics at www.nccs.urban.org, and/or The Nonprofit Almanac in your local library. In the field of foundations and grants, go to the Foundation Center with its wealth of information at www.fdncenter.org/onlib/index.html.

9. The Form 990 Nonprofit Accountability Collaborative (990-NAC) first met on October 14, 1998. Also known as the National 990-NAC, this collaborative develops sectorwide support to improve the quality of reporting on the Form 990. National 990-NAC participants include representatives from numerous nonprofit organizations, the IRS, state regulators, the accounting profession, and researchers. Lists of these and other organizations (with links) appear at www.qual990.org/nat_990_nac.html and www.qual990.org/participants_loc.html.

10. Eric Mercer is one individual who has compiled a series of Web sites such as www.muridae.com/publicaccess/accountability.html. The pages usually indicate a "last updated" date. All the links to other interested organizations and government sites worked for me. "The Internet Nonprofit Center is a project of The Evergreen State Society of Seattle, Washington. It offers information for and about nonprofit organizations in the United States" at www.nonprofits.org.

11. For example, see www.charitygift.com that provides for direct donations as well as gifts in honor of a friend or loved one.

12. See www.ftc.gov/bcp/conline/pubs/buspubs/donating.htm and www.ftc.gov/bcp/conline/edcams/giving/index.html.
13. See www.bbbonline.org.
14. Go to www.fraud.org/internet/intset.htm for a complaint form. For information on scams against business, see www.fraud.org/scamsagainstbusinesses.
15. See, for example, www.ftc.gov/bcp/conline/pubs/buspubs/donating.htm on public safety fundraisers, and also www.ftc.gov/bcp/conline/pubs/alerts/badgealt. htm on Public Safety Fund-Raising Appeals. Abuse can come from solicitors not really affiliated with the police, fire, and other public safety organizations. Solicitations relating to the September 11 terrorist attacks must also be investigated. See www.usdoj.gov/criminal/fraud/WTCPent-SpecRpt.htm.
16. See www.give.org/guide/index.asp.
17. Located at www.bbb.org/library/busgive.asp.
18. For city and county offices, see www.pueblo.gsa.gov/crh/state.htm.
19. For "Tips on Contributing Used Cars to Charity" go to www.bbb.org/about/usedcar.asp. Don't forget to use the appropriate IRS tax form, which can be found at ftp.fedworld.gov/pub/irs-pdf/f8283.pdf. You must have Adobe Acrobat Reader.
20. For a list of state attorneys general offices, see www.pueblo.gsa.gov/crh/state.htm or www.naag.org/ag/full_ag_table.cfm. For advice on "How to Help the Attorney General Handle a Complaint" see www.nonprofits.org/npofaq/npofaq/17/00.html.
21. See the National Association of Attorneys General at www.naag.org/about/ag.html.
22. A handy roster is provided by the National Association of Secretaries of State at www.nass.org/sos/sos.html.
23. See https://rn.ftc.gov/dod/wsolcq$.startup?Z_ORG_CODE=PU01. To complain by phone, call toll-free (877) FTC-HELP (877-382-4357) or T.D.D. (202) 326-2502. To complain by mail, send your concerns to the Consumer Response Center, Federal Trade Commission, 600 Pennsylvania Avenue, NW, Washington, DC 20580.
24. See www.irs.gov/exempt/display/0,,i1%3D3%26genericId%3D6867,00.html for directions and the address. The IRS does not have an e-mail complaint form but will accept e-mail complaints at tege.eo.ceo@irs.gov or you may write the IRS at: Internal Revenue Service, TE/GE Division, Customer Service, P.O. Box 2508, Cincinnati, OH 45201.
25. The volume of public inquiries helps identify which national charities will be the subject of a PAS Report. If you have a question about a specific national charity, check the Charity Reports Index (www.give.org/reports/index.asp). Even if the BBBWise Giving Alliance does not have information on the organization, the request will help alert it to national charities that it should review.
26. For charity complaints, go to www.give.org/inquire/index.asp.
27. See www.give.org/businesses/index.asp.

CHAPTER 6

Welcome to the Dark Side:
How E-Commerce, Online Consumer, and E-Mail Fraud Rely on Misdirection and Misinformation

Lysbeth B. Chuck

Computers and the Internet are the offspring of a simple duality: the zeros and ones of the binary number system and the way they are combined. Like other forms of commerce, e-commerce, made possible by the development of the Internet, is also a simple duality. Buyers and sellers in an ever-growing number of markets come together in a variety of technology-mediated configurations—some old, some new—to complete transactions. Like all things of a dual nature, there is a good side and a bad side to this activity, a bright side and a dark side. And the players on the dark side, whether buyers or sellers, frequently utilize the Internet to disseminate misleading, often totally inaccurate, information in order to deceive and snare their victims.

According to a University of Texas study done early in 2000, the online economy at that time generated $523 billion in revenue and employed 2.5 million Americans. According to other studies, it had also created $500 trillion in stock market value, and, if "Online" were an actual country, its economy would rank 18th in the world.

That, of course, is the bright side. Despite the recent, perhaps inevitable, dot-com shakeout, there's been spectacular growth in both the economy and in individual productivity, with little negative impact on the environment. There's also been a nurturing atmosphere for

113

innovation and an exponential increase in shareholder value. The World Wide Web has fostered this democratization of power and information through the "network effect," the Internet's enviable ability to take anyone with a PC, a modem, and an Internet connection, and make him or her part-owner of a multibillion-dollar telecommunications infrastructure, *and* give him or her equal stature with all other users, whether company presidents, senators, movie stars, society mavens along with con artists, pornographers, and master criminals. Those last three, of course, are the professionals. Along with them, the Net also enables fraudulent activity by rank amateurs, people that PC/Computing has called: "two-bit flimflam artists, small-time shysters, bunko bilkers, swindlers, filchers, bootleggers, purse snatchers, and scumbags of every persuasion."

Welcome to the Dark Side. As Hugh Stevenson, Associate Director of the Federal Trade Commission's (FTC) Bureau of Consumer Protection, told the Senate Finance Committee on April 5, 2001, "... fraud operators are always among the first to appreciate the potential of a new technology to exploit and deceive consumers." Indeed, where fraud is concerned, say the experts, the Internet is *the* growth area, and the underground economy it has produced may be as robust as its legitimate twin.

The Nigerian Letter: E-mail Brings a Deadly Worldwide Scam into Your Home

At least one tried-and-true international scam—the Nigerian Letter—has successfully made its way to the Internet, precisely because one of the wonders of the World Wide Web is that it's exactly what it claims to be—worldwide. As a result, few people are surprised to find e-mails from exotic places like Nigeria in their inboxes. Even fewer, it would appear from the latest statistics on online fraud, are aware that when they do get money-making offers in unsolicited e-mails from faraway places, what they're likely to be looking at is just a new twist on an old mail fraud and money-laundering confidence swindle, familiarly referred to as the Nigerian Letter.

Reportedly first appearing in the early 1980s, the original letter involved a request for help from an official of a government agency, usually the central bank, in Nigeria. Today, the country in question could be any one of a dozen, the agency could sport any official-sounding name, and the target company or individual receives the famous letter technologically, via either e-mail or fax.

These messages claim that the agency or bank in question has some really excessive funds, usually several million dollars, in a bank account due to some fluke, like a big overpayment made in error. The money needs to leave Country X for awhile or it will be lost to the letter writer. If the lucky-to-be-chosen addressee will please hide this extra money for a short period, preferably in his or her personal bank account, said addressee will get a sizable percentage of the hidden funds for their help. Not to mention the undying gratitude of Country X's government or central bank.

A recent twist on this old scam is an e-mail purporting to be from a member of the *"Secret Unit in charge of Diamond dealing for the Revolutionary United Front (RUF) of Sierra Leone."* In a twist made possible only by the Internet, and with an expert's eye for the power of information to legitimize and convince, the writer cites a number of names and incidents in Sierra Leone's recent history, all facts that can be easily verified at any Internet news site, thereby misleading an uninformed reader into thinking the letter is genuine. The writer then goes on to claim that he is "trapped with large quantity of unpolished diamond and millions of United States dollars that is in cash and because of the situation of things in my Country, the possibility of investing these funds here is highly limited, hence the decision to contact you arises. At this juncture, I am soliciting for your assistance to enable me legitimize and entrust in your care for investment US$12.5 million dollars (Twelve Million Five Hundred Thousand United States Dollars). I accept to concede some percentage to you for your materials and logistics involvement." A number of other examples are on view in the "Nigerian Scam Letters Gallery" at www.quatloos.com.

Once recipients show some interest in these offers, they are asked to pay for all kinds of things, e.g., advance fees, transfer taxes, performance bonds, or they're asked to extend credit or grant COD privileges. And once the victim agrees to that first payment, there are many complications, all of which require still more payments, including legal fees, expenses, and even bribes. Frequently, whole bank accounts are wiped out, with the money being sent, no doubt, to an account in some country like Nigeria, someplace with no extradition treaties and no government oversight of large financial transactions. Some targets have been invited abroad to collect their cut, then shaken down, or even held hostage, for more money. According to a 1998 story by the *Los Angeles Times*'s chief Washington correspondent, Jack Nelson, as many as 15 victims had been killed by then. In 2001, the Secret Service estimated that in the United States alone, losses to Nigerian Letter scams amount to more than $100 million a year.

There are a dozen or more permutations of this scenario, which for years was the poster child for "advance fee" mail fraud schemes, sometimes referred to as "419 scams" in reference to Section 419 of the Nigerian penal code, which prohibits the activity. Still, prohibitions or no prohibitions, 419 scams have become a worldwide industry. It's reported that the Financial Crimes Division of the Secret Service receives approximately 100 telephone calls from victims/potential victims of 419 scams, and 300–500 pieces of related correspondence per day. The Metropolitan Police Company Fraud Department in London estimates that over 3,000 letters a week are mailed or faxed worldwide, with over 50 percent sent to addresses in Great Britain or the U.S., which also happen to be two of the countries with the highest penetration of PC ownership and e-mail access.

In 1998, Postal Service inspectors in New York reportedly destroyed over 2 million paper-based Nigerian letters, just in New York. Since March of that year, they've seized a whopping 6 million letters tied to 419 scams. Combine this level of criminal activity with new Internet technologies like spamming software and virtually free e-mail, and you can easily see how the Web has facilitated the growth of fraud based on misinformation and deception. Although making up only 1 percent of online fraud documented by the Consumers Union in 2000, the Nigerian Letter had become so prevalent that the Union created a special category for their records that year. The Alliance Against Fraud in Telemarketing & Electronic Commerce, a coalition of government agencies, nonprofit public interest groups, businesses, and trade associations run by the National Consumer's League, issued a warning in 2000 that the scheme was indeed on the rise, this time via e-mail aimed directly at U.S. citizens.

Of course, the real question is: With all the resources of the Web available to most people and organizations with e-mail, why don't more folks uncover the history of this scam for themselves? You may well ask. There are sites all over the Web describing the Nigerian Letter in detail. Still, according to the 419 Coalition, a Nigerian-based group that actively fights the scam, the letter is reportedly the third largest industry in Nigeria, and has cost the world more than five billion dollars over the past 15 years. Not to mention costing at least 15 people their lives. Web of deception indeed.

Web-Based Fraud: You Can Even Get It Retail

Consumer fraud in the e-commerce arena cuts both ways: It sometimes seems that buyers cheat sellers almost as much as sellers cheat buyers. In both cases, the mechanism is the same: deceptive, misleading, or inaccurate information, which the seller provides about a product and his ability to provide it, or which the buyer provides about himself and his ability to pay.

It's obvious why attempts by unscrupulous consumers to defraud merchants should be of concern to merchants, but why they should be of equal concern to other consumers as well may not be as obvious.

Remember that merchants' losses are usually passed on to consumers in the form of higher prices, and efforts to contain future losses can raise prices and color the buying experience for everyone, so consumers should most definitely be concerned. It's also true that if consumer frauds continue to scare away potential online buyers, merchants will be deprived of new customers and new markets, and consumers will be deprived of the lifestyle benefits promised by this ecologically friendly and democratic technology.

Exact figures are hard to come by and there is a great debate over how bad online fraud really is, largely because research methodologies vary widely and because there are almost as many definitions of consumer fraud as there are of e-commerce. Still, according to Newton, Massachusetts-based financial consulting firm Meridien Research, fraud rates of 20 percent and up are common at retail Web sites. Meridien also claims that while only about 1 percent of bricks-and-mortar credit card transactions are allegedly fraudulent, when online that number may balloon to as high as 10 percent, a figure hotly disputed by credit card companies, which, it would be wise to remember, have a vested interest in promoting the safety of plastic on the Web.

Meridien reported that Internet credit card purchases in 2000 amounted to $45 billion worldwide and Internet payment fraud to $1.6 billion. Without widespread use of anti-fraud technology, it predicts that the $1.6 billion in losses could rise to $15.5 billion in 2005, when global Internet card purchases will also grow to more than $310 billion.

An earlier Gartner Group (Stamford, Connecticut) survey of more than 160 companies tends to back up Meridien's findings, as does a study commissioned by CyberSource (Mountain View, California). In the CyberSource study, online merchants estimated that anywhere from 5 to 25 percent of transactions at their sites were fraudulent. The Gartner study reported that 12 times more fraud does indeed exist on the Internet than in the traditional retail environment and, more importantly in terms of costs, that online merchants pay credit card discount rates 66 percent higher than traditional merchants.[1]

But consumers' perceptions may be more important than hard facts in the online retail world, and in early 2001, Jupiter Media Metrix (New York) reported that consumers *believe* that fraud is 12 times more prevalent online than off-line. In reality, according to the Jupiter study, the media, analysts, and computer security firms have exaggerated the problem and online credit card fraud is only about four times worse than "real" world fraud. Remember, many analysts, the media, and computer security firms have a vested interest in promoting the dangers of using plastic on the Web.

Whomever you choose to believe, it would appear from these studies that online sellers have taken a real monetary drubbing thanks to fraud. And, in the true spirit of duality, buyers have been hard hit as well, losing over $3.3 million to Internet fraud in 2000 and nearly a million dollars more in 2001—and that's just in incidents reported to the National Consumers League's (NCL) Internet Fraud Watch. According to the NCL, in 2000 the average online consumer lost as much as $636, up from $427 the year before, an increase of 49 percent.

Sometimes the "fraud" isn't so obvious. New Internet technology applications, using simple but deceptive devices known by absurd names like pagejacking (also known as cybersquatting) and mousetrapping, can produce revenues for fraudsters without the end-user ever reaching for his or her wallet.

Pagejacking occurs when legitimate Web pages are hijacked (copied to other sites) and their traffic is then diverted to those sites. The bogus site may rake in cash by charging higher ad fees based on the number of new visitors. The merchants dependent on the original site for e-commerce income lose cash because their products can't be purchased from the bogus site. They also lose customers who visited their sites hoping to buy state-of-the-art computer equipment or cheaper office supplies and instead found themselves linked to streaming media pornography.

Mousetrapping occurs when a small application is sent by a site to the user's PC to disable essential functions, like the "exit" and "back" buttons in the user's browser. The application essentially prevents the trapped user from leaving the site that placed the application, usually contributing to increased ad revenues for the site by extending the length of the user's stay or by getting the site a better placement in search engine results for the same reason. In a related trap, the user clicks on what looks like a system alert or system error message that suddenly appears on his screen. In reality, the alert is a banner ad, paid for by some merchant to take the user to the merchant's site. Adding insult to injury, the site may then mousetrap the customer in the manner described earlier. False alerts and mousetrapping also contribute to a legitimate consumer's discontent with the whole online experience and serve once again to deny merchants new customers, not to mention immediate sales.

Sometimes consumers are the victims of frauds tied directly to Internet use, such as Web page development scams or domain name registration scams. Sometimes they're the victims of indirect technological fraud perpetrated by merchants or services. Some comparison shopping sites tout technological advances that promise to guide buyers to the best available price, but only search retail sites that have paid fees to be included in the search, or they may return results that rank paying partners highest. In other words, the price "comparison" software puts pre-paid sponsors at the top of the returned list, regardless of the desired item's price. When these shopping "bots" were the hottest thing in e-commerce, Consumer Reports found that CNET, America Online, and Disney's Go Network all included only sites that paid to be included in the search. MySimon.com, which is still around, searches more widely, but gives placement preference to stores that pay.

Apparently, the sponsors of these sites hope that customers will assume the site has been supplier-neutral in finding the best available prices. In any case, finding a page on the site that spells out, in detail, just how the comparison software works, and who gets included in its lists and why, can be a daunting task.

Frequently, it's just such a lack of information that enables fraud. Several adult Web sites were recent targets of the FTC for illegally billing customer's credit cards for "free" virtual tours of their sites. The site owners, New York City-based Crescent Publishing Group, Inc.; its owner, Bruce Chew; and principal David Bernstein, were named as defendants in the federal complaint along with 64 affiliated corporations. They were accused of defrauding thousands of customers by obtaining their credit card numbers as "security" before the customers could begin their "free" tours. Then the site billed a recurring monthly membership fee ranging from $20 to $90 to the credit cards. The tour, it turns out, was indeed free, but only to "registered members" who paid monthly dues, a fact almost impossible to ascertain from information on the Web site. According to the complaint, this "free" tour Web site description used the Web to deceive and mislead, and generated income of $188 million.

Who's in Charge?

As these examples show, online buyers are "consumers" for many things in addition to traditional consumer products. Almost everything from investment and financial instruments to personal services can be bought on the Web, and the pitches for many of them are based on deceptive or misleading information. As a result, all types of criminal activities are booming in cyberspace. Along with traditional consumer fraud, the Department of Justice cites securities and commodities fraud, money laundering, financial institution fraud, telemarketing fraud, bankruptcy fraud, insurance fraud, the theft of identity, and the theft of technology and intellectual property rights as key concerns in keeping the Internet free of criminal activity.

What the Internet has done is to take many once selective areas of fraud, like securities and investments, and then level the playing field for criminals. A decade ago, the average citizen was not numbered among the population of serious investors. But today, anyone with a modem, an e-mail address, and a few spare dollars—the average consumer, in other words—can become an investor. And that means he or she can also become a "mark." Thanks to e-mail, chat rooms, and bulletin boards, the network effect is at work, greatly increasing a criminal's chances of reaching potential victims while greatly reducing the cost to do so. Some industry analysts even think that Internet fraud may be growing so rapidly simply because it is even more profitable than it is easy, and as we've seen, it is amazingly easy.

Specifically, just what *is* Internet consumer fraud? And why is it growing so fast? The Federal Bureau of Investigation (FBI) defines Internet fraud as "any fraudulent scheme in which one or more components of the Internet, such as Web sites, chat rooms, and e-mail, play a significant role in offering nonexistent goods or services to consumers, communicating false or fraudulent representations about the schemes to consumers, or transmitting victims' funds, access devices, or other items of value to the control of the scheme's perpetrators."

All of these Internet components cited by the FBI share several important characteristics for anyone bent on defrauding someone for profit. First, these elements are ubiquitous; anyone with a PC, a modem, and a telephone can visit any Web site or any chat room and can send and receive e-mail anywhere. Second, they're anonymous. Anyone can do those things, but no one has to own up to who they are when they're doing them. Screen names, aliases, and anonymous remailer technology protect the privacy of honest citizens and criminals alike. Third, they have no geographic boundaries, which may be one of the most important elements in the growth of cyberfraud.

The fact that cyberspace is decentralized presents a major obstacle to regulating it even where something as dangerous and destabilizing as fraud is concerned. There's an underlying assumption in all of the world's legal systems, the assumption that sovereign entities with the power to make laws, e.g., states, nations, cities, towns, counties, and territories also have the ability to enforce those laws within their borders. But the World Wide Web is, as we've mentioned before, truly worldwide. By its very nature, it is borderless. And even off the Web, as Thomas P. Vartanian, Chairman of the American Bar Association's Committee on the Law of Cyberspace, testified before a house subcommittee, "'Jurisdiction' is a word that makes even the most intense legal theoreticians' eyes glass over."

The first large-scale Internet case to test jurisdiction was brought by the FTC. It was financial in nature, and it's important because it highlights a government jurisdiction problem that is only exacerbated by the Internet. The question is: Who polices consumer affairs on the Internet? And the answer is: Depending on what is being sold and where and how it's marketed, or paid for or delivered, it could be the FTC, the FBI, the Department of Justice, the U.S. Postal Inspection Service, the U.S. Attorneys' offices, the Secret Service, the Securities and Exchange Commission (SEC), the Internal Revenue Service (IRS), any of the 50 state attorneys general, or local sheriffs and prosecutors.

In the case in question, FTC vs. Fortuna Alliance, L.L.C. et al., Civ. No. C96-799M (W.D. Wash., filed May 23, 1996), the defendant, Bellingham, Washington-based Fortuna Alliance, promoted what the FTC determined was an illegal pyramid scheme through an Internet Web site. Fortuna billed itself as "a new paradigm for financial independence," asking people to contribute to an "alliance" based on the mathematic phenomenon known as a Fibonacci series. The founders claimed the alliance would make every member wealthy. The FTC claimed it was a Ponzi scheme. Using the Internet and word of mouth, Fortuna had taken in an estimated $13 million from over 25,000 consumers, about half of them outside the U.S., by the time the FTC stopped them. A number of the principals in the case are still tangled in litigation, but the FTC did manage to close Fortuna down and freeze its assets, retrieving millions of dollars from offshore accounts and returning approximately $5.5 million to investors in the U.S. and 70 foreign countries.

Aside from the enormous amount of money netted from the gullible and greedy, what's important—and really scary—about the case is that Fortuna survived, at least for awhile, actually coming back on the Internet in 1997 as Fortuna Alliance II, claiming to be "a network marketing company" and the innocent victim of an FTC witch hunt. Fortuna returned despite the original federal restraining order that called for a complete shutdown of the company and the FTC's attempt to eliminate Fortuna from the World Wide Web. That order required all Internet Service Providers (ISPs) hosting promotional material for Fortuna to replace those pages with an FTC announcement, and a link back to the government site. But the FTC had no authority to enforce the order abroad and, for some time, links to Fortuna sites could be found on servers in foreign countries.

According to the *New York Law Review* (March 2000), "For the first time in history, there is an efficient channel of distribution that gives even the smallest of businesses access to a global marketplace." But whose laws rule in that marketplace? For ripped-off consumers looking for relief or revenge or both, questions of jurisdiction can be almost as frustrating as discovering they're the victim of fraud. So let's look at what can be done to protect against consumer fraud in cyberspace and at what's already being done and not done by federal, state, and local governments and some international bodies.

Whose Laws Apply?

Simply stated, anyone, merchant or customer, doing business in cyberspace needs to know what laws to obey, whether it's a question of what taxes are due and to whom, or what if any consumer protections apply to the sale of products or services there. Cyberspace may be virtual, but consumer protection laws are real, so how do we enforce real world regulations in a virtual space? It's a question with two important components: What are the mechanisms for enforcement and who has the jurisdiction to carry them out?

Many agencies are responsible for regulating activities in the area of e-commerce. The Food and Drug Administration (FDA) is responsible for policing health frauds on and off the Internet, and the FTC is the government agency actually charged with enforcing most federal consumer protection laws and regulations, as well as with regulating unfair competition in the marketplace, including "unfair or deceptive acts or practices in commerce that injure consumers." Other agencies have other responsibilities, and that's just in the United States at the federal level.

Internationally, even in areas where the law and who is responsible for applying it appear to be clear-cut, when the Internet comes into the picture, things tend to get muddled. Some drugs that are controlled in the United States, even some that are banned, are freely sold in Mexico. If a Mexican merchant offers them on a Web site, he's not in violation of Mexican law. If an American buys them off that Web site, it's not 100 percent clear that he is in violation of American law, which generally proscribes the sale or distribution, but not necessarily the use, of unapproved medications (as distinct from scheduled, or illegal, drugs).

On the other hand, there are some legal scholars who make the argument that, in the New World Order, the Mexican merchant just *might* be in violation of American law. This thinking was exemplified by the finding in a New York State case involving online gambling. The defendant's wholly owned Antiguan subsidiary was licensed to operate a casino in Antigua. The subsidiary developed interactive software, then purchased computer servers and installed them in the casino in Antigua. But users anywhere in the world could access the servers and gamble from their home computers. The casino was promoted through Internet and print ads accessible to New York residents.

The fact that these activities were undertaken by a company based in Antigua did not prevent the New York courts from ruling (July 2000 and upheld on appeal in August 2001) that the defendant had violated both state and federal gambling laws. According to State Supreme Court Justice Charles Edward Ramos, "It is irrelevant that

Internet gambling is legal in Antigua. The act of entering the bet and transmitting the information from New York via the Internet is adequate to constitute gambling activity within New York State."

Internationally, the same sorts of decisions about who controls activities on the Internet are also being made, although with many different outcomes. Other nations, for example, don't have a constitutional right to free speech, a legal defense frequently used by American companies involved in questionable commercial activities, or in promoting such activities. Witness a French court's decision in November 2000 requiring that Yahoo! block access in France to U.S.-based auction sites selling Nazi memorabilia and artifacts. It's hard to imagine a U.S. court delivering the same directive, no matter how odious it found the merchandise being sold.

What Can the Feds Do?

The American cases involve activities, gambling and selling drugs or medication, that have long been regulated in the United States at the state and federal level. There is currently no comprehensive state or federal legislation directed specifically at Internet activity specifically because it is on the Internet. Therefore, the application of existing consumer protection laws to online activities, when it can be made to stick, has up until now been the most effective and sometimes the only recourse for agencies seeking to regulate fraud in e-commerce.

It is more difficult to control online fraud partly because the federal government has deliberately adopted a hands-off approach to regulating Internet activity directly, relying instead on self-regulation by various industries in a number of areas. In fact, one reason fraud may have grown so quickly in cyberspace is because the policy of aggressively applying existing consumer protection laws to the Internet has only recently been undertaken by the FTC.

In May 2000, for example, the FTC issued a paper entitled "Dot Com Disclosures: Information About Online Advertising," providing advertisers with guidance about Internet advertising. For the first time, the document clearly confirms that the FTC considers online advertising to be well within its jurisdiction, and its prohibitions against unfair or deceptive advertising in traditional forms of media will apply to the Internet and will be vigorously enforced.

The FTC received almost 50,000 Internet fraud complaints in 2001—roughly 42 percent of the 118,000 fraud complaints logged into its Consumer Sentinel complaint database by various organizations. This number is well over the 25,000 online fraud complaints received in 2000. To put this in perspective, in 1997, the FTC received fewer than 1,000 complaints related to Internet fraud.

Consumer Sentinel is an example of fighting fire with fire, an Internet-based, online system for fighting Internet-based, online fraud. It's a tri-national (the U.S., Canada, and Australia), multistate database that can be accessed by over 300 law enforcement organizations and contains nearly 475,000 consumer complaints about telemarketing, direct mail, and Internet fraud. As of January 1, 2002, 112,990 of those related to Internet Fraud specifically. The Better Business Bureau's (BBB) offices also provide consumer complaint data, the U.S. Postal Inspection Service shares appropriate consumer complaints from its Mail Fraud Complaint System, and all fifty state Attorneys General are signed up as members. The FTC database is a collection of information about known or suspected frauds. Then, using Consumer Sentinel data, the FTC may refer potential cases to a wide array of law enforcement agencies, or those agencies may claim the cases depending on jurisdictional determinations. The responsible agencies then undertake investigating the complaints.

Still, despite the success of Consumer Sentinel, by early 2002 the FTC has brought a little over 300 enforcement actions, and only 211 actual cases, against Internet companies and online services since its first Internet case in 1994.

It is true that in those cases the FTC addressed a wide variety of consumer protection issues from fraudulent business opportunities to pyramid schemes and telephone scams, from billing practices of online services to Year 2000 investment schemes, and from credit repair to work-at-home rip-offs. Yet the agency has had to be even more careful than usual in selecting cases for prosecution given the lack of specific laws and regulations governing Internet commerce. Hence there is a dearth of case law on many of the issues where online fraud is concerned as well as a dearth of regulations. That means legal relief for victims is usually a long time away. Redress still comes in old-fashioned calendar time, not in accelerated Web years.

What Can—or Can't—the States Do?

Because the Commerce Clause of the U.S. Constitution, Article I, Section 8, specifically grants to Congress the authority to regulate commerce "among the states," there is a significant obstacle to states themselves regulating Internet activity, which definitely takes place among the states. A corollary, the "dormant commerce clause," actually limits the ability of states to impede the flow of interstate commerce. In short, intrastate regulations that purposefully discriminate against interstate commerce are typically held to be invalid, unless they are justified because such regulations further a legitimate state interest and the burden on interstate commerce is outweighed by the local benefit derived from the statute. The Internet, of course, is the most interstate medium around, but the federal government has declined to regulate it directly, and the states are limited in what they can do to regulate it. It's a con artist's idea of heaven.

States are still trying, however, to regulate the Internet. Though not concerned specifically with fraud, American Library Association vs. Pataki, 969 F.Supp. 160 (S.D.N.Y. 1997) is of interest as one of the first cases to address state regulation of Internet conduct under the Commerce Clause. In it, the U.S. District Court for the Southern District of New York held a section of the New York Penal law to be unconstitutional because the statute imposed an undue burden on interstate commerce. The statute at issue made it a crime to use a computer system to communicate or transmit materials harmful to minors or to engage in sexual communications with minors.

Despite the fact that the statute targeted deplorable and harmful—not to mention illegal—behavior that most people would willingly put a stop to, the court found that, given the nature of the Internet, the impact of the statute could not be limited to purely intrastate communications and that it impermissibly regulated conduct occurring outside the state of New York. Thus it imposed an undue burden on interstate commerce that exceeded any local benefit.

All of which brings up another problem with global access: It's not just a question of who has jurisdiction, but also of how each court interprets the reach of that jurisdiction. Note how differently the Pataki decision interprets the idea of sovereignty than does the French ruling in the Yahoo! case. Pataki says that New York cannot regulate activity *inside* its own state boundaries if such regulation affects citizens *outside* its state boundaries, yet the French court decision says that Yahoo!, a company in the U.S., must block customers in France from accessing sites in the U.S. that sell Nazi memorabilia.

Around the World Wide Web with Credit Card ... and Caution

Let's say you want to buy from an overseas vendor. Are there any protections if you run into problems? Is it safe to transmit credit information overseas via the Internet? Are taxes or duties routinely added to the price? How long should deliveries take? It is also complicated with problems with global connectivity between merchants and consumers, making multicurrency settlements, overcoming language barriers, and—to repeat—the legal uncertainties about jurisdiction over the transaction.

The United States and 28 other countries, working together as members of the Organization for Economic Cooperation and Development (OECD), have signed on to new international guidelines to help answer those and other questions. According to the FTC, the guidelines will help accomplish the following:

- Set out principles for voluntary "codes of conduct" for businesses involved in electronic commerce.

- Offer guidance to governments in evaluating their consumer protection laws regarding electronic commerce.

- Give consumers advice about what to expect and what to look for when shopping online.

The goal is to ensure that consumers are just as safe when shopping online as off-line, no matter where they live or where the company they do business with is based. The OECD says that the guidelines will ensure that e-businesses use fair business, advertising, and marketing practices; that they provide truthful, accurate, and complete information to consumers; avoid deceptive, misleading, or unfair claims, omissions, or practices; and that they will be able to back up all claims about how well a product works or how quickly a product will arrive. The guidelines also require that advertising and marketing material be easily identifiable as such and, when appropriate, that it identify its sponsor.

That's what the OECD hopes. But the guidelines aren't in place yet, and the organization has no enforcement authority itself, and, as we've seen, determining who does have the authority to enforce standards or guidelines is difficult just within a single country.

However, the OECD is calling on participating governments to help boost consumer confidence in the electronic marketplace right now by encouraging governments themselves to evaluate their current consumer protection laws and most importantly to make sure they specifically extend to online shopping and consumers have some kind of legal recourse if they are dissatisfied. Finally, they also recommend that governments work together to combat cross-border fraud and help establish a healthy climate for electronic commerce. Governments that sign on to the guidelines are presumed to be committed to evaluating their current consumer protection laws and, most importantly, making sure they do cover online shopping and that conned consumers do have some kind of legal recourse. Finally, the OECD also recommends that governments work together to combat cross-border fraud and help establish a healthy climate for electronic commerce.

At the time of this writing, the following countries were signatories to the agreement:

Australia	Korea
Austria	Luxembourg
Belgium	Mexico
Canada	The Netherlands
Czech Republic	New Zealand
Denmark	Norway
Finland	Poland
France	Portugal
Germany	Spain
Greece	Sweden
Hungary	Switzerland
Iceland	Turkey
Ireland	United Kingdom
Italy	United States
Japan	

The OECD also provides an "Inventory of Consumer Protection Laws, Policies and Practices Applied to Electronic Commerce," which the organization claims is a "comprehensive inventory of existing consumer protection laws, fair business, fair marketing and disclosure requirements." It can be found on the Internet by going to www.oecd.org, selecting "Consumer Policy," then selecting "Related Links and Documents."

In addition to the OECD, the G-8 nations several years ago created the Lyon Group of Senior Experts on Transnational Organized Crime, whose work also covers fraud. According to the Lyon Group, organized crime is taking advantage of new technologies, especially the

Internet, to conduct a number of criminal activities, including serious fraud and attacks on critical infrastructures. Many of these activities are financial in nature, but they contribute to rising costs and destabilized economies, all of which hurt the world's consumers. Basically, the G-8 ministers have assigned the Lyon Group to help countries combat high-tech crime by working to accomplish the following, while maintaining the delicate balance between security and freedom:

- Set up a 24-hour contact point in each country to ensure swift cooperation at any time.

- Train and equip police.

- Make sure the law keeps pace with technology.

- Take high-tech crime into account when thinking about how countries can help each other.

- Ensure that evidence and computer data are always accessible and that transborder searches can take place.

- Make sure everyone investigating a crime can get the information they need.

- Use new technology to collect and keep evidence.

- Use the telephone, fax, or e-mail to offer urgent assistance when needed.

- Develop reliable and secure telecommunications and data processing systems.

- Set international standards for retrieving electronic data and making sure it is authentic.

- Look at ways of tracking down criminals who use new technology to steal money or information, commit fraud, or deal in illegal material.

- Build partnerships with industry to guarantee that the most up-to-date crimes are being tackled by the most up-to-date methods.

Finally, on the international front, the BBB is working globally to get the three components in place that it thinks most important for providing consumer protection on the Internet: trust marks, business codes, and alternative dispute programs to protect consumers (more about those efforts later).

What to Watch Out For

So, just how successful are scams like the Nigerian letter? In the first ten months of 2001, they were third overall in the top five Internet frauds perpetrated on Americans, both off- and online, according to the National Consumer's League. The top five reported Web scams, in order of magnitude, were the following:

1. Online auctions—63%

2. General merchandise sales—11%

3. Nigerian money offers—9%

4. Internet access services—3%

5. Information adult services—3%

Other scams reported included:

6. Computer/Equipment/Software—2%

7. Work at Home—2%

8. Advance Fee Loans—1%

9. Credit Card Issuing—.6%

10. Business opportunities/Franchises—.4%

Most importantly, the amount of money lost to online fraud is increasing. According to the National Consumers League, losses rose overall to $4,371,724 in 2001, up from $3,387,530 the year before. And the average loss per person rose from $427 to $636.

On the other hand, it would appear that existing consumer protections are beginning to be effective in cyberspace, and one reason may be that a great many Internet consumer fraud schemes are familiar scams all dolled up in electronic clothing: pyramid schemes, chain letters, bogus business opportunities, fake franchises, warped work-at-home scams, phony prizes and sweepstakes, over-hyped merchandise, and services promised yet never delivered.

The problem, as mentioned earlier, is in determining how criminals can be legally prosecuted. If a criminal sends the Nigerian letter through the mail, there are several ways he or she can be prosecuted under the mail fraud statutes. But the U.S. Postal Service isn't responsible for e-mail, and, unless the law is changed or new laws are written, applying mail fraud regulations to e-mail activity is an example of how tricky the business of regulating the Internet can get.

Going, Going, Gone for Good

As the online auction proves, the Internet has also bred some tricky businesses of its own. A relative newcomer on the fraud scene has claimed the spotlight. The online auction, not around pre-Web, was the number one Internet consumer fraud in both 1999 and 2000, sky-rocketing from a mere 106 complaints to the FTC (in 1997) to 13,901 in 1999, then dropping slightly to 10,872 in 2000. That up and down movement is confirmed by Internet Fraud Watch figures, which show that online auction fraud increased from 68 percent of all online frauds (reported in 1998), to 87 percent in 1999, and then declined to only 78 percent in 2000. It dropped to 61 percent for the first 10 months of 2001.

In only five years, Internet auctions became one of the hottest phenomena on the Web. They offer something for everyone, buyer or seller. Millions of items are available, and the vast majority of transactions are trouble-free. But Internet auctions are an easy way for fraud-minded scammers to make a fast buck—in most cases a buyer sends a personal check, a cashier's check, a money order, or a credit card number to someone they don't know for a product they've seen via computer. It got so bad, so quickly, that in February 2000, eBay, perhaps the largest and best known of all the Internet auction sites, joined the many organizations feeding their fraud complaints directly into the FTC's Consumer Sentinel database.

In most auction fraud complaints, auctioneers either offer goods they don't have, accept payment for goods they can't deliver, provide goods that are not what they're advertised to be, or fail to deliver the goods in a timely manner if at all. In a few cases, the seller has complained that the buyer didn't pay, paid with a bad check, or—worst case scenario for the seller—paid with a stolen credit card.

But, according to the FTC, there may be other explanations besides just a rise in fraudulent activities to explain the increase in complaints. One big problem is that, despite their popularity, many consumers don't fully understand how Internet auctions work, that there are different kinds of auctions available, and how to participate in them as responsibly and safely as possible. To help educate consumers about Internet auctions, the FTC has published "Internet Auctions: A Guide for Buyers and Sellers," which offers tips to help online auction buyers protect themselves against fraud:

- Identify the seller and check the seller's feedback rating.

- Do your homework. Be sure you understand what you're bidding on, its relative value, and all terms and conditions of the sale, including the seller's return policies and who pays for shipping.

- Establish your top price and stick to it.

- Evaluate your payment options. If possible, use a credit card. It offers the most protection if there's a problem. Consider using an escrow service if the seller doesn't accept credit cards.

And, in good dual fashion, it suggests that sellers follow this advice:

- Provide an accurate description of the item you're selling, including all terms of the sale and who will pay shipping costs.

- Respond quickly to any questions bidders may raise during the auction.

- Contact the high bidder as soon as possible after the auction closes to confirm details of the sale.

- Ship the merchandise as soon as you receive payment.

The Dirty Dozen

While many scofflaws are actively out on the Internet looking to make money no matter how illegal it may be, there are a number of ways the average honest citizen can be pulled into a Web-based scam. According to Internet Fraud Watch, 82 percent of fraudulent solicitations on the Internet in 2000 were via Web sites, and 4 percent through newsgroups (up from just .5 percent the previous year). And the Web's killer app, e-mail, was used as the method of initial contact in 12 percent of reported Internet scams in 2000. That, too, is up since e-mail was used for only 9 percent of initial contacts the year before. In 2001, 78 percent of fraudulent solicitations were via Web sites, 18 percent via e-mail, and only 2 percent through newsgroups. In 1998, the FTC identified a full "Dirty Dozen" scams that were "most likely to arrive via bulk e-mail in your e-mail box," a list that's still distributed by the FTC as an up-to-date handbook on how to recognize fraudulent solicitations in your e-mail.

The online auction, 2000's number one venue for Internet fraud, doesn't appear on this FTC list because most auctions don't actively solicit bidders via e-mail. In other words, most people find the auction sites by themselves, frequently because the sites engage in some small-time marketing fraud by embedding often-searched-for words like "sex" or "restaurant" in their Web sites so more search engines will index them.

Here are the FTC's Top Twelve candidates for "Scam in a Spam," tempting offers that the FTC says are *most likely* to generate a "You've got mail" message. Don't forget to add the Nigerian letter scam and all its cousins.

1. Business Opportunities Scams

These are offers that claim you can start a business or earn piles of money without hard work, making lots of sales, or risking any cash. They are based on misleading or deceptive (or totally inaccurate) information. Most are illegal pyramid schemes, sometimes masquerading as multilevel marketing (MLM) organizations. In a true MLM company, you make your money by selling products or services. In a pyramid scheme, people pay money for the right to sell a product or service and for the right to benefit by recruiting others into the organization.

Pyramid schemes usually have the following characteristics:

- Claims that you can make thousands of dollars in a very limited amount of time

- A significant commitment on your part to bring other people into the organization

- An emphasis on continued recruiting vs. selling a product/service

- A requirement to buy substantial amounts of inventory for membership or promotion, usually with no clear "buy back" policy

Like the Nigerian letter, many of these "opportunities" require some kind of advance fee for the right to participate, or even to learn more, and other financial charges frequently follow.

Often short on details and long on promises, many e-mails touting business opportunities include a telephone number to call for "more information." This opens the door to two additional scams, one where the call back number is actually in a pay-per-call area code. The call charges then wind up on your existing phone bill, and you may not even know you've been scammed. Modems can even be induced to dial back for dollars. Some e-mails include a link to a "better" viewer or "better" soundcard that you can download for "free." But the downloaded software could hijack your modem, disconnect the PC speaker, hang up from the local ISP, and dial a high-priced international modem connection, which stays open even when the user leaves the site. Again, the charges come through on your phone bill.

A second scam is when you call the number as requested and leave your name and phone number, which the caller then sells to telemarketing firms. The call you get back is from a salesperson with a pitch.

2. Make Money by Sending Bulk E-Mail

These people want to sell you millions of e-mail addresses, along with either the spamming software or services to send spam on your behalf to these same millions of addresses. Even if you have a legitimate product to sell and think your target market's inbox is the best place to sell it, be aware that sending bulk e-mail violates the terms of service of most ISPs, so your ISP may shut you down.

Some spamming programs allow you to insert a false return address into your solicitations, which can land you in legal hot water with the owner of the address's domain name. Several states have laws regulating the sending of unsolicited commercial e-mail, and sending bulk e-mail of any kind *may* violate those laws. Spammed advertising may be legal in some jurisdictions, but, as mentioned, ISPs usually prohibit it. Matters are further complicated since, in many jurisdictions, advertising via unsolicited fax is illegal, which raises the question: Shouldn't it also be illegal to send unsolicited e-mail (spam), since it can be argued that the modem connected to your computer makes it virtually identical to a fax machine? So far, there has been no real legal test.

3. Chain Letters

Here is the most famous scam of all, ready for another millennium. All you do is send a small amount of money, or some item, to four or five names at the top of a list, and then forward the message on, sometimes via bulk e-mail, making sure to include your name at the bottom. Nearly all these letters include an impassioned claim that they are legal, but they're not. Here's what the Post Office has to say about chain letters: "Chain letters are a form of gambling, and sending them through the mail (or delivering them in person or by computer, but mailing (payments or items) to participate) violates Title 18, United States Code, Section 1302, the Postal Lottery Statute." Chain letters are illegal if they request money or items of value, and promise a substantial return to participants, even if a product, like a report on Internet businesses, is involved.

According to the FTC, nearly everyone who participates in a chain letter involving cash or merchandise loses money. Actually, the whole premise of chain letters, the promise of ever-growing returns which makes it sound so workable, is mathematically flawed. If you start by sending money or merchandise to five people, who each have to send money or merchandise to five other people, it takes just 15 interactions for the total number of participants to reach 6 billion. It took until November 1999 for the earth's entire population to hit that number.

4. Work-at-Home Schemes

Work-at-home schemes have proliferated on and off the Internet. They accounted for about 5 percent of the complaints in the FTC's Consumer Sentinel database in 2000 and are the fourth most prevalent Web scam. The most common scheme, of course, is earning money for stuffing envelopes. You can earn as much as $2.00 per envelope, according to some e-mails. Except that what happens is you pay the sender for the right to stuff the envelopes, at which point you're instructed to send the same envelope-stuffing ad (frequently via bulk e-mail) to others, who will also be asked to pay for the privilege.

Again, it takes only a simple calculation to figure out that, in order to make $1,000, you'd have to stuff 500 envelopes. If you figure 30 seconds an envelope, it would take you 4 hours. That's $250 an hour. Would someone really pay that for doing mindless work that goes for below minimum wage in the real world? Don't quit your day job yet.

Craft or assembly work schemes are another popular work-at-home offer. These usually require an investment of hundreds of dollars in equipment or supplies. According to the FTC, if you actually do work for one of the fraudulent outfits, they could refuse to pay, claiming that your work isn't up to their standards of quality. You should also know that it is illegal to do certain types of work at home, and the Department of Labor strictly enforces its prohibitions on those activities.

5. Health and Diet Scams

Like business opportunities that claim you can make money without working, there are people on the Web who claim you can lose weight without eating less or exercising more, that you can cure yourself by paying them, not your doctor, for expertise. Almost always pitching "scientific breakthroughs" or "secret formulas," they offer cures for everything from hair loss to acne to obesity. Some even offer $99 "ultimate cures" for cancer or AIDS, not to mention home abortion and self-sterilization kits. In June 1999, the FDA issued a warning against buying such products because they posed "significant, possibly life-threatening health risks." Trust the FDA on this.

Also consider that, while not all health and diet product pitches on the Web are scams, many of the product sales sites may prove to be harmful in more subtle ways. Even if you order something relatively harmless from a site that also carries the already mentioned life-threatening products, or that sells medications not approved by the FDA for sale in this country, you're consciously supporting a commercial activity that has an uncertain interest in the long-term well-being of its patrons.

6. Effortless Income

Not exactly a "business opportunity," this is a new get-rich-quick scheme that offers unlimited profits exchanging money on the world currency markets. You put up the seed money, the perpetrators put up the expertise. If they're such experts, why aren't they rich? What do they need your money for? Don't let them bilk you out of your hard-earned cash.

7. Free Goods

Pay a modest amount of dues to belong to a buying club, bring in a certain number of other dues-paying members, and you'll get expensive items such as computers for "free." These are disguised pyramid schemes. The "free" merchandise is just a come-on for you to drag in more friends. It seldom materializes, or it's a tacky "gimme" if it does, and you and your buddies are out the cash for the dues, with only expensive and time-consuming litigation as a recourse to get it back.

8. Investment Opportunities

Sky-high returns at "no risk." Most investment scams, on- or off-line, are Ponzi schemes that pay early investors with money from later investors, fooling the early investors into believing that the system works, and encouraging them to invest more money, which they eventually lose. Sales pitches in these e-mails tout high-level financial connections, inside information, and ironclad "guarantees." The North American Securities Administrators Association has cited bad Internet deals as a dangerous scam, singling out "Internet fraud involving small stocks whose value is being inflated," along with bogus offshore "prime bank" notes and the ever popular pyramid schemes. Don't fall for it.

9. Cable De-Scrambler Kits

Again, you're offered something for nothing, i.e., cable transmissions without paying any subscription fees. First of all, it's illegal to steal service from cable companies, and most cable companies are aggressively prosecuting theft of service. Second, most of these kits don't even work! If you really want cable television, pay the cable company for service.

10. Guaranteed Loans or Credit, or Easy Terms Scams

These run the gamut from home equity loans that don't require any equity, to credit extended in the form of a loan or a credit card that disregards your credit history and to offshore bank loans. Sometimes they're combined with pyramid schemes that pay you for attracting other participants. You pay a "small" advance to qualify for the services, and then the loan doesn't come through, or the credit cards don't arrive. Be smart about these offers and make sure you read the fine print. If there is none, walk away.

11. Credit Repair Scams

These scams promise to erase accurate negative information from your credit file so that you can illegally qualify for loans, mortgages, or credit cards. Many of them make their money by charging you for an explanation of how you, too, can commit fraud and violate federal laws by lying on loan or credit applications, misrepresenting your

Social Security Number (SSN), or getting an Employer Identification Number (EIN) from the IRS under false pretenses.

12. Vacation Prize Promotions

Congratulations! You've "won" a fabulous vacation! You've been "specially selected" for a great opportunity! Send money to cover administrative expenses. And then wait and wait and wait for your tickets. Or else pay for an upgrade to your "free" cruise, and arrive to find that the ship is nothing like what was advertised and that you've been had.

Other FTC Activities

In addition to the Consumer Sentinel database, the FTC built an Internet fraud lab that scans the Internet for deceptive business practices. It is equipped to electronically "secure" any evidence that is discovered on the Web, which will help the agency in future prosecutions. In the past, the ability to change, destroy, or disguise digital data has made most evidence of fraud ephemeral.

The FTC also regularly holds "surf days," during which commission staff, attorneys general, and other regulators across the country scan the Net for potential scams. In March 1999, they sponsored the first one, called "Business Opportunity Surf Day," which turned the e-mail tables on scammers by sending 200 warnings via the Web to businesses that had exaggerated claims on their Web sites or in their e-mails.

The FTC now has a roster of focused "Surf Days" that are run at irregular intervals. These are some of the more recent ones:

- International Health Claim Surf Day: The FTC led 80 organizations from 25 countries in a surf of 1,200 Internet sites to find false advertising claims about the treatment or prevention of six major diseases, including cancer, arthritis, and HIV/AIDS.

- Investment Opportunity Surf Day: The FTC, along with over 30 state and federal agencies and two national associations in the United States and Canada, surfed over 400 sites to find bogus investment promotions.

- Environmental Marketing Claims Surf Day: Finally, some good news. A surf of 150 Internet sites using environmental advertising found that most of them were in compliance with the Guides for the Use of Environmental Marketing Claims.

- Coupon Surf Day: The FTC and the Coupon Information Center identified over 50 Internet advertisements as potentially fraudulent coupon-related schemes.

- Jewelry Guide Compliance Surf: FTC staff surfed 100 Web sites advertising jewelry to determine compliance with the FTC's recently updated Jewelry Guides.

In fact, officials from 27 countries and 45 states participated in one massive sweep of the Internet for "get-rich-quick" schemes and scams. The "Get-Rich-Quick.Con" program uncovered more than 1,600 sites that made promises like "surf the Net and earn $100 an hour," touted pyramid schemes, made outrageous product claims, or were otherwise fraudulent.

The FTC also employs the power of the Web to lure the gullible into giving up their hard-earned cash, and then turns it on its head and uses it to educate the potential victims. It runs a number of "sting" pages in cyberspace, sites that provide a typical come-on, but that instead of taking the potential victims' money carry a warning on their last screen explaining just why these people are potential victims.

And the FTC is hot on the trail of new ploys that have surfaced since January 2000, particularly the bulk e-mail scams designed to collect e-mail addresses and other information about individuals for resale to spammers. These include phony Microsoft giveaways, free pre-Initial Public Offering (IPO) stock in Internet companies, e-mail gift certificates, calls for political action, and bogus surveys. The most common address-collecting trick recently was an e-mail tracking system giveaway, purportedly from Microsoft and Disney, in which people are promised money for each e-mail address they add to a circulating list. E-mail addresses are also collected this way by scammers claiming to lobby for specific legislation or circulating surveys or polls on "hot" social issues.

You may have put the nail in your own coffin if you responded to an instruction common to spammed messages. "If you no longer wish to receive messages on this topic, just send a blank reply." If you do so, you've just confirmed that the spammers have a valid e-mail address in their list, making the list even more valuable when they go to sell it to other spammers.

P.T. Barnum's famous words still hold true, with a twist. Barnum was referring to suckers when he said, "There's one born every minute." In the Internet age, it's also true of con artists on the Web.

Countermeasures

Laws can protect our society from fraud, quackery, criminal behavior, venery, and other scams but only to a point. The resources of our law enforcement agencies and courts are finite, and the sheer amount of illegal activity in our society today is close to overwhelming. Add the exponential effect of the Web, and your best bet is to avoid being taken for a ride in the first place. Some tried-and-true rules to help you sort the wheat from the chaff in the virtual world follow.

1. Never pay money to get money.

It is possible that you actually inherited something from a long-lost relative, in which case taxes or probate fees may be due. But always check with a reputable probate or inheritance lawyer to be sure the firm contacting you, and the fee or tax being asked for, is legitimate. If they are, ask that the fee or tax be subtracted from the amount you have coming. In every other case, remember that a bird in the hand is worth two in the bush.

2. Never use credit cards for ID or age verification.

Credit cards aren't meant to be ID cards. They're meant to be credit cards. The information they contain about you is not information anyone needs to identify you. Credit card theft is easily translated into identity theft, which was the leading category of complaints in the Consumer Sentinel database in 2000, accounting for 23 percent of all reported consumer fraud, and increasing to a whopping 42 percent in 2001. Nationwide, there were nearly 86,000 complaints of identity theft. The Internet, it seems, has made this particular fraud a lot easier.

Still, despite the frenzy kicked up by the privacy hawks, credit cards may be the safest way to pay for items you do buy on the Internet because there are laws that limit your liability as a consumer in the event that you are scammed. Ironically, the FTC issued an alert late last year warning consumers about credit card "loss protection insurance" scams being promoted via telemarketing and e-mail. Consumers are buying worthless credit card loss protection when all they need to do is follow the card companies' procedures, i.e., check your bills carefully, don't pay unauthorized charges, and know how to dispute them.

3. Do not rely on guarantees or warranties on the Internet.

Guarantees originating in other states or countries can only sometimes be enforced, usually by costly civil litigation if there are any guarantees. On the Internet, however, you have no "guarantee" in the first place that the people you're dealing with are who they say they are.

4. Do not rely on the law, especially local law, to insure your safety or rights.

City, state, provincial, or federal laws in your country may offer you some protection on the Internet, but you should probably assume that all your Internet transactions and activities are currently "at your own risk." Lawmakers in every country are enacting laws of every imaginable description, but these may not be enforceable in any other jurisdiction. Be as informed as possible about the country, the company and the product in question. In particular, don't rely on the law to help you in Nigeria!

5. If you are thinking of buying into an MLM plan, consider these tips from the FTC:

- Avoid any plan that includes commissions for recruiting distributors or claims that you will make money through the continued growth of your "down-line."

- Beware of plans that ask new distributors to buy expensive inventory or establish a minimum monthly sales quota.

- Avoid plans that claim to sell "miracle" products or promise enormous earnings. Ask the promoter to substantiate all claims.

- Evaluate the product or service to determine if there's a market for it and if it's competitively priced.

- Beware of testimonials from people who claim to have earned large sums through the program. They may be "shills" paid by the program's promoters.

- Resist pressure to buy in. Take your time to think over your decision and your investment. Discuss it with a friend, accountant, or lawyer.

- Before signing up for any program, call the BBB and state Attorney General where you live as well as where the company is based to see if there's a history of complaints against the organization. While a complaint record may indicate questionable business practices, remember that a lack of complaints doesn't necessarily mean that the program is legitimate.

- Be leery of any plan that makes claims that seem too good to be true.

6. *If you think you've found a legitimate low-cost travel or vacation package, remember the following before you buy it:*

- Know whom you're dealing with. If you're not familiar with a company, get its complete name, address, and local telephone number. Be wary if the names of the seller and travel provider differ. You may be dealing with a telemarketer who has no further responsibility to you after the sale. As for a company that wants to send a courier for your payment or asks you to send your payment by overnight delivery, it may be trying to avoid detection or charges of mail or wire fraud.

- Check out the company's track record. Contact the Attorney General, consumer protection agency, and BBB where you live and where the company is based to see if there is a history of complaints on file. Keep in mind that while a complaint record may indicate questionable business practices, a lack of complaints doesn't necessarily mean the company is legitimate. Unscrupulous dealers often change names and locations to hide a history of complaints.

- Get the details of your vacation in writing and a copy of the cancellation and refund policies *before you pay*. Ask the business if it has insurance and whether you should buy cancellation insurance. Don't accept vague terms such as "major hotels" or "luxury cruise ships." Get the names, addresses, and telephone numbers for the lodgings, airlines, and cruise ships you'll be using. Call to verify your reservations and arrangements.

- Use a credit card to make your purchase. If you don't get what you paid for, you may be able to dispute the charges with your credit card company. However, don't give your account number over the phone unless you know the company is reputable. Some telemarketers may claim they need your account for identification or verification. They don't. Your account number should be used only to bill you for goods and services.

- Investigate charter flights. If your trip involves a charter flight, get the charter operator's name and address and check the operator's registration by writing to: U.S. Department of Transportation, Office of Consumer Affairs, I-25,

Washington, DC 20590. Also, call DOT's Public Charter Office at 202-366-2396 to see if the operator has filed to operate a charter flight from the planned departure city to the planned destination. Charter packages can't be sold until DOT approves the filing.

- Learn the vocabulary. "You've been specially selected to receive our spectacular luxury dream vacation offer" doesn't mean you'll get a free vacation. It means you'll be offered an opportunity to pay for a trip that may or may not fit your idea of luxury. "Subject to availability" means you may not be able to get the accommodations you want when you want them. "Blackout periods" are blocks of dates, usually around holidays or peak seasons, when no discount travel is available.

- Watch out for "instant travel agent" offers. Some companies may offer to sell you identification that will "guarantee" you discounted rates from cruise lines, hotel companies, used car companies, or airlines. In reality, the companies that sell this identification have no control over discounts. Only the actual supplier of the services can extend professional courtesies.

Checklist for Consumer-Friendly Web Sites

Don't buy through Web sites you've never used before unless it's easy to find the following information:

1. Exactly what kind of business is being operated

2. The physical business address, including the country, an e-mail address, and a telephone number

3. What the site is selling, with enough details that you can make an informed buying decision

4. What the actual costs will be to you and how you will be expected to pay:

   • A list of total costs collected by the merchant (including taxes) and, on international sites, duties collected and the currency used

   • The existence of other routine costs

   • Any restrictions or limitations on the sale

   • Any warranties or guarantees associated with the sale

   • An estimation of when you should receive the order

   • Details about the availability of convenient and safe payment options

5. A return policy, including the following:

   • An explanation of how a consumer can return an item, get a refund or credit, or make an exchange

   • Where the consumer should call, write, or e-mail with complaints or problems

   • The opportunity for consumers to keep a record of the transaction

   • The site's policies on sending unsolicited e-mail solicitations to consumers, including an opportunity for consumers to decline these offers

   • Information about easy-to-use and affordable dispute resolution programs the site participates in

6. A notice about the site's information collection practices, such as what personally identifiable information is

collected, how it's used, and whether or not and with whom it's shared:

- The ability for you to choose how personally identifiable information is used and shared with others (opt-in or opt-out options)
- Procedures to ensure accuracy, including allowing consumers reasonable access to their information

7. Information on security measures appropriate to the transactions—a clear identification of advertising, marketing materials, and sponsorship of ads

8. Finally, Web site rating symbols from BizRate and the BBB

The BBB has the largest trust-mark program on the Internet right now. It actually has two programs, BBBOnline Reliability and BBBOnline Privacy, each with its own trust mark, which is a seal displayed on a company's Web site that ensures consumers the company is complying with BBB Online guidelines.

Companies must make a commitment to a series of standards, to truthful and accurate advertising, to resolving any dispute that might come up if there is a problem with a product or service that's purchased on line, and to a third-party arbitration to be part of the Reliability program. Currently, several thousand businesses participate, covering more than 10,000 Web sites.

BBBOnline Privacy, on the other hand, covers over 750 Web sites. According to the BBB, the trust marks are supposed to do "what Better Business Bureaus have always done—help people find reliable companies that have committed to business standards."

Like everything on the Internet, trust marks are not without their problems. The BBB itself estimates that there may be as many as two dozen programs in the Internet consumer protection industry and maybe a dozen concentrating on privacy. That can really become confusing to the online consumer and to businesses. There's a danger that consumers can be misled if they expect the same amount of protection from each one, and a danger that businesses may go to the easier trust mark that doesn't require them to do much.

Despite all of the considerations outlined earlier, the online shopping experience has a great deal to offer consumers: more choice, easier access, sometimes better prices, and frequently greater convenience. In short, it's just one more option for buying things, whether in person, from a catalog, over the phone, or via the Web. That choice can be dictated by many things, e.g., time, need, level of comfort, convenience, or by completely unrelated considerations, such as stopping by a friend's on the way to the supermarket or getting a kick out of a Web site's graphics. The difference is that shopping on the Web is a little like shopping on the frontier. It's a little more lawless and a little more prone to the unexpected. In short, it's a place where the alert and prepared consumer will survive, and the naïve and the greedy will become statistics. So, strap on your credit card, fire up your modem, and always remember to use your head—not to mention using the Internet itself to check up on the free offers, special sales, and almost-too-good-to-be-true offers that land in our e-mail boxes with increasing frequency.

Where to Go for Help

1. Internet Fraud Watch at www.fraud.org (*not* at www. Internetfraudwatch.com). This service is provided by the National Fraud Information Center, which was established by the nonprofit National Consumers League to fight fraud by improving consumer prevention and enforcement. When you reach the home page, click on "Internet Fraud." The site provides tips, articles, and sources regarding Internet fraud. For people who wish to report possible fraud, they also have an Online Incident Report Form. At the home page, click on "How to Report Fraud and Ask Questions," and then on the "Online Incident Report."

2. Consumer Sentinel database at www.consumer.gov/ sentinel. An innovative, international law enforcement fraud-fighting program. Use the site "to get the facts on consumer frauds from Internet cons, prize promotions, work-at-home schemes, and telemarketing scams to identity theft; report your fraud complaints so they can be shared with law enforcement officials across the U.S. and around the world; learn how U.S., Canadian, and Australian law enforcers work together with private sector companies and consumer organizations to combat fraud; and see trends and the types of complaints consumers file. Or, use it to report a suspected scam you'd like investigated.

3. Computer Crime and Intellectual Property Section at www.usdoj.gov/criminal/fraud/internet.htm. Part of the Criminal Division of the Justice Department that is designed to resolve issues relating to Internet fraud.

4. Internet FAQs, at www.crblaw.com/faqs/fraud.htm. A well-designed and informative set of Web pages maintained by the Washington, DC, telecommunications law firm of Cole, Raywid, and Braverman, designed to describe Internet fraud and the statutes that govern it.

5. Introduction to Net Scams and Hoaxes, this site, a taxon- omy of Internet scams, used to be at kryten.eng.monash. edu.au/netscams.html, but that URL is dead. The document can still be retrieved by entering "Introduction to Net Scams and Hoaxes" in Google, however.

6. The Official Internet Blacklist at www.blacklist.com. This site bills itself as being about "alleged" Internet fraud. Visitors can make anonymous reports of scams and bogus sites, but be aware that reports are not verified or in any way validated by the Blacklist or its owners or operators. The list is solely an unmoderated forum for people to express their opinions regarding online companies and their practices. Neither the Official Internet Blacklist or its owners or operators make any claims or knowledge of claims regarding the validity of the reports. And the Blacklist appears to be the victim of an Internet scam. The Web page's title has been sprinkled around on a lot of adult sites so that people using search engines to find the Blacklist wind up looking at pornography.

7. Federal Trade Commission, at www.consumer.gov, the agency's newest Web site, which is designed as a clearinghouse for government information online. The site includes excellent advice regarding online shopping, Internet fraud, and identity theft.

8. Quatloos, at www.quatloos.com,[2] a private Internet Website hosted by First American Global Advisors that warns the public about various sophisticated tax frauds and financial frauds.

9. The World Wide Scam Network at www.worldwidescam. com. An overly busy "bulletin board"-style Web page that provides ongoing reports about current scams. There's no way to discover who owns the page or is responsible for its content, but it contains some good stuff, like a list of business addresses and phone numbers for the National Association of Attorneys General.

References

1. It's important to understand that credit companies treat the two markets differently, generally absorbing some of the cost of fraud for traditional merchants but letting Web merchants bear the liability and costs of e-commerce credit card losses. This is largely because online transactions lack a physical receipt signed by the customer that can later be verified. Selling online is therefore riskier and online merchants eat the cost of all chargeback disputes. In fact, online merchants spend about four times more to resolve and process chargebacks than do traditional merchants. So, for merchants, fraud is a very big worm in an otherwise delicious apple.

2. "Quatloos" are defined as "farcical units of currency which poke fun at ridiculous business offers."

CHAPTER 7

Make Sure You Read the Fine Print:
Legal Advice on the Internet

Carol Ebbinghouse

Your car's speedometer probably informs you that the highest speed it can reach is 120 miles per hour. The posted speed limit in your area probably varies from 25 to 35 miles per hour. The local interstate probably allows up to 65 miles per hour, at most. Right? Just because a car can go 120 miles per hour doesn't mean it's a good idea to drive it that fast. However, you can certainly safely exceed the posted speed limit at times without endangering anyone, including yourself. This is the same with professional advice on the Internet. Just because it's there doesn't mean it's a good idea. But, you can certainly safely use the Internet to find quality resources without endangering anyone, including yourself. Good judgment is called for. As LaJean Humphries will state in Chapter 8: How to Evaluate a Web Site, don't check your common sense at the door.

For the sake of simplicity, this discussion will focus on legal advice on the Internet although there are analogies for medical and other professional advice as well. The reason we include it in a discussion of misleading information or deception is that searchers may be lulled into thinking that what's there is all they need. Without the benefit of professional advice, searchers using professional advice sites may be misled and deceived about what *isn't* there.

As with the business world, lawyers are embracing the Internet in an effort to expand the services available to their clients and potential clients. According to Peter Jaffe in the *National Law Journal* (June 19, 2000, "Legal Practitioners Take Note: Virtual Lawyering Has Arrived"):

> ... legal Web sites allow individuals to better understand complex legal issues that may be affecting their lives. The support of the legal community will be integral to the determination

of which models will succeed and which ones will fail. Sites offering inaccurate or outdated legal information will fall prey to market rules that require a high degree of quality. Similarly, sites that provide faulty resources will not, over time, support user traffic sufficient to remain in business. On the Web, word of mouse is a powerful tool.

He goes on to give examples of people who either researched a legal problem online or got good advice from communicating with a lawyer on the Internet. Waxing poetic on the subject, he gushes:

In addition to this free and understandable legal information, consumers can also use the Internet to customize simple legal documents to fit their unique needs, find a nearby attorney who specializes in their particular legal need and even "chat" with a lawyer who can answer their questions and guide them toward practical solutions.

It takes him forever to get his reality check:

These Web sites, however, cannot eliminate the need for professional legal services—and they should not aim to do so. In fact, the opposite is true. They won't supplant the need for counsel, but they will make it less unnerving for consumers. Well-informed consumers will be more comfortable and much less intimidated when seeking high-quality professional legal advice. The attorney can, in turn, devote more attention to actually solving the client's legal problems, without having to spend a good deal of time explaining the basics.

He also recommends "Surf's Up" at www.nlj.com for "a listing by category of helpful locations on the Net for a variety of practice areas."

So which is it? Can consumers with legal issues do it all on the Internet? Will more legal information on the Net mean more, not less business for attorneys? And do the "ask an attorney" services on the Internet provide quality information? It is too early to tell. The one certain thing is that consumers are looking to the Web for legal information and more people (including attorneys) are putting information up for them.

What's wrong with consumers finding their own legal forms and getting their legal advice through a free "chat" room discussion with an attorney? While a lot of things can go right, potentially lots of things can also go wrong. For instance, the "legal" form provided might not be valid in the state where the consumer is located. The "chat" attorney may be a law student or an attorney not licensed to practice law in the consumer's state. The advice may be incompetent, but without a retainer agreement, the consumer will have a difficult time proving a claim for malpractice especially with no proof of an established attorney-client relationship. Finally, the "chat" in which the consumer tells the attorney all, perhaps confessing to a crime or disclosing trade secrets, "insider," or highly personal information in the course of describing the legal problem may be open for all on the Internet to see. With no attorney-client relationship, there is no confidentiality, no privilege against the "attorney" testifying against the consumer, and no protection whatsoever for the layperson. A lawyer's idle responses to anonymous chat room participants may in fact constitute a conflict of interest, should the attorney be discussing legal issues with an individual who is contemplating filing a lawsuit against one of the attorney's existing clients. Even worse, the alleged attorney in a chat room may be deliberately promoting the legal position or business interests of a client, rather than giving objective advice. In most, if not all of these scenarios, the "word of mouse" described earlier would not protect searchers with no legal background, and would not help them to evaluate the "legal" Web site or chat room participant's qualifications, honesty, or expertise.

Attorneys with Web sites must, at minimum, note in which jurisdictions they are licensed to practice. While the seven signs of cancer do not change from state to state, statutes of limitation for filing a lawsuit, the elements of a claim, and many other legal issues *do* change with each jurisdiction. What if the advice given causes the layperson to lose the lawsuit or causes financial harm? The courts will ask: Was it reasonable for this person to rely upon the advice of a Web site, from an alleged attorney he or she never met and who may or may not be licensed to practice in that state, after "clicking" through multiple disclaimers? The alleged attorney(s) may be vulnerable to action by the state bar association of any jurisdiction where they practice or where their advice went if, indeed, it was an attorney who gave the advice. The attorney may face the state bar's wrath for the following: unauthorized practice of law (if not licensed to practice in that state); false, deceptive, untruthful, or misleading advertising; conflicts of interest; inadvertent attorney-client relationships; violation of client confidences and secrets; and unconscionable fees and other potential ethical issues. If it was an attorney who gave the advice, and if an attorney-client relationship is determined by the court to have been created, it is possible that the malpractice insurance carrier will not cover the consumer's losses.

A traditional attorney-client relationship is based on an established relationship between a consumer and an attorney appropriately licensed in the jurisdiction and qualified to handle the particular legal need. There is a one-on-one relationship where the consumer can disclose everything to the attorney, secure in the knowledge that it will be held in strict confidence and that the attorney will never testify against the client. The attorney is bound by the rules of professional conduct (ethical rules) of the jurisdiction where they meet, and the client has legal remedies (e.g., can sue in court or look to the bar to discipline the attorney) in the event of malpractice or malfeasance of any kind.

Whenever you seek advice from an attorney or law firm Web site, scrutinize the street address on the home page, determine in which jurisdictions the attorneys are licensed, and check for compliance with recognized services relating to privacy, security, etc. Then read all the disclaimers and terms and conditions. If the information is just posted, look for date of the last update. Be aware of any advertising and whether there might be a conflict of interest between your information needs and the advertising that pays for the "free" information you will get. If you still want to communicate with a lawyer online, there are several services if you don't care about privacy or keeping your situation confidential. Make sure to read the list that follows on evaluating professional advice on the Internet. It bears repeating: Do your homework.

Attorneys and bar associations have begun working out new rules for client confidentiality in the age of e-mail and fax machines. Among the issues that they want to resolve is whether a lawyer's or law firm's Web site is "advertising" or free information. If it's advertising, attorneys should already be admitted to practice in any state in which they advertise. But Internet sites can be accessed from anywhere in the world, and this makes it seem like the attorneys are licensed to practice law wherever users are accessing them. This is not necessarily the case, so you must always inquire as to where the attorney is licensed to practice law. Potential problems arise because those who "practice law" in states where they have not been admitted (or licensed) can be found guilty of unauthorized practice of law. Hence, you see the disclaimers on the legal Web sites. Finally, if legal Web site information seems out of date, one-sided, oversimplified, or erroneous, consumers may have no remedy unless they can establish an attorney-client relationship, and you can't have an attorney-client relationship with someone who isn't an attorney in your jurisdiction.

In the world of legal advice, you get what you pay for. The free information may be brilliant and right on point, but you won't know unless you double and triple check it. You may find satisfaction in just getting background information and enough legal vocabulary or terminology to enable you to discuss your issue with your own "real" lawyer more efficiently. But what if you decide to go it alone and get the wrong form for your jurisdiction, use it, and lose your (civil or criminal) case? What if mistaken forms or bad advice voids the inheritance you thought you were providing your children in a trust? The stakes can be quite high, making the Web a place where deceptive data lurks, just waiting for unsuspecting victims.

How to Locate Legal Information on Your Own

Many articles in the news review legal Web sites, such as those specifically devoted to the "legal do-it-yourselfer" like Nolo Press's Web site. A good example is by Marci Alboher Nusbaum, on the *Wall Street Journal Interactive* (May 11, 2000, "Untangling the Legal Maze by Surfing the Web"). Cornell Law School's Legal Information Institute is probably the most extensive legal reference tool online. And there are sites where you can ask questions of a lawyer, or "legal expert" (whatever that means), for free or a fee.

Once you find a legal site that you trust, you will need to keep updating the information you have received. There are several ways to do this, but one effective way is to use LISTSERVs, sites where subscribers share information with each other on a particular topic. There are several directories of legal and law-related LISTSERVs, and you should locate at least two on your target topic. You will find LISTSERVs covering every side of an issue, and by subscribing to several, you have a better chance to find not only information to support your cause but the ammunition the other side may try to use against you. Consider the difference between pro-choice and anti-abortion groups and their newsletters. The same is true of Web sites. Consider the different information you will get on the Copyright Clearance Center's Web page as opposed to the Stanford University Web site on fair use (Stanford is an online journal publisher). Use good judgment though. Even *.org* and *.edu* extensions on a Web address do not guarantee the absence of a hidden agenda.

The principles that operate in the tangible world function in the virtual world as well. Get second opinions on everything you find relating to the law and your rights. Bring what you have found to an attorney who can answer your questions. Gather advice tailored to your needs and your jurisdiction. The more you have riding on a decision, the more you should get advice from someone held to the highest standards in the jurisdiction where you live.

Medicine and law are professions with knowledge bases beyond most people's reach due to the long years of education required. In these two professions, practitioners must pass licensing examinations before they can practice and acquire more education and experience, and sometimes pass more examinations before they can practice as specialists. Both disciplines use highly technical vocabularies to communicate. Just to search databases in these fields, one needs a specialized thesaurus and dictionary.

These obstacles would challenge a graduate student in that field, so the plight of Internet searchers is daunting. Do you need a "live chat" with a "legal expert" who may or may not be a lawyer? Is the information you want going to be independent of the commercial concerns that support the site? Are the authors real lawyers, who specialize in the particular field? Are they bar certified? And what if you compare the information you get from two different sites? Is that enough? Or should you seek a third online opinion? It all depends.

At least in the case of medical information sites, there are standards if the site wants to follow them. In the legal field, there are no standards. Most of the criteria for good medical information sites apply equally to legal information sites. (See Chapter 2: Charlatans, Leeches, and Old Wives: Medical Misinformation.) Legal Web sites can help consumers but can also lead them astray. In law, as in medicine, there are professional ethical problems with advertising on the Internet in jurisdictions where you cannot practice your profession. There are confidentiality issues unique to the profession of law. These issues have not yet been effectively resolved. The information people seek can, after all, affect their personal, legal, and often financial well being be they members of families and/or businesses. Would you trust your personal, private legal questions to a nonprofessional, one who could be forced to testify as to your communication, or worse yet, someone who can post your question and the answer for all to see?

Another consideration regarding legal advice on the Internet: Every legal issue is dependent upon unique facts. Packaged "legal advice" can't ask the interactive questions and elicit the answers necessary to make sure that the lawyer is tailoring advice to the facts at hand and the client is getting advice tailored to his or her needs.

On the other hand, there is a certain amount of convenience in visiting sites to find an encyclopedia to define a term that you don't understand or explain the relative merits of one form of a particular type of contract over another. These types of visits can help you to prepare to meet with your professional, give you access to the vocabulary of law, etc. However, even when used carefully and conservatively, the site may still track your every move, every question, and then peddle your interests and e-mail address (and any "registration" information you gave) to vendors of every type of product imaginable.

The next time you go to a legal site, look at the sponsors and look at the banner ads. Investigate the qualifications of the "advisors" who will answer your personal question for free or a set fee. If they are not *really* lawyers within your own state, then take the "advice" with a pound of salt.

Question authority, even if you're over 30. Trust no one on the Internet as the sole source of your legal rights. Go for second and

third Internet opinions if you want, but if you find something that dis-
turbs you, check it out with a trusted professional advisor. Go to your
own lawyer. Professional lawyers have your best interests at heart,
and if you don't feel comfortable talking with one of them, then
switch to another lawyer with whom you do have some rapport.

How to Evaluate Professional Advice Sites on the Internet

1. Where possible, seek information from several sources, especially from organizations, persons, or institutions with which you are familiar and already have some confidence. Don't let any Internet advisor prevent you from seeking competent professional advice from a lawyer in your own jurisdiction.

2. Know who sponsors the Web site.

   - The sponsors should provide name, street address, phone, fax, and e-mail information. It is even better if you can "click" and send the sponsor(s) a message from any page. If the sponsorship is not clearly indicated, go to another site.

   - If an organization sponsors a site, see if it identifies itself along with affiliations and financial interests.

   - If the sponsor is an individual, look for his or her credentials and use other sources such as print media to check on those credentials. Make sure that it is a lawyer that is in charge or giving the advice. If it is a layperson, this individual may have an ax to grind. Verify that this isn't a "revenge site" built to get back at a company.

   - There should be biographical information for individuals contributing to or managing the Web site, including an e-mail address.

   - If the sponsor is a corporation, it may be selling something to you (legal forms, a directory or legal software, etc.) or wants your business in some way. Check the advertisements to determine if there might be any bias in the collection or presentation of information. Does the corporation provide the information for the site, or control the content in any way? If there are editors, do they have independent editorial policy and practices with the authority to reject advertising they consider inappropriate?

3. See if the site acknowledges that some issues are controversial and makes good faith efforts to present all reasonable sides fairly and in a balanced way. See if it lists

alternative methods of dispute resolution described such as negotiation, arbitration, and mediation.

4. Look to see who is writing and/or updating the Web site. If not all the information and advice is given by professionals (doctors, lawyers), look for a clear disclaimer or other statement that the information is offered by nonprofessionals. Look for references to the sources of all articles mentioned. Make sure the articles are signed and check if the authors are professionals (doctors and lawyers licensed in your state) or if they are students, librarians, or laypeople. Check if the original articles are reviewed by an advisory board, subject to peer review by professionals, or certified by somebody. If the articles are posted from some other source(s), see that they provide complete articles or at least complete citations to the originals.

5. Check the extension on the URL. While a .org, .edu, or .gov might indicate a noncommercial environment, that does not mean that the site doesn't have a hidden agenda to support a particular position.

6. Check the date of the information on each page so you can tell whether it is current information and that the page itself has been updated recently.

7. If there are hyperlinks to external Web sites, be aware when you have left the host site and whether you know if the links are provided for information only or if they endorse the other site(s).

8. If there are banner ads on the Web site and they are a source of income to the site, make sure the advertising policy is clearly displayed so you can evaluate it yourself.

9. You may not have much choice about the terms and conditions on the site, but here are some considerations. If they are truly unacceptable, don't use the site. Regarding privacy and security, remember everything you read in Chapter 4: Internet Users at Risk: The Identity/Privacy Target Zone.

   • If any online advice is provided, make sure you know in advance what fees, if any, will be charged for online consultation and how payment for services is made.

   • Look for any clearly disclosed sponsorships, financial incentives, or other information that might affect you or a prospective client's perception of professional independence.

- The provider should clearly and accurately describe the constraints of online analysis and recommendations for action since the online provider cannot meet the "client."

- Look for the disclaimers against liability for the legal advice. Any disclaimers should come up on every entry to the Web site and should require the consumer to click "I understand and agree" each time the site is accessed.

10. The Web site should seek to comply with self-regulation. Checking these sites can help.

- TRUSTe at www.truste.org

- BBB Online at www.bbbonline.org

11. Opportunities for providing feedback easy for users are an important barometer of quality. If complaints from users aren't reviewed promptly and with timely responses, this should set off an alarm.

12. Warnings! Avoid sites that claim to constitute the sole source of information on a topic or sites that are disrespectful of other sources or established organizations. Also avoid sites that include undocumented case histories claiming "amazing" results, a fantastic jury award, or a quick cure-all for a wide range of ailments.

13. Feel free to ask your lawyer to recommend some authoritative Web sites in his or her field.

How to Evaluate Web-Based Directories of Professionals

A number of directories of professionals appear online. Several can be searched based on languages spoken, states in which the attorneys are licensed, etc. Most have some kind of consumer center with information on the hiring, care, and feeding of a lawyer once you have hired one. At least one such site also has a list of support groups with social workers for those involved in emotionally sensitive issues such as adoption, divorce, grief and loss, and employment discrimination, to name but a few. If the Web site is a directory of professionals, asking these questions helps evaluate the quality of the source:

- Is it a directory of all professionals within the jurisdiction listed, only those who pay several thousand dollars, or only those who agree with the Web sponsor? Obviously, this can affect whose listings you get to see.

- How do attorneys get into the directory? If the directory is a listing of all members of a professional association and is indexed by specialty and jurisdiction, it is more likely to be of use to you. If attorneys need to pay for listings, perhaps they won't choose to list themselves. If there is a political or other known bias to the Web sponsor, perhaps certain attorneys won't want to be affiliated with the directory.

- Is there any evaluation of the quality of the services or the qualifications of the legal services provider? Do other attorneys evaluate them for quality of services? Can consumers post their evaluations of the advice they received? This is of obvious importance to you as a client.

- Are they listed by specialty or practice area, and if so, are they certified specialists, with advanced education, experience, etc.? Or, do they just pay extra for multiple listings under different specialties? Here, too, if money is the operative factor you may not get the best information from the directory.

- Do you have complete contact information on each listed attorney? Name, street address, phone, fax, e-mail, and Web site(s) are essential. You also need to know the states where each has been licensed.

- How much information is provided? Look for date of birth, date of graduation, name of alma mater, date license to practice awarded, specialization certification, list of publications, languages spoken, etc.

- Look for links to the state bar association to check on the disciplinary record of an individual.

Recommended Reading

Lawyers Meet the Net

David M.M. Bell, "Ethics and the Internet: In a Chaos Dot Com World, Internet Use Presents Many Practical, Ethical and Regulatory Questions for Lawyers," *California Bar Journal*, July 2000, p. 12+. An overview of professional ethics and liability issues for attorneys under California law.

Joan Rogers, "Cyberlawyers Must Chart Uncertain Course in World of Online Advice," reprinted from the March 15, 2000 issue of *ABA/BNA Lawyers' Manual on Professional Conduct* www.bna.com/prodhome/bus/mopc.html. This excellent special report analyzes the terms, conditions, disclaimers, and types of services available on the Internet today. If you want an in-depth look at individual services and the issues of quality and service surrounding their use, this article is first rate. It also reviews live and e-mail, fee and free legal advice services, as well as "virtual law" communities.

Legal Advice Sites

Try www.FreeAdvice.com, or the "Ask a Lawyer" feature at www.lawyers.com. Don't forget to ask "Auntie Nolo" at www.nolo.com. There you can find a legal encyclopedia and other services and information, as well as order information for the California-based publisher's legal self-help books. This is not a recommendation for these sites. They just exemplify the types of services one can find. The quality of the information in any case remains in the eye of the informed beholder. However, www.law.cornell.edu works for lawyers, librarians, law students, and anyone interested in the law.

Searcher magazine ran a series of articles on legal awareness tools in 1997 by Carol Ebbinghouse: "Current Awareness in the Law: Legal Periodical Information and Online Services Offering Legal Information," *Searcher*, vol. 5, January 1997, pp. 49+ and "Current Awareness in the Law: Legal Listservs," *Searcher*, vol. 5, March 1997, pp. 49+.

The premier site for law-related discussion lists is produced by Lyonette Louis-Jacques: www.lib.uchicago.edu/~llou/lawlists/info.html or the keyword searchable version of the continuously updated file at www.lib.uchicago.edu/cgi-bin/law-lists. Also visit the LawGuru site with a variety of mailing and discussion lists at www.lawguru. com/subscribe/listtool.html.

An "Ask a Lawyer" feature at www.uslaw.com/ask-a-lawyer provides good disclaimers. A competitor, FreeAdvice Live!, also seems to require consumers to read and understand the disclaimer before getting the advice, at http://freeadvicelive.com/live.htm as does TheLAW.com, with its disclaimer at www.thelaw.com/sections.php? op=viewarticle&artid=3.

The Findlaw site, http://consumer.pub.findlaw.com/lawyers/hire. html, has a section on hiring a lawyer in the "Consumer Center." The Lawyers.com site, www.lawyers.com, has the Martindale-Hubbell directory of law firms and lawyers. West Publishing's lawyer directory is now at http://directory.findlaw.com as well as its original www.lawoffice.com. Most sites include e-mail addresses, links to attorney and law firm Web sites, biographies, published works, languages spoken, and sometimes representative cases.

Privacy Concerns

In the article "Privacy and Legal Research on the Web," (*The Legal Intelligencer,* June 7, 2000, pp. 8+), Bobbi Cross and Michelle Ayers point out, "There are tools to help with the challenge. A cookie manager called Privacy Companion helps your browser know the difference between first-party cookies from, say, the *New York Times*, to let you into the site and third-party cookies from ad companies that track your habits while you're there (www.idcide.com/html/prod/prod.htm). Complete cloaking tools like Anonymizer and Freedom can cloak the identity of a user in a broader way by hiding everything from your e-mail address to your computer's IP address (www.anonymizer.com/3.0/index.shtml and www.zeroknowledge.com)."

Evaluating Legal Web Site Quality

The following sites will assist you in evaluating the quality of a site: From Ballard Spahr Andrews & Ingersoll LLP, www.virtualchase. com/quality/checklist.html, and from the American Association of Law Libraries, www.aallnet.org/committee/aelic/criteria.html.

CHAPTER 8

How to Evaluate a Web Site

LaJean Humphries

Everything you've read in this book tells you why it's important to know how to evaluate an Internet site. You've been reminded that just because you find information on the Internet or on a computer does not mean that the information is current, correct, or reliable. The quality, accuracy, and reliability of information may be good, bad, or anywhere in between, so it behooves you to follow the adage, "Buyer beware."

This does not mean that everything on the Internet is unreliable. It does mean that, as with any other resource, you must carefully evaluate the material you find. We evaluate information every day, from which color to paint the living room to which new book to read. Use the same skills to evaluate Internet sources. Continue to use the good judgment you've already developed when evaluating and using electronic information.

There's a fair amount of deceptive and misleading information on the Internet that is posing as truth, as you've seen in each of the chapters. How do you tell the difference? First, always be skeptical. Never believe anything you read or see at first glance. Question everything. And most important: Don't check your common sense at the keyboard.

Factors to Consider

1. Who wrote it?

2. Who published it?

3. Is the information current, accurate, and complete?

4. Is the information presented in an objective manner?

5. How often is the site updated?

6. Is the document well written?

165

1. Who wrote it?

Internet users might ask how one compares Web authors. It's easy for almost anyone to put up a Web site today. There is no peer review or government-sanctioned approval process. A Web author does not have to have a certain level of education, obtain a certificate or license, meet any professional criteria, or pass a test in order to create a Web site. All a Web author needs is a little Internet technology skill and a small amount of money for an Internet account from any of the many Internet Service Providers (ISPs). Sometimes it is not even clear who really is the author of a Web page. If you cannot determine the author and the author's authority, you may want to question the information on that Web page.

You can believe the claims a person makes or you can verify those claims. If the author claims to have invented something (or many wonderful somethings), go to the U.S. Patent and Trademark Office Web page at www.uspto.gov. Click on the Searchable Databases link, read the instructions for searching, do a search, and see how often the person turns up as an inventor. There is no charge connected with the USPTO site.

Jakob Nielson is a well-known name to many Internet users. He has been called one of the Web's 10 most influential people and the guru of Web page usability. He has written extensively on Web usability. Visit his Web site at www.useit.com. In the spring of 2002, a search of the name "Jakob Nielson" in the USPTO Web database revealed that he holds 64 patents, a result that implies something positive about Nielson's skills and qualifications. One can feel safe in assuming that if he is writing in his area of expertise, one can believe in his writings. On the other hand, if Nielson were writing about raising roses, be more skeptical unless there's proof that he is also an expert on roses. There is an unfortunate tendency today to consider anything posted by the rich, beautiful, or famous as gospel. It just isn't so.

You may not have access to *Books in Print*, but if you have Internet access you can search a number of library catalogs and online bookstores. Your library may not have any books by Nielson, but you will likely find some libraries that have his books. Remember that popularity is not a measure of quality. Just because a book is a best-seller does not mean that it's a great book. Also be aware that the people writing the "reviews" on bookseller sites such as those of Amazon.com and Barnes and Noble are readers like you, not professionals in that field. For serious reviews of his work, you should rely on the ones in *Publishers' Weekly* or the professional journals about the virtual world. Book reviews are more reliable than sales figures when determining quality.

Suppose the author of the Web site you are viewing isn't well known. How do you verify the credentials? Has the author written some articles? Most local or county public libraries provide access to at least one general magazine and newspaper database that can be accessed online using a library card number as a password for access and searching. A simple search turns up articles by or about a given name. If the author provides a resume or list of writings on the Web site, check that list by doing some searches in the various library magazine or periodical databases available. Can you find a copy of those articles through another source? Different libraries provide different resources. If you have trouble locating a database or doing a search, stop by your local library and ask for help. Librarians are there to help you find information.

2. Who published it?

Some publishers have excellent reputations. They employ highly skilled and competent editors. You can rely on the content of books and/or journals with their imprint. Many university presses are renowned for the quality of their publications. The same is true of Web sites. Some of the best and most reliable Web sites, with high-quality information, are published by government agencies, universities, major trade associations, and publishing companies that are familiar names in the nonvirtual world.

Much government information is in the public domain and is free. The *Federal Register* is the medium for notifying the public of official federal agency actions, and all regulations must be published there. Many other sites may post information from the *Federal Register*; however, when you want *Federal Register* information go to the source, GPO Access, the Government Printing Office Web site at www.access.gpo.gov/su_docs/aces/aces140.html. GPO is the official publisher of the *Federal Register*. It is usually better to rely on the official publisher instead of a secondary publisher, who is republishing the data, as errors can be inadvertently introduced in a number of ways. This is also where intentional errors can be slipped in, making it deceptive as well as incorrect.

3. Is the information current, accurate, and complete?

Currency may not matter for some things. If one needs a good recipe for making jam, a 5-year-old recipe might be just as good as a 5-day-old recipe. On the other hand, if one is responsible for the salaries of contract workers on a federally funded or assisted construction project, the proper prevailing Davis-Bacon wage determination is critical. Last week's wage rate or last month's wage rate is not necessarily current and not good enough to keep an employer out of serious trouble. The wage rate found on the Internet may be accurate as of the date it was posted, but if it is not current, it may be a problem to rely on it. When looking at a site, ask yourself when the information was first written or when was the Web page first posted. Is there a date to indicate when it was last revised? Is there any indication of how the material is kept current? Are there incomplete dates and e-mail links that go nowhere? If so, that's a major clue that the content of that site may not be of the best quality.

Sometimes you may find current and accurate information, but the information on the Web site is only part of the story. Perhaps you are looking for a nursing home or assisted adult living situation for an elderly parent. You find three great sounding places on the Internet. The pictures of the rooms are lovely; the descriptions of the staff sound like your beloved aunt and favorite doctor. The site states that the information is current as of yesterday. This sounds good. But, what about the rates? Do they take people with Alzheimer's? Is there adequate medical care if needed? What else do you need to know? Do the sites provide checklists of information to consider? Does the site encourage you to compare? Sometimes you need complete information.

4. Is the information presented in an objective manner?

Some sites clearly state, "Our mission is ..." or "Our purpose is to ..." You should not have to guess at the purpose of a Web site. There are many types of Web sites: personal, informational, news, educational, commercial or marketing, and advocacy. The purpose of the Web site should be obvious. Whose judgment are you about to trust? A site that clearly says our mission is "to foster a secure and reliable energy system that is environmentally and economically sustainable" or a site that rambles about "meeting client needs" and "providing a range of services" without ever being specific about those needs or services? You might not agree with a site that states that "our goal is to persuade you to vote this way because ... ," but at least you know where the sponsor of that site stands on the issue.

Is the information provided as a public service or is there an ulterior motive? How easy is it to determine? Is there advertising? If there is advertising, is it clearly differentiated from the informational content of the site? Many reputable sites have an "about us" link that clearly identifies the author, publisher, and/or source of the information, a clear mission statement, at least one name, address, and telephone number in addition to an e-mail address. An e-mail address alone, without other contact information, should make you suspicious.

There is nothing inherently wrong with an advocacy or consumer site. It can provide accurate, current, and useful information. An advocacy site, like any other Web site, should clearly state its purpose and provide information that can be verified in other sources.

5. How often is the site updated?

First, there should be dates on the Web page. Ideally, there will be a date of creation or a date when the page was first placed on the Web and the date the page or site was last revised. Charts and graphs are often an effective method of presenting statistical data. However, there should be a clear indication of when the data was gathered. The Web site may have been created or updated yesterday, but if the data in the chart was compiled ten years ago, then it is historical and not current.

6. Is the document well written?

A bit of elitism goes a long way when evaluating a site. What you say represents who you are. Sloppy writing indicates sloppy thinking. It's fine to be casual, but misspellings, grammatical errors, and lack of punctuation indicate that the author is careless and unreliable at best. Text is a superior communication medium for most people. High-quality writing conveys the meaning of the text clearly and easily. Not all high-quality writing reflects accuracy, reliability, and currency, but the lack of it is a good clue in evaluating the content as well.

Looks Can Be Deceiving

Many reputable government bodies at all levels of government have been putting information on the Internet. With regard to legal documents particularly, most post a disclaimer to the effect that the text on the Internet is not the official text of the law. One of the reasons for such caution is the ease with which text may appear differently on different computers. The American Association of Law Libraries hosts The Compleat Internet Researcher, which illustrates this point quite well. This site (www.aallnet.org/products/crab/margin.htm) demonstrates how space and appearance do matter, according to Elliot Chabot, an attorney in Washington, DC, and for many years head of the automated legal support team of the House Information Resources staff of the U.S. House of Representatives. At the site, you view two versions of a specific United States Code section. The only difference between the versions is the location of the left margin in one sentence. Those few spaces make a multimillion dollar difference in the meaning of the text. Take a look at not only the specific margin page but at the entire The Compleat Internet

Researcher site, as listed down the left column of that page. It is not new, but the advice is timeless.

Sources of Web Reviews

There are excellent sources of Web page reviews just like there are excellent sources of book and movie reviews. Some personal favorites for learning about high-quality Web sites include: Librarians' Index to the Internet, http://lii.org; *The Scout Report* (ISSN 1092-3861), http://scout.cs.wisc.edu, from Internet Scout Project, located in the University of Wisconsin-Madison's Department of Computer Sciences; and *Free Pint* (ISSN 1460-7239), www.freepint.co.uk, a free newsletter written by information professionals who share how they find quality and reliable information on the Internet. You may sign up for free e-mail notification from each of these sources.

Sites to Help You with Evaluation

The following sites provide useful checklists and tutorials and can help you learn how to evaluate Web pages critically. ICYou See: T is for Thinking, at www.ithaca.edu/library/Training/hott.html, is maintained by John R. Henderson. Henderson, a reference librarian at the Ithaca College Library, has been involved in Web development and articulation issues since 1994. He is an active member of STUMPERS-L, an e-mail discussion list through which some of the best reference librarians in the world plus other researchers seek or supply answers that have others puzzled. Henderson has six suggestions for examining Web pages. Henderson also created the University of Santa Anita site, at http://147.129.1.10/library/research/AIDSFACTS.htm, as a training tool for critical thinking about Web sites. He has the user visit the Santa Anita site and the Center for Disease Control site at www.cdc.gov/hiv/dhap.htm. The comparison of the two sites is striking. As Henderson points out, it takes real effort to distinguish among magazines, trade journals, and peer reviewed journals, especially when all you can see is the full-text transcript and not the lurid cover or staid publisher responsibility statement.

Evaluating Quality on the Net, at www.hopetillman.com/findqual.html, is an educational site from Hope Tillman, the Director of Libraries at Babson College in Babson Park, Massachusetts, who has been active in library associations for many years. In this excellent article that has been on the Web since 1995, and updated as of May

30, 2000, she points out that the inclusion of promotion and advertising can make it difficult to evaluate information on the Net. The piece covers relevance of existing criteria for other formats, looking at the continuum of information on the Net, generic criteria for evaluation, the current state of evaluation tools on the Net, her own key indicators of quality, and more.

Alastair Smith teaches in the Library and Information Studies group of the School of Communications and Information Management at Victoria University of Wellington, New Zealand. Smith maintains two Web sites that will help searchers evaluate Internet information, Criteria for Evaluation of Internet Information Resources www.vuw.ac.nz/~agsmith/evaln/index.htm and Evaluation of Information Sources www.vuw.ac.nz/~agsmith/evaln/evaln.htm.

Smith maintains the WWW Virtual Library section on Evaluation of information sources, the Criteria for Evaluation site, and is on the editorial board of *Library and Information Science Research*. The Criteria site, like the Tillman Evaluating Quality site, has detailed descriptions of what to look for regarding scope, content, purpose, workability, and cost. The Evaluation site has numerous links to other sites on evaluating Internet sites.

Genie Tyburski, research librarian at Ballard Spahr Andrews & Ingersoll, LLP, maintains The Virtual Chase, A Research Site for Legal Professionals at www.virtualchase.com. Visit her section on Evaluating the Quality of Information on the Internet, at www.virtualchase.com/quality/index.html, for checklists, interactive tutorials, and more.

Usable Web, at http://usableweb.com, has a collection of links that are useful to anyone interested in what makes a Web site work well. This is where you can learn more about design, speed, navigation structure, and standards. Keith Instone, an Information Architect for IBM, who maintains the site, says that is a collection of links about information architecture, human factors, user interface issues, and usable design specific to the World Wide Web.

The Critical Factor

Even worse than poorly written sites are sites that present opinion as fact or draw illogical conclusions. Beware of extremes. There is much to be said for the scientific method. If you slept through biology or never took a math class after 8th grade, you might benefit from a brief refresher on the scientific method. Some people tend to believe anything they read or anything they see on television or the Internet even though it flies in the face of scientific fact.

For example, all child molesters probably drank milk as very young children. Do you really believe that drinking milk causes one to become a child molester? There has been a 100 percent increase in the number of women over age 60 in rural areas developing AIDS. That may be true if last year two women had AIDS and this year four women have AIDS. Does it mean anything? Is it significant? It depends on a lot of other factors. Be careful in drawing conclusions. Don't be fooled by big words or outrageous statements. Careful appraisal of Internet sites is a must. Question, compare, and verify. Do *not* believe everything you see!

You Decide

Take a look at the following sites, and you decide if these are informational or advocacy sites. Is the information presented accurate, complete, unbiased, and reliable? Can it be verified through other reliable sources? Note: Some of these sites may be offensive or even very offensive. Use your judgment and the criteria listed above.

- American Cancer Society
  www.cancer.org

- Halloween, its origins and customs
  www.jeremiahproject.com/halloween.html

- Health Research: Women's Health: Fetal Alcohol Syndrome
  www.wineinstitute.org/res_ed/health_research/fas.html

- Martin Luther King, Jr.
  www.martinlutherking.org

- The White House
  www.whitehouse.net

- The White House
  www.whitehouse.gov

- The White House
  www.whitehouse.com

CHAPTER 9

This Is What I Asked For?
The Searching Quagmire

Susan Feldman

Information seekers are an intrepid lot. We set out across uncharted, unlit territory, willing to endure the bumps and surprises that flailing around in the dark will surely yield, for finding anything in cyberspace remains a challenge. Electronic information is invisible, and the contents of a collection of electronic documents offer none of the visual cues that humans rely on to locate either what they seek or where they stand in this invisible space. Under such conditions, searching may often seem like a quagmire, with patches of hidden quicksand ready to snatch the unwary. In this unknown expanse, search engines provide our only entry point.

If the inner workings of a search engine are a mystery, then it feels as if we are being led blindfolded. It comes as no surprise, then, that search engines are viewed with some suspicion. Are they leading us astray? Can they skew results and select data based on hidden agendas? In this chapter about search engines, we will discuss the problems stemming from confusion by well-intentioned users as well as "anti-user" policies of search engine companies.

Deceptive Advertising Practices

It seems that there is some truth to our suspicions. Among the issues we face are advertising practices that are misleading to most online searchers. On July 16, 2001, Commercial Alert filed a complaint with the Federal Trade Commission (FTC) against some major search engine companies charging them with deceptive advertising for placing ads in search engine results without clear disclosure that the ads are in fact ads. The complaint named AltaVista Co., AOL Time Warner, Direct

175

Hit Technology, iWon Inc., LookSmart Ltd., Microsoft Corp., and Terra Lycos S.A. This does not constitute evidence that these parties are guilty, but be forewarned that the FTC may look into these practices and require appropriate labeling. The complaint said, in part:

> This concealment may mislead search engine users to believe that search results are based on relevancy alone, not marketing ploys. ...
>
> For years, search engine companies have incorporated advertising into their websites [sic] that do not affect search results, such as banner ads. But some search engines have recently adopted three advertising practices which may affect search results: paid-placement, inclusion and submission. ...
>
> Paid placement is advertising that is outside of the editorial content of the search results, sometimes above or below the editorial content, or in a sidebar. Paid inclusion is advertising within the editorial content of the search results, though it does not necessarily guarantee a certain position within the results. Paid submission is the practice of requiring payment to speed up the processing of a listing though it rarely guarantees that a site will in fact be listed by the search engine.
>
> In some search engines, disclosure of paid placement or inclusion in some search engines is either non-existent or obfuscatory.

The complaint limits itself to the practices of paid placement and paid inclusion. It also makes clear that not all search engines are guilty of these deceptive practices. At the Jupiter Media Metrix Online Advertising Forum, held in New York in August 2001, Ted Meisel, the CEO of Overture.com (then known as Goto.com), which makes no secret of its pay-for-placement policy, claimed that it isn't important to the searcher whether search engines tell users which listings have been paid for by advertisers as long as useful results are displayed. However, this deceptive practice still exists and we should take it into account when we search the Web. *Dow Jones Newswire* (August 8, 2001) quotes Meisel, "Users don't care how they're made. Most search is influenced by payments in one form or another."

According to the *Online Journalism Review* (July 23, 2001), Danny Sullivan, editor of *Search Engine Watch*, said, "This is like one day opening your newspaper and finding it filled with nothing but ads." A *Search Engine Watch* survey in early 2001 showed that some of the largest search services are providing results in which more than half their listings are paid links.

While differing in the definitions a bit, Gary Price clarifies why this is a problem in his article in *Searcher* (October 2001).

> Pay-Per-Placement, Pay-Per-Click allows a person or company to buy a keyword or keywords and have their results at the top of the results list when that word or words are searched. GoTo.com (now Overture.com) is just one of many examples of this type of search engine. The extra challenge with GoTo and others is that in addition to searching at GoTo.com they also sell their database to other search engines for them to brand as their own. For example, GoTo.com "powers" NBCi and Go.com (formerly Infoseek). So if a user tells you that NBCi is his or her engine of choice, in actuality they are searching GoTo.com material. Various "flavors" of this type of branding exist in the Web search world. To get an idea of how many of these engines are online, check www.payperclicksearchengines.com.

The Danger of Hidden Assumptions

In any relationship, expectations about the other party can lead to misunderstanding and anger. Searchers have been outraged to discover that some search engines sell higher rankings to sites that pay for being returned. Spamdexing (manipulation of metatags and text by Webmasters) in order to obtain high rankings or inappropriate listings also makes searchers (and search engine companies) irate. These are intentional efforts to mislead. However, the hidden assumptions by searchers and search engine designers may in the long term create more inaccurate results than any of the intentional misrankings for commercial purposes.

Finding incomplete or wrong information can have profound effects on the bottom line of a company or, worse, the life of the searcher. In a summary of their research, Steve Lawrence and C. Lee Giles (www.wwwmetrics.com) stated, "Search engine indexing and ranking may have economic, social, political, and scientific effects. For example, indexing and ranking of online stores can substantially effect economic viability; delayed indexing of scientific research can lead to the duplication of work; and delayed or biased indexing may affect social or political decisions."

In order to avoid these inherent biases, searchers need to know how their tools work. While each search engine may select its results slightly differently, it should announce its priorities to the world. Is it tuned for precision at the expense of recall? Does it use metadata to determine page ranking? (Metadata describes a document but is not part of it. For instance, metadata may be a tag that tells the program "what follows is a headline" or "what follows is the author's name.") Does it offer its own pages first? How does it select which pages to crawl? Does it collect personal information in order to improve a search? Where is this information stored, who has access to it? Search engine owners may feel reluctant to give away too many secrets. However, with hundreds of search engines on the Web, this kind of differentiation may be an advantage. Search engines will lose users who don't find the information they need. Anything that they can do to help the user understand how a search engine works and to improve their search results will make happier, repeat customers. Information seekers also share part of the blame for poor information finding. Like tools in the nonvirtual world, search engines can make your life harder or easier. Using a spackling knife to hammer in a nail is probably futile. Do you blame the spackling knife for not being a good hammer or do you learn how to use each tool appropriately? Perhaps the cyberworld is more like reality than we think.

What's Going On Behind the Curtain?

Not all inexplicable results are due to misleading or deceptive advertising practices, however. More likely our mistakes come from confusion about how search engines do what they do. Since search engines have become the entry point to the Web, this discussion will explain why we sometimes get results that don't make sense to us, no matter how high our IQ.

Search technology is based on logical and easily understood principles. Web search engines are just computer software, machinery obeying instructions. This limits their intelligence and probably explains why most of the hurdles they present to the user are sins of omission rather than commission. That is, they do not intentionally mislead the user, but misunderstandings on the part of the user and also within the model of how a search engine matches documents to a question create suspicion or frustration for the user. We expect search engines to know everything and to find everything. We expect them to understand what we are looking for and to match their idea of what is relevant to our own. Instead, their capabilities are bounded by how fast they can index and search, how big an index they can build and maintain within a reasonable amount of time, and what their programmers have defined as the important information to gather. Each of these practical limits on their omniscience introduces the possibility of failing to find information.

Web search engines select the Web sites they cover not only based on such common selection principles as popularity of the topic or site and importance of a source but also by the automatic selection of pages that are linked to other pages. In other words, Web crawlers cover the Web by following the existing path of links. A site that is not linked is isolated until it gets linked by another site, is submitted to a search engine manually, or is stumbled on by the Web search engine's crawler. Once we decide that as a practical matter we can include some but not all Web pages, the possibility exists that information will also be left out.

Selection is also the process that determines which results are displayed first in answer to a query. Matching the user's idea of what is a good match to the multitude of possible good matches in a results set is a combination of statistics, linguistic analysis, and in some cases, good guessing. A document is only useful to a searcher if it contains the specific answer to the information need that stands behind a query. This differs from one searcher to the next. If you type in the name of a drug, you may want to know about its safety or about where you can buy it online. And, much to the frustration of many information seekers, even if the perfect document is retrieved for a user's question, if it is more than 30 hits from the top of a results list, it might as well be nonexistent.

Search engine companies are well aware of this dilemma. They are also under pressure to compete with other Web search engines and to bring in enough revenue to survive as businesses. Therefore, each Web search engine strives to distinguish itself by size, by speed, by the kinds of Web sites it searches, by accuracy or comprehensiveness of results, and, for its advertisers, by the number of users it can deliver to the advertiser's Web site. Sometimes these goals war with each other. If you are accurate in offering a few well-chosen hits to the user, can you also be comprehensive? If an advertiser is paying by the number of users who click to the Web site, do you want to bury that hit too deep in the "results" list? From a purely altruistic point of view, can you decide, based on a one- or two-word query, what the user really wants to know? What is THE most relevant Web site for a query like "travel"? A search engine's lot is not a happy one.

Outside Influences: Pernicious and Otherwise

To compound the problem, a state of war exists between some Webmasters who will use any means, fair or foul, to boost their site's rankings in a list of search results. While most discussions of searching consider the search process as an interaction between the user and the search engine, the Webmasters' relationship to search encounters on the Web complicates the retrieval process. The author of either the document or the metadata or the Web page design wants and needs to be noticed by the world. There is no sense in creating a Web site if it doesn't attract readers or customers. We usually assume that pages are selected to match queries based on the content of each and that mismatches stem from faulty technology, faulty queries, or both. Mismatches can be caused by a Webmaster's deliberate attempts to attract attention as well.

Web search engines dance a wary minuet with the sites that they index. Webmasters (and authors) know that unless their page appears in the top ten retrieved by the search engine, most users will never see their listings. They are driven, therefore, to "optimize" the presentation of their content in order to get a high ranking.

Search engines, on the other hand, want to serve up the "best" documents, those most likely to seem both pertinent and valuable to a searcher. Webmasters often optimize, some might say skew, the metadata to appear highly relevant to several popular topics. Search engine designers catch on and develop methods for identifying and countering these efforts, possibly by installing link analysis or popularity rankings to validate the trustworthiness of sources. Webmasters discover the change and start boosting their page's rankings by creating dummy sites to point to their content. And so it goes, round after round.

Misconceptions That Lead Us Astray

Nor is our life as a searcher easy. Searching for information is a complex undertaking in the best of circumstances. In a perfect world, we would know the nature of the content in the database being searched and understand all the particulars of the search engine we were using. We would be as expert in searching for a subject as the authors who write about it. The terms that we chose for searching would match the expert's choice of terminology. This is rarely possible on the World Wide Web. Faced with the invisible and hidden aspects of Web searching, it is not surprising that most of us labor under some common misconceptions (see Figure 9.1).

1. The whole Web is crawled.

Let's start with a quick overview of how Web search engines search the Web. In order to search, a search engine must have an index of terms to search against. This index is created by gathering the text of millions of Web pages and then creating an alphabetical list of words with pointers to their locations in each Web page indexed. This is known as an inverted index. It is this index that is searched by the Web search engine, not the original pages. In order to

To the usual problems of online searching, the Web adds several others: lack of consistency among materials searched, no indication of what may or may not be indexed within a Web search engine's collection of documents, and a pervasive mystery about what happens when the user launches a query. In such elusive situations, people build an explanation, or mental model, for what is happening. Sometimes these models are accurate. Too often, in the case of cyberspace, they omit some important pieces and, therefore, lead to some common misconceptions. Web searching is rife with these and they can doom the searcher's attempts to failure. Here are some that we have run into in the past five or six years: These general statements are all substantively false. If you have always thought them true, you're in trouble.

1. The whole Web is crawled.

2. All search engines search the same set of Web pages.

3. AND should find more results than OR.

4. All search engines work the same.

5. Search engines search the actual page at the time of searching.

6. "Advanced" features (i.e., Boolean queries) are the best way to search and will get you everything that is relevant to your question.

7. Directories and search engines are the same thing.

Figure 9.1 Some common Web searching misconceptions.

create this index, each Web search engine sends a *crawler, spider*, or *bot* out to forage on the Web. Usually the crawler starts with a list of known pages and then follows links from those pages to add others. But there are over a billion pages on the Web, and to make matters more complicated, those pages appear and disappear with no warning. The sheer quantity of Web pages makes building an effective Web search engine a Sisyphean endeavor.

To add to the confusion, about 50 percent of the World Wide Web is not publicly or easily available. And that is a conservative figure. Some pages are hidden behind firewalls or protected by a file that prohibits crawlers from indexing the site. Others cannot be crawled because spiders index only text, and that text must appear in HTML, the coding language of the Web. Therefore, any words displayed as a graphic, such as many corporate logos, are not indexed. Any text formatted as a flat ASCII file or contained inside a database will also not get indexed. Unfortunately, as sites with deep rich archives of information go online, this is an increasingly common design for Web sites: Pages are stored in a database as plain text and dynamically turned into HTML only after retrieval by the site's search engine. This collection of inaccessible materials that are still technically part of the Web is called the *invisible Web*. The invisible Web is rarely searched by one of the large search engines, although each separate site with a dynamic database offers it own search engine for its collection. Some format barriers have begun to fall, e.g., Google and Northern Light have announced that they now target PDF documents. However, a large percentage of the most valuable materials are still hidden from most search engines.

Search engines must also make some decisions about how often to crawl a site. Even if we only consider the publicly crawlable Web, there are still billions of pages. In order to keep up with the newest pages, Web search engines often take submissions from owners or designers of pages so they will know what addresses to look for as they crawl. They also have gathered, over the years, a list of sites that they crawl regularly. Even so, only a small percentage of the Web pages are crawled, as it isn't feasible to crawl them all. Here the question of selection creeps in. If crawlers cannot cover the entire Web in any reasonable length of time, then what pages should they crawl? How often? A newspaper site crawled once a week would miss six days of news until crawled again. Issue-oriented Web sites, on the other hand, may change once a month or even once every six months.

Faced with this monumental task, each Web search engine has been programmed to index what and when. These decisions reflect the demand for particular topics or types of pages, as well as the philosophical bent of the search engine designers. Each search engine, therefore, searches a different database, which is one reason why results can differ so wildly. And, since pages appear and disappear but the index reflects the crawler's last visit to them, we often end with broken links or links to pages no longer relevant to a search since the site owner has changed the content in the interim. To add to the confusion, as search engine designers continue to adjust their systems to improve results, the changing algorithms may change how pages are ranked. Whatever the reason, this constant flux mystifies users who may launch the same search two weeks later and receive entirely different results.

2. All search engines search the same set of Web pages.

Studies by Greg Notess (www.notess.com) and by Steve Lawrence and C. Lee Giles (www.wwwmetrics.com) have demonstrated that each search engine searches a fraction of the Web. These separate slices of the Web rarely overlap between search engines. Notess estimated that overlapping coverage between any two search engines was probably no better than 20 percent. This means that searchers who do not find the information they need quickly on one search engine should try another search engine, preferably several, or even a metasearch engine. However, since many metasearch engines do not cover some of the largest Web search engines, there is no way to search everything on the Web from a single entry point. The lesson remains, however: if you are not finding the information you need, look somewhere else.

3. AND should find more results than OR.

Although professional searchers don't usually confuse the effects of AND and OR, many Boolean queries that the search engines receive appear to have the two operators backward. Many searchers expect that AND will yield more results than OR, since that is the way that we use those words in plain English ("one Dog AND one Cat = two Pets."). But in Boolean searching, the AND requires that all connected terms must occur in the same document. Therefore, "one document mentioning Dog AND one document mentioning Cat *may* = zero documents" since neither document mentioned both animals. To insure the broadest coverage, use the OR connector. OR pulls up documents that mention only Dog, documents that mention only Cat, as well as documents that mention both. Better yet, don't use connectors at all, and let the advanced search algorithms of the engine calculate what to return. Second-guessing modern search engines is fraught with danger. Even search engine designers have told us that they avoid using any Boolean commands when they do their own searching. Make sure when you get results from a search engine that you determine whether its default is AND or OR so you can be more precise in future queries.

Since the sheer size of the Web usually retrieves a mass of results for almost any query, searchers who opt for AND are often more satisfied because their results appear more precise. What they don't realize is that they are finding at best 20 percent (usually less) of the materials relevant to their search when they choose precision. Therefore, searchers must not believe that they have found "all" the relevant results. At best, they have found a sampling.

4. All search engines work the same.

While most Web search engines are based on similar principles— for example, that if a query term appears frequently in a document, then that document must be about that topic—each search engine implements that concept differently. Some believe that "precision" or maximum relevance of results to a query is more important than "recall" or assuring comprehensive results. Precision-minded search engines may choose to offer only exact matches to a query. Others expect that users need help and clues, so they may return any document even remotely related to the query, if only to help educate the user on terminology and concepts.

Most plot a middle course, returning exact matches, and then the closest matches. The matter of AND vs. OR illustrates this point. Some search engines default to an AND search, and others to an OR. Google, for instance, achieves its precise results in part because Google is programmed to insert an AND between query words. Northern Light is fairly precise because it returns a "fuzzy" AND, i.e., an AND with some latitude for finding additional good matches.

Some search engines index the whole Web page, while others only index the first 500–1000 words. Some use the number of links pointing to a page to boost its ranking in a results set. To make matters worse, by the time this book is printed, the choices that all of these search engines have made will have changed. AND may have switched to OR on one service while another will have gone from OR to a fuzzy AND. Full-text indexing may be added or subtracted. And, of course, many more Web pages will be crawled, URLs dropped, and dynamic databases added. Ranking algorithms will be subtly altered. Each of these will affect the outcome of a given search.

Knowing such basic design decisions can help users choose an appropriate search engine for each information need. However, other design decisions also determine which document is returned and which is not, decisions that the user will probably not find in the search engines' Help or FAQs. These include:

- Whether or not the system includes metadata in its ranking or weighting

- The importance given to term proximity in the weighting algorithm

- Whether the search engine uses built-in clusters of synonyms or categorization in order to improve searching

- Whether the designers take the query term's position in the document into consideration

Does the search engine look at the document as a single work, or does it "chunk" the document so that paragraphs are considered separately? Sometimes, a single paragraph in a longer work can contain the perfect answer to a question. Unfortunately, most of these decisions are proprietary to each search engine. What is a poor searcher to do? The answer is inelegant: If you haven't found the information you seek in the first 30 or so documents, or it appears that the search engine has misinterpreted your question, then change the query or change the search engine you use. It is quite possible that you are seeking information that is not indexed by that particular search engine.

5. Search engines search the actual page at the time of searching.

Search engines search their index, not the actual page that appears on the Web, when they answer a query. It would take too long for them to go to each page and search it separately. Consequently, if a Web page has been moved or removed, the fact of its nonexistence may not be discovered for weeks or even months, until the search engine's crawler does its next crawl. This assumption led one less than technically proficient business to sue its previous Internet Service Provider (ISP) because the business's previous Web page kept being retrieved after it had already moved to another ISP. The business was so irate that it was ready to sue all the search engines as well. It demanded in court that the ISP should write a letter to force all search engines to update their indexes. This misunderstanding of how things work cost the business money, as well as useless anger.

6. "Advanced" features, (i.e., Boolean queries), are the best way to search and will get you everything that is relevant to your question.

Web search engines were designed to improve Boolean searching. The idea is that most people are searching for something that they have trouble describing because they don't know very much about the topic. If you are an expert and you know what you are looking for, a Boolean query can be the right approach. However, tests over the years show that a good query that uses many synonyms can often be more successful, even if you are looking for a specific title, so try that approach first.

By and large, Web search engines should be allowed to work without meddling. No pluses, no minuses, no other commands or parenthetical nesting, other than specifying a phrase as a unit. These search engines need more query text to crunch to help them match a description of an idea in the searcher's head to descriptions of topics in a document. So, expand the query. Add synonyms. Use lots of words to describe the idea.

7. Directories and search engines are the same thing.

There are several different valid approaches to looking for information. Browsing and searching can yield good results and are often used in tandem. One's natural searching style, browser or searcher, probably stems from cognitive style and training, but a good searcher learns to adjust personal style to suit the question and the resources used to answer it. Browsing works best when the required information is still a vague idea. Searching works best when the idea has been formulated and fleshed out. However, most users browse and search together. First, people send in a broad query. Then they browse through the results to find additional clues on how to improve their search query. Using whatever additional terminology they may find, they refine the query and may repeat this cycle many times.

Directories are browsing tools. They are organized hierarchical guides to the contents of a collection of information. They enable users to browse from the broad to the narrow and then up again to start at the beginning of another hierarchy. Directories encourage serendipity, the process of meandering through a collection until one reaches a likely source. Usually, they contain a collection of manually selected sites that represent a topic well. Therefore, they offer a much smaller collection of sites of higher quality.

In the case of Yahoo!, the best known directory on the Web, experts select sites on a subject and organize the listings according to a subject scheme that groups together related topics. Directories are a good approach to helping people find information in an invisible information space like the Web because they describe the contents of the collection at a top level. They are good navigation tools. However, directories like Yahoo! cannot possibly contain the number of sites that the Web does nor would one want them to. The strength of a directory lies in its selections. Search engines, on the other hand, yield direct answers to specific questions.

Search Engine Assumptions About Searchers

The common misconceptions about Web searching previously discussed lead people to expect that a Web search engine will find everything on the Web, that all search engines search the same collection, and that Yahoo! covers as many sites as any of the search engines does. Often they give up, confused, frustrated, and angry because they expect one finding aid—directory or search engine—to work as well as any or all of the others.

Search engines make some assumptions about the people who use them as well. If you do not fit the profile of a typical Web searcher, then they may misinterpret your query. For search engine and searcher to work well together, their underlying assumptions about what is important must match.

In selecting what to crawl and what to display first, Web search engines all make the following assumptions:

- The documents that contain the most occurrences of a query term are the most likely to be relevant to that query.

- Rare terms are more important than common terms in determining what a document is about.

- If all the words in the query appear close to each other in the document, the document is more relevant.

- Plural and singular forms of nouns should be treated the same.

In addition, some search engines use the following criteria to determine ranking:

1. Popularity of the site: as indicated by the number of links to it or by the choices that people make in selecting a site to view from a results page.

2. Link analysis: Google, Northern Light, and many other search engines use link analysis as one of the factors that may boost the ranking of a page. The system designers have assumed that if more pages point to a site, then those pointers represent "selections" by real experts on a topic. That may or may not be true. By and large, the greater the number of links to a site does seem to indicate that the site has valuable information.

3. Collaborative filtering: The choices others with the same query have made, such as what pages people choose to go to and how long they stay there, may also be used to boost a page's ranking. This is called "collaborative filtering," the technology used by Direct Hit.

4. Exceptions to popularity: While popularity may be a good indicator of the relative merits of a site, there are certainly exceptions. New sites, for example, will have fewer links to

them until they are discovered. Thus, the newest research on a topic may not come to the top of the list if link analysis is used too heavily. Conversely, one new form of "spamming," or the attempt by a Webmaster to boost the ranking of a site, is to create dummy sites that link to the original page. This is intended to fool the search engine into thinking the page is popular.

5. Boosting ranking by type of site (e.g., .com vs. .edu): Some engines assume that people are more interested in products than in academic treatises; some assume the reverse. Giles and Lawrence at NEC (www.wwwmetrics.com) have found that content of the Web is heavily skewed towards commercial sites. In 1999, they said, "83 percent of sites contain commercial content and 6 percent contain scientific or educational content. Only 1.5 percent of sites contain pornographic content." Even though this balance may reflect the state of the Web, some search engines make a special effort to crawl academic and research sites, while others are more product oriented.

6. Sources of search engine revenues: As discussed at the beginning of this chapter, these revenue factors include pay-for-ranking, as well as various partnerships and alliances with other enterprises. Overture.com was the first search engine to announce it would boost a site's ranking based on how much site owners are willing to pay for a listing. It assumes people will prefer pages that have been paid for to be displayed because those are the "serious" players in the field. This is akin to using the Yellow Pages and scanning for boxed ads or at least ones in bold face.

7. Information skewing: Business relationships or advertisements can skew the information offered more subtly. While other search engines besides Overture.com claim they do not allow revenue production to tamper with search results, many search sites now offer related information in an adjoining column on the "results" page. This may provide links to other related sites, to advertising partners who sell related products, or to collections about the topic being searched. For instance, WebMD is the sole source for the medical information section on Lycos. It pays Lycos for this privilege since Lycos generates traffic to the WebMD Web site. WebMD is a good, authoritative source of medical information, but it isn't always the best one. This ignores the contents of competitors' sites, although the

other sites may show up in a straight search if they have been indexed.

8. Metadata and classification schemes: Some search engines use the metadata tags on a page to improve their understanding of a page. Metadata single out the important concepts. Classification schemes group similar documents together by concept. Metadata or a classification scheme may improve the quality of the search. But metadata and classification schemes are based on the world as we know it. New information can end up forcibly shoved into an ill-fitting box because the system found nowhere else to put it. The flexibility of the taxonomic scheme and the efforts devoted to keeping it and the metadata current determine the prevalence of this problem. In addition, metadata are often manipulated by Webmasters in order to improve the ranking of a Web page.

9. Context and personalization: The more a search engine knows about the searcher, the better it can perform its job. One of today's trends is to "personalize" products to fit the needs of the individual better. However, a little personalization can go a long way. Determining font size, or even predilection for academic instead of popular information, may be useful. When we begin to personalize by topic or behavior, however, we may find that the search is led astray.

For example, all search engines struggle to decide which of a word's multiple meanings matches the user's actual intent. Most words have many meanings. We determine which is appropriate by examining the context in which we find the word. Since many searches consist of a single word, though, most queries do not give a search engine the context it needs to determine which meaning is the right one. Does the user mean "java" the coffee, Java the geographic home of the coffee (an island in Indonesia), or Java the programming language? Perhaps if we know that past searches from this user have focused on computer programming, that will help to clarify or determine the appropriate meaning by using what we know about a user's interests as the context for a new search. This seems reasonable until we realize that a biologist could be interested in financial institutions (banks) even though he or she might also want to know about river-banks. The idea of using a person's past interests to provide context to a search becomes even more perilous when that person is an information intermediary who puts on and takes off the many hats of his or her clients as he proceeds from one search to another. In any case, the danger persists that tracking people's interests under the guise of improving search results could lead to privacy violations. Users must be wary about too much probing into their interests for what is presumably a good purpose. While improving search is laudable, the data collected could easily end up in the hands of the search engine's marketing partners.

What Are We to Do?

It is the early days for the Web. Standards for what constitutes quality and trustworthiness do not yet exist. Those developed for the print world resulted from a long history of standards discussions. Discussions of quality and good data, like this one, are just beginning. We need to establish what we mean by good data. We want accuracy, timeliness, trusted, expert authors, and the verification of a certain level of quality that a well-known publisher lends to a work. Yet, the Web is a free-for-all, and all we can say at this point is "buyer beware." If, as is increasingly the case, we make critical decisions based on what we find by using search engines on the Web, then we must establish some markers of quality.

Search engines are intermediaries. They match queries to documents. But they also have clout because they lead users to documents that want to be found. Can we ask the companies that own them to use this clout to improve the quality of the material we retrieve? We need

- to know the identity of the metadata source,

- to identify if that source can be trusted or not—for quality or for truthfulness, and

- to monitor and publicize the behavior of Web information or metadata sources over time to establish reputations for responsible or irresponsible information behavior. We may want to leave that one to information professionals.

One hopes that search engine companies cooperate in pushing for better information. They will need protection so that they can cooperate without showing their hands—the algorithms that are their intellectual capital. That's a tall order, but the need is taller.

Recipes and Recommendations for Better Searching

- Know if the search engine uses AND or OR as its default setting.

- Use phrases rather than single terms to search, and indicate that they are phrases to the search engine by using quotation marks when necessary.

- Describe a question fully with synonyms and multiple concepts. This will not narrow the query. It will focus it.

- Demand that search engines be less mysterious. They should, at a minimum, post their policies in broad terms. For the cognoscenti, they should be able to display how they interpret a search.

Is It Bias or Selection?

All of the strategies below influence which information is delivered in a user's search results list. Most are genuine attempts to improve the quality of the information returned. Can they backfire?

- Partnerships: If WebMD is licensed by Lycos as its exclusive source of health content in its medical information section, and it pays Lycos for that privilege, will users always get the best medical information available? Do users know that WebMD is the only source of this information?

- Sticky features: The more views a search engine gets, the more ads they can serve, increasing their revenues. Does this serve the user as well as displaying the best match first?

- Decisions on what to crawl and when: Search engines want to keep their most used information up to date first. This may force them to ignore more obscure but outstanding sites.

- Collaborative filtering: Yep.com rates sites based on how quickly they load and how other visitors have rated them. These rankings boost or lower the position of a page in a results set. Direct Hit uses the popularity of a site to boost its ranking. How many people are looking for the same thing you are?

- Spamdexing: Webmasters manipulate metatags and text in order to gain a top ranking.

- Changes in weighting algorithms: Atomz.com, Thunderstone, Verity, and most other search engines used by individual sites give a site the capability to "tweak" the rankings in order to offer the documents they consider most important first. But this can mean that a site's documents are always displayed first even if other documents are better matches.

- Pay-for-ranking: Overture.com sells high rankings to the highest bidder. It is quite open about this practice of accepting payment for placement. However, it is up to the searcher to read policy statements and to understand how they may affect the results of a search.

- Name resolution: Finding a company's home page is often difficult. Many search engines have tried to resolve such searches ahead of time by selecting the "right" page for each product. Several, including MSN (Microsoft Network), use

RealNames for this purpose. RealNames promises to select the one right home page site for each product, but it collects fees from each vendor or manufacturer to resolve those names. Would this bias it in favor of Optio, the optometrist's site, instead of Optio Software, if it receives payments from one but not the other?

A Quick Guide to How Search Engines Rank Pages

- Term Frequency: The number of times your search term appears in a document.

- Location of search terms: Proximity of query terms to each other in a document. Words in the title or lead paragraph. URL or metadata often are given higher weight in the rankings.

- Link analysis and source of information: The number of links to a Web page or whether that page is commercial or from a research institution may change the ranking of a Web page.

- Date of publication.

- Proper nouns: These are commonly sought and may be given a high weight in a search.

- Unpredictable factors: Popularity (Direct Hit), whether the site has paid for its ranking (Overture.com), or whether the site has paid to be selected as the first choice when a user types in a corporate or product name (Real Names).

Games Webmasters Play

Metadata has become one pawn in the game. Good metadata that really reflects the content of a page is invaluable. It can determine not only the core topics of the document but also the real meaning of ambiguous terms. Good categorization, using metadata as well as classification by the search engines, helps improve searching. However, there are several questions that must be answered before metadata can be accepted at face value:

- Who wrote the metadata? Are they skilled information professionals or subject experts? Perhaps it's someone who can't submit a document without a topic, so he or she picks one out of a hat.

- What is the purpose of the metadata? Is it to specify what the document is or to trick the search engine into serving up an irrelevant page?

- What is the source for the metadata tags used? Is it a controlled vocabulary or well-established taxonomy or thesaurus? Or just some terms snatched out of thin air?

Page substitutions are another tool to trip the unwary. In order for a crawler to index a page, it must send a request using the HTTP protocol to a server. The request identifies the crawler as a search engine. Pages tailored to search engine crawlers can thus be readily substituted for what the unwitting user may see. Sometimes this is useful since Web crawlers index only text while Web sites may want to present words as graphics, e.g., corporate logos; the search engine page may add a text version. However, this technique can also substitute pages that might "hijack" a user from the page he wants to see to a competitor's site or to a page that slams the competitor.

Invisible text can also trip a search engine. When Webmasters found out that search engines base their rankings on the number of times a search term appears in a document, they began repeating the same term over and over in the metadata, which the user doesn't see displayed. Search engines figured this out quickly and began to reject repetitions over a certain number. To counterattack, Webmasters began incorporating invisible text, white text on a white background, that boosted the number of times that a search term appeared in a document.

CHAPTER 10

How a Search Engine Works

Elizabeth D. Liddy

Many Internet nomads are confounded when they enter a search query and get back a set of over 10,000 "relevant" hits, viewable in batches of 10. There are occasions when the intrepid searcher will plow through the list hoping to find the perfect link, but as Sue Feldman has shown us in Chapter 9, many times there are other factors at work that cause inappropriate results to rise to the top of the list. One of the factors that can lead to this type of misinformation may be erroneous assumptions by searchers as to what's really going on "behind the curtain." As a public service to all those who are curious to know, we offer this explanation for what happens after you enter a search query into the little box.

"Search engine" is the popular term for an Information Retrieval (IR) system. While researchers and developers take a broader view of IR systems, consumers think of them more in terms of what they want them to do, namely search the Web, an intranet, or a database. Consumers would actually prefer a finding engine, rather than a search engine.

Search engines match queries against an index that they create. The index consists of the words in each document, plus pointers to their locations within the documents. This is called an inverted file. A search engine or IR system comprises four essential modules:

- A document processor

- A query processor

- A search and matching function

- A ranking capability

While users focus on "search," the search and matching function is only one of the four modules. Each of these four modules may cause the expected or unexpected results that consumers get when they use a search engine.

Document Processor

The document processor prepares, processes, and inputs the documents, pages, or sites that users search against. The document processor should perform some or all of the following steps:

1. Normalize the document stream to a predefined format.
2. Break the document stream into desired retrievable units.
3. Isolate and meta-tag subdocument pieces.
4. Identify potential indexable elements in documents.
5. Delete stop words.
6. Stem terms.
7. Extract index entries.
8. Compute weights.
9. Create and update the main inverted file against which the search engine searches in order to match queries to documents.

Steps 1–3: Preprocessing

While essential and potentially important in affecting the outcome of a search, these first three steps simply standardize the multiple formats encountered when deriving documents from various providers or handling various Web sites. They serve to merge all the data into a single consistent data structure that all the downstream processes can handle. The need for a well-formed, consistent format is of relative importance in direct proportion to the sophistication of later steps of document processing. Step 2 is important because the pointers stored in the inverted file will enable a system to retrieve various sized units, either site, page, document, section, paragraph, or sentence.

Step 4: Identify Elements to Index

Identifying potential indexable elements in documents dramatically affects the nature and quality of the document representation that the engine will search against. In designing the system, we must define the following: What is a term? Is it the alphanumeric characters between blank spaces or punctuation? If so, what about noncompositional phrases (phrases where the separate words do not convey the meaning of the phrase, like "skunk works" or "hot dog"), multiword proper names, or interword symbols such as hyphens or apostrophes that can denote the difference between "small business men" vs. "small-business men?" Each search engine depends on a set of rules that its document processor must execute to determine what action is to be taken by the "tokenizer," i.e., the software used to define a "term" suitable for indexing.

Step 5: Deleting Stop Words

This step helps save system resources by eliminating from further processing, as well as potential matching, those terms that have little value in finding useful documents in response to a customer's query. This step used to matter much more than it does now when memory has become so much cheaper and systems so much faster, but since stop words may comprise up to 40 percent of text words in a document, it still has some significance. A stop word list typically consists of those word classes known to convey little substantive meaning, such as articles (*a, the*), conjunctions (*and, but*), interjections (*oh, but*), prepositions (*in, over*), pronouns (*he, it*), and forms of the "to be" verb (*is, are*). To delete stop words, an algorithm compares index term candidates in the documents against a stop word list and eliminates certain terms from inclusion in the index for searching.

Step 6: Term Stemming

Stemming removes word suffixes, perhaps recursively in layer after layer of processing. The process has two goals. In terms of efficiency, stemming reduces the number of unique words in the index, which in turn reduces the storage space required for the index and speeds up the search process. In terms of effectiveness, stemming improves recall by reducing all forms of the word to a base or stemmed form. For example, if a user asks for *analyze*, he or she may also want documents which contain *analysis, analyzing, analyzer, analyzes*, and *analyzed*. Therefore, the document processor stems document terms to *analy-* so that documents that include various forms of *analy-* will have equal likelihood of being retrieved, which would not occur if the engine only indexed variant forms separately and required the user to enter all. Of course, stemming does have a downside. It may negatively affect precision in that all forms of a stem will match, when, in fact, a successful query for the user would have come from matching only the word form actually used in the query.

Systems may implement either a strong stemming algorithm or a weak stemming algorithm. A strong stemming algorithm will strip off inflectional suffixes (*-s, -es, -ed*) and derivational suffixes (*-able, -aciousness, -ability*), while a weak stemming algorithm will strip off only the inflectional suffixes (*-s, -es, -ed*).

Step 7: Extract Index Entries

Having completed Steps 1 through 6, the document processor extracts the remaining entries from the original document. For example, the following paragraph shows the full text as sent to a search engine for processing:

> Milosevic's comments, carried by the official news agency Tanjug, cast doubt over the governments at the talks, which the international community has called to try to prevent an all-out war in the Serbian province. "President Milosevic said it was well known that Serbia and Yugoslavia were firmly committed to resolving problems in Kosovo, which is an integral part of Serbia, peacefully in Serbia with the participation of the representatives of all ethnic communities," Tanjug said. Milosevic was speaking during a meeting with British Foreign Secretary Robin Cook, who delivered an ultimatum to attend negotiations in a week's time on an autonomy proposal for Kosovo with ethnic Albanian leaders from the province. Cook earlier told a conference that Milosevic had agreed to study the proposal.

Steps 1 through 6 reduce this text for searching to the following text:

> Milosevic comm carri offic new agen Tanjug cast doubt govern talk interna commun call try prevent all-out war Serb province President Milosevic said well known Serbia Yugoslavia firm commit resolv problem Kosovo integr part Serbia peace Serbia particip representa ethnic commun Tanjug said Milosevic speak meeti British Foreign Secretary Robin Cook deliver ultimat attend negoti week time autonomy propos Kosovo ethnic Alban lead province Cook earl told conference Milosevic agree study propos.

The output of Step 7 is then inserted and stored in an inverted file that lists the index entries and an indication of their position and frequency of occurrence. The specific nature of the index entries, however, will vary based on the decision in Step 4 concerning what constitutes an "indexable term." More sophisticated document processors will have phrase recognizers, as well as named entity recognizers and categorizers, to insure index entries such as *Milosevic* are tagged as a Person and entries such as *Yugoslavia* and *Serbia* as Countries.

Step 8: Term Weight Assignment

Weights are assigned to terms in the index file. The simplest of search engines simply assign a binary weight: 1 for presence and 0 for absence. The more sophisticated the search engine, the more complex the weighting scheme. Measuring the frequency of occurrence of a term in the document creates more sophisticated weighting, with length-normalization of frequencies still more sophisticated. Extensive experience in Information Retrieval (IR) research over many years has clearly demonstrated that the optimal weighting comes from use of term frequency/inverse document frequency (tf/idf). This algorithm measures the frequency of occurrence of each term within a document. Then it compares that frequency against the frequency of occurrence in the entire database.

Not all terms are good discriminators; that is, they don't all single out one document from another very well. A simple example would be the word "THE." This word appears in too many documents to help distinguish one from another. A less obvious example would be the word "antibiotic." In a sports database, when we compare each document to the database as a whole, the term "antibiotic" would probably be a good discriminator among documents, and therefore would be assigned a high weight. Conversely, in a database devoted to health or medicine, "antibiotic" would probably be a poor discriminator, since it occurs very often. The tf/idf weighting scheme assigns higher weights to those terms that really distinguish one document from the others.

Step 9: Create Index

The index or inverted file is the internal data structure that stores the index information that will be searched for each query. Inverted files range from a simple listing of every alphanumeric sequence in a set of documents/pages being indexed along with the overall identifying numbers of the documents in which that sequence occurs, to a more linguistically complex list of entries, their tf/idf weights, and pointers to where inside each document the term occurs. The more complete the information in the index, the better the search results.

Query Processor

Query processing has seven possible steps, though a system can cut these steps short and proceed to match the query to the inverted file at any of a number of places during the processing. Document processing shares many steps with query processing. More steps and more documents make the process more expensive for processing in terms of computational resources and responsiveness. However, the longer the wait for results, the higher the quality of results. Thus, search system designers must choose what is most important to their users—time or quality. Publicly available search engines usually choose time over very high quality because they have too many documents to search against.

The steps in query processing are as follows (with the option to stop processing and start matching indicated as "Matcher"):

1. Tokenize query terms

2. Recognize query terms vs. special operators

   ----------------------------> Matcher

3. Delete stop words

4. Stem words

5. Create query representation

   ----------------------------> Matcher

6. Expand query terms

7. Compute weights

   ----------------------------> Matcher

Step 1: Tokenize

As soon as a user inputs a query, the search engine, whether a keyword-based system or a full Natural Language Processing (NLP) system, must tokenize the query stream, i.e., break it down into understandable segments. Usually a token is defined as an alphanumeric string that occurs between white space and or punctuation.

Step 2: Parsing

Since users may employ special operators in their query, including Boolean, adjacency, or proximity operators, the system needs to parse the query first into query terms and operators. These operators may occur in the form of reserved punctuation (e.g., quotation marks) or reserved terms in specialized format (e.g., AND, OR). In the case of an NLP system, the query processor will recognize the operators implicitly in the language used no matter how they might be expressed (e.g., prepositions, conjunctions, ordering).

At this point, a search engine may take the list of query terms and search them against the inverted file. In fact, this is the point at which the majority of publicly available search engines perform their search.

Steps 3 and 4: Stop List and Stemming

Some search engines will go further and stop-list and stem the query, similar to the processes described in the Document Processor section. The stop list might also contain words from commonly occurring querying phrases, such as "I'd like information about ..." However, since most publicly available search engines encourage very short queries, as evidenced in the size of query window they provide, they may drop these two steps.

Step 5: Creating the Query

How each particular search engine creates a query representation depends on how the system does its matching. If a statistically based matcher is used, then the query must match the statistical representations of the documents in the system. Good statistical queries should contain many synonyms and other terms in order to create a full representation. If a Boolean matcher is utilized, then the system must create logical sets of the terms connected by AND, OR, or NOT.

An NLP system will recognize single terms, phrases, and Named Entities. If it uses any Boolean logic, it will also recognize the logical operators from Step 2 and create a representation containing logical sets of the terms to be AND'd, OR'd, or NOT'd.

At this point, a search engine may take the query representation and perform the search against the inverted file. More advanced search engines may take two further steps.

Step 6: Query Expansion

Since users of search engines usually include only a single statement of their information needs in a query, it becomes highly probable that the information they need may be expressed using synonyms, rather than the exact query terms, in the documents that the search engine searches against. Therefore, more sophisticated systems may expand the query into all possible synonymous terms and perhaps even broader and narrower terms.

This process approaches what search intermediaries did for end-users in the earlier days of commercial search systems. Then intermediaries might have used the same controlled vocabulary or thesaurus used by the indexers who assigned subject descriptors to documents. Today, resources such as WordNet are generally available, or specialized expansion facilities may take the initial query and enlarge it by adding associated vocabulary.

Step 7: Query Term Weighting (Assuming More Than One Query Term)

The final step in query processing involves computing weights for the terms in the query. Sometimes the user controls this step by indicating either how much to weight each term or simply which term or concept in the query matters most and *must* appear in each retrieved document to ensure relevance.

Leaving the weighting up to the user is uncommon because research has shown that users are not particularly good at determining the relative importance of terms in their queries. They can't make this determination for several reasons. First, they don't know what else exists in the database and document terms are weighted by being compared to the database as a whole. Second, most users seek information about an unfamiliar subject, so they may not know the correct terminology.

Few search engines implement system-based query weighting, but some do an implicit weighting by treating the first term(s) in a query as having higher significance. They use this information to provide a list of documents/pages to the user.

After this final step, the expanded, weighted query is searched against the inverted file of documents.

Search and Matching Functions

How systems carry out their search and matching functions differs according to which theoretical model of IR underlies the system's design philosophy. Since making the distinctions between these models goes far beyond the goals of this explanation, we will only make some broad generalizations in the following description of the search and matching function. Those interested in further detail should turn to R. Baeza-Yates and B. Ribeiro-Neto's excellent textbook on IR (*Modern Information Retrieval*, Addison-Wesley, 1999).

Searching the inverted file for documents that meet the query requirements, referred to simply as "matching," is typically a standard binary search no matter whether the search ends after the first two, five, or all seven steps of query processing. While the computational processing required for simple, unweighted, non-Boolean query matching is far simpler than when the model is an NLP-based query within a weighted, Boolean model, it also follows that the simpler the document representation, the query representation, and the matching algorithm, the less relevant the results, except for very simple queries, such as one-word, nonambiguous queries seeking the most generally known information.

Having determined which subset of documents or pages match the query requirements to some degree, a similarity score is computed between the query and each document/page based on the scoring algorithm used by the system. Scoring algorithms base their rankings on the presence/absence of query term(s), term frequency, tf/idf, Boolean logic fulfillment, or query term weights. Some search engines use scoring algorithms not based on document contents, but rather, on relations among documents or past retrieval history of documents/pages.

After computing the similarity of each document in the subset of documents, the system presents an ordered list to the user. The sophistication of the ordering of the documents again depends on the model the system uses, as well as the richness of the document and query weighting mechanisms. For example, search engines that only require the presence of any alphanumeric string from the query occurring anywhere, in any order, in a document would produce a very different ranking from one by a search engine that performed linguistically correct phrasing for document and query representation and that utilized the proven tf/idf weighting scheme.

However the search engine determines rank, the ranked results list goes to the user, who can then simply click and follow the system's internal pointers to the selected document/page.

More sophisticated systems will go even further at this stage and allow the user to provide some relevance feedback or to modify his or her query based on the results retrieved. If either of these are available, the system will then adjust its query representation to reflect this value-added feedback and rerun the search with the improved query to produce either a new set of documents or a simple reranking of documents from the initial search.

What Document Features Make a Good Match to a Query

We have discussed how search engines work, but what features of a query make for good matches? Let's look at the key features and consider some pros and cons of their utility in helping to retrieve a good representation of documents/pages.

1. Term Frequency

How frequently a query term appears in a document is one of the most obvious ways of determining a document's relevance to a query. While most often true, several situations can undermine this premise.

First, many words have multiple meanings or are polysemous. Think of words like "pool" or "fire." Many of the nonrelevant documents presented to users result from matching the right word but with the wrong meaning.

Also, in a collection of documents in a particular domain, such as education, common query terms such as "education" or "teaching" are so common and occur so frequently that their ability to distinguish the relevant from the nonrelevant in a collection declines sharply. Search engines that don't use a tf/idf weighting algorithm do not appropriately down-weight the overly frequent terms, nor do they assign a higher weight to appropriate distinguishing (and less frequently occurring) terms, e.g., "early-childhood."

2. Location of Terms

Many search engines give preference to words found in the title or lead paragraph or in the metadata of a document. Some studies show that the location, where a term occurs in a document or on a page, indicates its significance to the document. Terms occurring in the title of a document or page that match a query term are, therefore, frequently weighted more heavily than if they occur in the body of the document. Similarly, query terms occurring in section headings or the first paragraph of a document may be more likely to be relevant.

3. Link Analysis

Web-based search engines have introduced one dramatically different feature for weighting and ranking pages. Link analysis works somewhat like bibliographic citation practices, such as those used in the Science Citation Index. It is based on how well connected each page is, as defined by Hubs and Authorities. Hub documents link to large numbers of other pages (out-links) and Authority documents are those that are referred to by many other pages, or have a high number of "in-links" (J. Kleinberg, "Authoritative sources in a hyperlinked environment," *Proceedings of the 9th ACM-SIAM Symposium on Discrete Algorithms.* 1998, pp. 668–77).

4. Popularity

Google and several other search engines add popularity to link analysis to help determine the relevance or value of pages. It utilizes data on the frequency with which a page is chosen by all users as a means of predicting relevance. While popularity is a good indicator at times, it assumes that the underlying information need remains the same.

5. *Date of Publication*

Some search engines assume that the more recent the information is, the more likely it will be useful or relevant to the user. They, therefore, present results beginning with the most recent to the less current.

6. *Length*

While length per se does not necessarily predict relevance, it is a factor when used to compute the relative merit of similar pages. So, in a choice between two documents containing the same query terms, the document that contains a proportionately higher occurrence of the term relative to the length of the document is assumed more likely to be relevant.

7. *Proximity of Query Terms*

When the terms in a query occur near each other within a document, it is more likely that the document is relevant to the query than if the terms occur at greater distance. Though some search engines do not recognize phrases per se in queries, some search engines clearly rank documents in results higher if the query terms occur adjacent to one another or in closer proximity, as compared to documents in which the terms occur at a distance.

8. *Proper Nouns*

Sometimes proper nouns have higher weights, since so many searches are performed on people, places, or things. Useful as this may be, if the search engine assumes that you are searching for a name instead of the same word as a normal everyday term, then the search results may be peculiarly skewed. Imagine getting information on "Madonna" the rock star when you were looking for pictures of madonnas for an art history class.

Summary

The above explanation lays out the range of processing that might occur in a search engine, along with the many options that a search engine provider decides on. The range of options will help clarify users' frequent surprise at the results their queries return. Until now, search engine providers have mainly opted for less, vs. more, complex processing of documents and queries. The typical search results therefore leave a lot of work to be done by the searchers, who must wend their way through the results, clicking on and exploring a number of documents, before they find exactly what they seek. The typical evolution of products and services suggests that this status quo will not continue. Search engines that go further in the complexity and quality of the processing they perform will be rewarded with greater allegiance by searchers, as well as financially rewarding opportunities to serve as the search engine on more organizations' intranets.

Searchers should keep watching for the best and pursuing it.

CHAPTER 11

Getting Mad, Getting Even, Getting Money: Remedies for Intentional Misinformation

Carol Ebbinghouse

If you have suffered damages due to fraudulent information, omission of information, misinformation, or commercial fraud on the Internet, it is small consolation that there were ways to have prevented your damages, even if only to your pride. So, now we are going to look at remedies that may be available to you in the event you or your employer is significantly harmed by deliberate misinformation on the Internet: Getting mad, getting even, and getting money.

Getting Mad: Where and How to Complain
The First Place to Complain

The first place to complain to is the source. Whether the misinformation came from a broker, an investment e-newsletter author, a charity, a corporation Web site, or an e-mail message containing information that you believe defamed you or your organization, go to the source.

First, make sure that the Web site belongs to the person, organization, or company you think it does. One of the most surreptitious methods of deceiving and misinforming Internet users is to cybersquat on a corporate or trade name (take a real company or product and register a Web site using that name with a "dot anything" extension), or similar misrepresentation. This is now illegal in certain states, so double-check to see if you live in one of them. Other misleading domain names are based on common misspellings of legitimate corporate and nonprofit organization names. This practice is called "typosquatting."

To verify a Web site's ownership, check for a live link to the Better Business Bureau's (BBB) Reliability Seal, go to www.checkdomain.com or Register.com at www.register.com. Key in the URL address of the Web site in question. It will show who has registered the site and may also give the address, contact name, and a phone number. While parts of it are outdated, you may also find the Electronic Frontier Foundation's "Cybersquatting and Internet Address & Domain Name Disputes" (www.eff.org/pub/Intellectual_property/Internet_address_disputes) archive useful.

If the misinformation came from a posting or e-mail message, you can respond to the sender. However, with anonymous mailers, the return address that you think belongs to Person A may really be Person B making his message look like a message from Person A. Domain names are not the only things that can be deceiving.

When you make contact, keep a copy of your correspondence (either hard copy or saved e-mail archive). Describe the problem; give the source the opportunity to correct the information. Take notes (see the SEC form for taking notes on phone calls relating to Internet activity at www.sec.gov/complaint/callform.htm). Talk to someone higher up in the corporate food chain if you are not satisfied, e.g., the branch manager, regional director, or compliance department. Ask them to respond to you in writing within 30 days or 24 hours, whatever, but be specific.

Alternative Dispute Resolution

Fortunately, the next step need not be hiring an attorney, though if the sum at issue is significant, that might be a good investment.

There are several services that support the resolution of disputes without litigation. The BBB has a Dispute Resolution Division described at www.bbb.org/complaints/aboutResolution.asp. Training in conciliation, arbitration, and mediation are all provided to local BBB dispute resolution programs. Go to the www.BBB.org Web site or contact your local BBB.

Another dispute resolution program is the Uniform Domain-Name Dispute Resolution Process (UDRP) from the Internet Corporation for Assigned Names and Numbers (ICANN). Designed to resolve cases of alleged cybersquatting quickly, efficiently, and cost effectively, UDRP can save a minimum of three to four months to get a legal resolution and lots of money, as well. "In fact, the tack appears to be highly effective. More than 80 percent of the 2,000-plus UDRP complaints filed have resulted in either the transfer or cancellation of a domain name," reports Zak Muscovitch, publisher of the Domain Name Law Reports, a volunteer organization that helps legal experts research UDRP cases effectively. As he also notes, however, "To prove a person has wrongfully registered a domain name under the UDRP, the owner must prove all of the following:

1. The domain name is identical or confusingly similar to a company's trademark.

2. The respondent(s) has no rights or innate interest in the domain name.

3. The domain name has been registered in bad faith.

'Proving bad faith is the toughest of all three,' says Joelle Thibault, eResolution's vp, [sic] mediation and arbitration services." (See www.joinwow.org/newsletter/16/fa5).

Using this system, "a trademark owner brings action against a domain-name holder through ICANN and chooses one of four ICANN-approved arbitration providers: The World Intellectual Property Organization (WIPO), eResolution, the National Arbitration Forum, or CPR Institute for Dispute Resolution. Filers typically incur costs that range from $750–$2,000 for each domain dispute and the cost of an arbitrator from one of the four groups." That is less than the cost of litigation and is significantly faster.

The services of WIPO as an approved arbitration provider have become the most popular. "WIPO has handled 1,500 cases filed by universities (e.g., University of Nebraska, University of Oxford), celebs (e.g., Sting, Julia Roberts, Jimmy [sic] Hendrix), sports figures (e.g., six members of the Dutch football team) and companies (e.g., eResolution, AltaVista, Pizza Hut)," reports Francis Gurry, WIPO's assistant director general and legal counsel. "Approximately 80 percent of WIPO's cases favor the trademark holder," says Gurry, "Fifteen percent of all cases don't even require a decision—the respondent simply gives up the name."

If the direct approach does not work, and dispute resolution is either unavailable or has failed to meet your needs, you can complain to the misinformer's Internet Service Provider (ISP). After an investigation, the ISP may remove the misinformation or terminate the offender's access. It works about the same as going to the advertising manager of a publication that runs a fraudulent or erroneous ad; the advertising manager will investigate and take action.

If the information still remains, you can consult an attorney about the possibility of filing suit and seeking an injunction ordering the Web site to remove the postings. This has occurred in cases where getting postings off of a Web site mattered greatly to the subject of the misinformation. According to the *Wall Street Journal Interactive* (February 7, 2000), after a libel lawsuit against a particular stock-discussion Web site was filed, the court ordered the site to remove three postings made by the defendant, at the request of the company that had sued the writer for defamation. Before the court order was issued, the Web site had refused to remove the postings.

Complaining to the Agencies

Myriad federal and state regulatory agencies, nonprofit organizations, and others provide forums for complaints, but effective help and action may not follow from all agencies. Below are contacts for many of the leading organizations to which you may turn if burned.

1. For Securities or Corporate Misinformation, Consumer, or Mail Fraud

The SEC maintains a Web site that includes a complaint form to report Internet fraud and deceptive practices (see www.sec.gov/complaint. shtml or www.sec.gov/investor/pubs/howoiea.htm). If you are not online, then contact the Enforcement Complaint Center, U.S. Securities & Exchange Commission, Mail Stop 8-4, 450 Fifth St. N.W., Washington DC 20549-0213 or phone: (202) 942-7040, fax: (202) 942-9634, or e-mail to enforcement@sec.gov. If you need a complaint form, call (800) SEC-0330.

The National Association of Securities Dealers (NASD) has a complaint program. Go to www.nasdr.com/2100.htm to get two types of forms:

- The "Customer Complaint" form for customers or persons acting on their behalf who feel they have been subjected to improper business practices involving their broker or brokerage form.

- The "Regulatory Tip" forms for investors, industry members, or professionals aware of instances of unfair practices, fraud, or abusive conduct involving brokers or brokerage firms.

The states have agencies that enforce securities regulations. Locate the agency for your state and contact the complaint department by visiting the North American Securities Administrators Association (NASAA) (www.nasaa.org/nasaa/abtnasaa/find_regulator.asp). The NASAA is made up of the regulators from all fifty states. Its Web site includes the names, office addresses, phone numbers, fax numbers, and Web site addresses for the appropriate agencies and, usually, the e-mail addresses of the appropriate persons.

2. For Trade, Retail, or Consumer Misinformation or Fraud

The Federal Trade Commission (FTC), located at www.ftc.gov, has many powers and a number of possible actions that it can take, including

Remedies for Intentional Misinformation 213

court action for consumer redress.[1] The complaint form is located at www.ftc.gov/ftc/complaint.htm.

3. Complain to Nongovernmental Agencies and Organizations

Internet Fraud Watch at the National Consumer League's National Fraud Information Center (www.fraud.org) accepts complaints from consumers and has a special area on its Web site for scams against businesses. The complaint form is at www.fraud.org/info/repoform.htm.

4. Bring in the Cavalry

The Internet Fraud Complaint Center (www.ifccfbi.gov) solicits e-mail complaints from consumers. The site is designed to take complaints from consumers and other Internet users, determine jurisdiction, and identify the best agency/agencies (local, state, federal, administrative, etc.) to investigate and prosecute fraudulent schemes on a national and international level. *This is the modern day cavalry.* It is not just the FBI, but the National White Collar Crime Center, which involves the 50 state Attorneys General, the FTC, local law enforcement, over one hundred BBBs, the National Consumer League's National Fraud Information Center and Fraud Watch, as well as Canada's "Project Phone Busters."[2] Don't forget that if the mails were used, there might be criminal actions for mail fraud, etc., and if the telephone or fax were used, there might be actions for wire fraud.

It isn't up to you to discover all the laws that might have been violated by the purveyor of misinformation; the government and other agencies are perfectly capable of using every piece of ammunition of which you are aware and some you never heard of. According to the Web site at www.ifccfbi.gov/strategy/wn050800.asp:

> Victims can go directly to the secure IFCC Web site to submit complaint information, making it a fast and efficient forum to file an Internet fraud complaint. IFCC's trained personnel log complaints filed online, analyze them to determine the jurisdiction of the complaint, conduct the appropriate level of analytical and investigative work that is necessary, and disseminate the information to the appropriate local, state, and/or federal law enforcement agencies for criminal, civil, or administrative action, as needed. The IFCC will adequately identify and track new fraudulent schemes on the Internet on a national and international level.
>
> The IFCC has been developed to identify, track, and assist in the prosecution of fraudulent schemes on the Internet on a national and international level. This partnership will allow law enforcement and the private sector to

address and eradicate this growing problem," according to then FBI Director Louis Freeh. As of spring 2001, "A new Web site is currently under development for the Internet Fraud Complaint Center (IFCC). This new site should reduce your efforts to file a complaint and better allow us to serve you.

Remember, they don't promise to investigate every case, just to forward the complaint to the most appropriate agency. Their interest lies in investigating and stopping those who defraud—not in providing individuals with a satisfactory remedy.

Getting Even: The Revenge Web Site

So, what if you feel burned, frustrated by the perpetrator, but can't or don't want to bring suit for some reason, and you are unsatisfied with the responses of government agencies and business self-regulation organizations? For some people, the preferred battleground for alleged misinformation on the Internet is the "revenge Web site."

There are a number of fairly well known revenge Web sites that have been successful in changing a company's behavior. For instance, the "flamingFords.com" site maintained by the Goldgehns was created after Mr. Goldgehn watched his Ford Ranger pickup burn to a twisted pile of metal on his driveway because of a faulty ignition switch. After researching the switch defect and learning that Ford conducted a recall of Canadian cars with the switch, but not American cars, he got really mad. The Web site contributed to a recall of over 8.7 million cars and trucks in the United States that cost Ford $200,000,000.

In another case, Carla Virga, a secretary and mother of four, set up a Web site at www.syix.com/emu/index.htm to complain about Terminix, the nation's largest termite and pest company, and its mishandled inspection of her home in Yuba City, California. In addition to her Web site, Mrs. Virga contacted state regulators and posted other consumers' complaints against the company. Terminix filed suits against Virga in her home state of California and in Tennessee, alleging that she engaged in trademark violations, deceptive practices, and unfair competition. The company sought to bar her from using the names of Terminix and its sister companies to steer traffic to her Web site. To date, the actions were either dismissed or withdrawn.

While revenge Web sites may make you feel better, they won't necessarily get you remuneration for damages caused by misinformation or fraud. Revenge site creators have been sued, in multiple jurisdictions, by their targets, and litigation is not cheap. However, it makes some people feel better to join or create a forum to vent their frustrations and to share the complaints of others in some kind of cyberbonding experience.

This is not a recommendation. If you really insist on creating one of these revenge sites, make sure to double and triple check your information, refrain from hyperbole, avoid defaming the trade name of a business or the reputation of individuals. Make sure that you don't become the defendant in a suit for misinformation, libelous information, or fraud—by you! If you insist on this approach, remember to be fair and factual.

But, while the romance of revenge may sound like it would taste sweet, companies don't always give people money to take down such sites. They may sometimes just ignore them as the exercise of free speech, yet more often these days, they are suing where the communications are defamatory, disseminate confidential or proprietary information, violate trademarks, use copyrighted material, or constitute false advertising.

By creating a revenge Web site, you can help turn the federal, state, and/or local law enforcement agencies onto a company that has defrauded you, then use the results of the criminal prosecution in a civil suit to establish that you (and maybe others) were indeed defrauded by the company and establish a basis for your damages. If the company has assets, the lawsuit is a better remedy because you may be able to seek more than mere restitution. You can sometimes go for punitive and other damages, but the revenge Web site should be your last resort. If you are really that angry and all else has failed, and you still need to vent, it may be second only to picketing the business yourself. It is a poor course of action because it gets you nothing, and costs you time, aggravation, Internet fees, and opens you up to a lawsuit.

However, that doesn't mean you can't use someone else's revenge site to get assistance. Remember to check the Web for a "get even" Web site against a company that you feel defrauded you as a consumer or mistreated you as an employee. Make your own contribution to the site if it makes you feel better. Of course, use judgment in posting to these sites, as they may be counterfeit sites themselves.

Getting Money: The Court Is Now in Session

If you aren't an attorney, you might want to skip this section entirely. For the intrepid and hearty souls who continue, this is not a mini-law school session on theories of recovery, the necessary elements of different causes of action, or elements of proof. It is simply an overview.

The principles of law governing recovery for fraud and deception are part of our common law; that is to say they are found in judicial precedents. In some cases, statutes have been written that codify basic common law principles in this area. They vary from state to state. However, there are some concepts that are basic to the law of fraud. The following sections of The Restatement (Second) of Torts describe how these concepts apply to our concerns in this book.

- §525 (1977) dealing with "Liability for Fraudulent Misrepresentation" provides that, "One who fraudulently makes a misrepresentation of fact, opinion, intention or law for the purpose of inducing another to act or to refrain from action in reliance upon it, is subject to liability to the other in deceit for pecuniary loss caused to him by his justifiable reliance upon the misrepresentation." Stated in plain English, this describes intentional stock touting and other securities schemes, charity frauds that bilk generous people out of money in the name of legitimate charity, and many of the other illustrations of misleading information in this book.

- §536 provides: "If a statute requires information to be furnished, filed, recorded or published for the protection of a particular class of persons, one who makes a fraudulent misrepresentation in so doing is subject to liability to the persons for pecuniary loss suffered through their justifiable reliance upon the misrepresentation in a transaction of the kind in which the statute is intended to protect them." This applies to corporate reports, banking or insurance or any other information required by state or federal statutes.

- The Restatement also provides for missing information. §529 states: "A representation stating the truth so far as it goes but which the maker knows or believes to be materially misleading because of his failure to state additional or qualifying matter is a fraudulent misrepresentation." This is true in some states but not in others.

- The general rule, as stated in §531 reads: "One who makes a fraudulent misrepresentation is subject to liability to the persons or class of persons whom he intends or has reason to expect to act or to refrain from action in reliance upon the misrepresentation, for pecuniary loss suffered by them through their justifiable reliance in the type of transaction in which he intends or has reason to expect their conduct to be influenced." However, there are rules that determine whether the recipient of the misrepresentation is justified in relying upon it (see §§537–545). The person bringing suit must establish that the defendant knew that the information was false (see §§526–527). This is written in complicated language but means that you have the burden of proving that the person you want to sue did in fact intend to misinform you or misrepresent the information.

- Finally, the Restatement covers misrepresentations made to third parties (persons other than the person to whom the misrepresentation was initially communicated). §533 provides:

"The maker of a fraudulent misrepresentation is subject to liability for pecuniary loss to another who acts in justifiable reliance upon it if the misrepresentation, although not made directly to the other, is made to a third person and the maker intends or has reason to expect that its terms will be repeated or its substance communicated to the other, and that it will influence his conduct in the transaction or type of transaction involved." §534 extends that rule to more than one person or class of persons.

• The legal causation rule requires that "§548A. A fraudulent misrepresentation is a legal cause of a pecuniary loss resulting from action or inaction in reliance upon it if, but only if, the loss might reasonably be expected to result from the reliance." One must look to the "foreseeable risk of harm" at the time of the misrepresentation.

• The standard measure of damages for fraudulent misrepresentation is covered in §549. "(1) The recipient of a fraudulent misrepresentation is entitled to recover as damages in an action of deceit against the maker the pecuniary loss to him of which the misrepresentation is a legal cause, including (a) the difference between the value of what he has received in the transaction and its purchase price or other value given for it; and (b) pecuniary loss suffered otherwise as a consequence of the recipient's reliance upon the misrepresentation (2) The recipient of a fraudulent misrepresentation in a business transaction is also entitled to recover additional damages sufficient to give him the benefit of his contract with the maker, if these damages are proved with reasonable certainty."

• The rule for concealment and nondisclosure of material information is "subject to the same liability to the other for pecuniary loss as though he had stated the nonexistence of the matter that the other was thus prevented from discovering." (See §§550–551.) This also differs from state to state. There are other rules relating to those harmed due to a fraudulent misrepresentation that involves an unreasonable risk of physical harm to another (§557A) which might arguably cover those harmed by fraudulent medical and/or drug information. [See also §§310–311.]

If you have been harmed, and it is significant enough in your mind to justify a lawsuit, speak with a lawyer. A lawyer can evaluate the facts you have and conduct a preliminary investigation to gather any other facts needed to do the following:

- Investigate whether and which court (state or federal) may have jurisdiction over the defendant (i.e., where the defendant can be sued).

- Determine what law will be applied (on the Internet, this may not be obvious).

- Determine whether, under the statutes and cases, you do or do not have a cause of action.

- Assess whether filing a lawsuit will be worth the time, money, and aggravation.

Evaluating Your Chances for Success

There are insurance policies for Internet-related risks.[3] Chances are that a business has a policy against such risks, Internet-related or not, and whether the business appears profitable or not. Individuals may have supplemental liability insurance or may be covered under a home-owner's policy rider. If you have been harmed, your business has been damaged, or you have lost money, do not let a "poor looking" defendant deter you from investigating the merits of filing suit. How the defendant will pay restitution is not your problem. Your attorney may discover hidden assets and insurance policies.

So, can you sue? Sure, anyone can file a lawsuit. The real question is whether you can recover, or even get your case heard in your local courts, or whether you will have to travel halfway across the world to present your case.

Where to File Suit?

As one author commented, "Having a website [sic] is dangerous because people can sue businesses located anywhere. With the explosion of commercial activity on the Internet, both business-to-business and business-to-consumers, courts across the country are facing the challenge of adapting established jurisdictional principles based on notions of territorial sovereignty to new technologies not limited by geographic boundaries. Businesses using the Internet risk suit almost anywhere in the world."[4]

If the source of the misinformation is not from your state, check the terms and conditions, disclaimers, choice of law and forum provisions, etc., on the Web site. To do this, check the allegedly deceitful Web site for national, branch, regional offices, affiliated corporations, local offices or stores, etc., for any reference to doing business in your state. Of course, you should have done this *before* relying on Internet information. At this point, you want to find anything that limits your right to sue in your local court of choice. Choice of forum and/or binding arbitration clauses are two of the more common types of contract provisions that you should look for. Bring prints of these with you when you go to your attorney. It will help speed the analysis of whether and where you can sue. If there are no such clauses, or they were not brought to your attention at the time you relied upon the information, look for evidence that the company intended to do business in your state or jurisdiction or not.

Establishing jurisdiction will be your first hurdle. Personal jurisdiction is the power of a court over the parties. If the defendant is not present in your state, then you must look for some behavior to bring the individual or corporation within the power of your local court. Perhaps the defendant has consented to jurisdiction in your state in previous lawsuits, has offices in your state, or created some other voluntary "presence" that might lead one to conclude that the defendant intended to solicit business there. Remember that on the Internet, traditional acts that would establish jurisdiction, such as where the contract was signed or where the tort or injury occurred, just don't exist. The court will still look to the acts of the defendant to establish a basis for jurisdiction. But it will be different evidence (than geographical physical presence), of intent to solicit business, or contributions, or benefits from residents of the state, to demonstrate some consent to the jurisdiction of your state's courts.

The acts that establish a basis for personal jurisdiction over the defendant(s) are unique in each case, however they fall on a continuum, as shown in Figure 11.1. First are the passive Web sites, then the interactive Web sites, and finally direct solicitation.

A passive Web site with static information is not likely to be amenable to suit outside of its own jurisdiction. However, an active Web site that takes orders online, does not block orders from your state, provides an "800" number, and so forth, just may be subject to a lawsuit in your jurisdiction. Other elements the court may look to in determining whether it can assert power over the defendant include the volume of business transactions, and/or the number of "hits" from your state. Unfortunately, since you probably won't have access to this information, you will usually have to file suit before you can get this kind of information out of the defendant.

A new type of court, the "cybercourt," is being created or at least considered by a number of states. Cybercourts would permit companies in the state to litigate in a special high-technology court over the Internet. Lawyers would not have to be in the state, much less the courtroom, documents could be filed online, and high-technology cases could be fast-tracked to save litigants time and money. The lawyers, parties, and witnesses could be anywhere—along with the

Least likely to get jurisdiction outside of defendant's state or country of residence.	More likely to have court in your state or country assert jurisdiction over the out-of-state defendant.	Most likely to have courts assume jurisdiction over the out-of-state defendant.[6]
Plaintiff discovers the Web site on his or her own, through links, search engine, or broswer. Defendant does not advertise the site.	Defendant advertises and/or promotes the Web site. Invites commercial transaction or solicits donations.	Direct solicitation by defendant through unsolicited e-mail (e.g., spam), advertisements on newsgroups or LISTSERVs.
No interaction. Information just sits on the site.	Plaintiff is invited to interact, subscribe (e.g., to a corporation's LISTSERV), participate, upload comments, receive e-mail offers, etc.	Plaintiff is invited to buy a product or service, enter a contract, etc.
There is little or no contact information available to be able to interact with the host of the site.	Often has a link to e-mail the site host, along with an "800" number, fax number(s), and other ways to contact the defendant. There is no indication on the Web site that defendant will not do business with residents of your state or country.	Includes ways to purchase the product or service, through "800" phone number(s), fax, e-mail, online order form, etc.

Figure 11.1   Personal jurisdiction continuum.

viewing public, although the proposals only provide for a trial by a specially trained judge (no jury).

Check your state's Web site for the latest legislation. If no terms and conditions or disclaimers or provisions exist on the Web page relating to "not doing business" in your state nor any jurisdictional limitations on where suit may be brought, you can go to whatever expense you feel necessary. Certainly, if you have been significantly damaged and can prove it was due to purposeful misinformation, deceit, or fraud, you should go for the gold in a civil suit. Significant damage or not, you can report the transaction to government agencies (e.g., FTC, FDA, IRS, SEC), industry groups (trade and/or self-regulation organizations) to which the perpetrator might belong (like the BBB or TRUSTe), and criminal prosecutors.

In many cases you should go to the government, industry, and criminal bodies *before* going to trial in a civil action because a prior reprimand, consent decree, injunction, fine, or conviction may help prove your civil case. Aside from being probative of wrongdoing, you may be able to take advantage of nonconfidential investigations conducted by these agencies and/or organizations to help gather your own facts and proof. These investigations, especially if performed by the government, are likely to be much more far ranging and technologically sophisticated than what your own resources could provide.

Prior investigation(s) may reveal a pattern of deceit involving many potential plaintiffs. In such a case, a class action might be warranted, and through such disclosure you would discover the names and contact information necessary to reach these potential plaintiffs, something you could hardly do on your own. This is doubly important if, because of a forum selection clause, you must file suit in the jurisdiction where the defendant is situated. You might find it difficult to know where to turn for legal advice and/or specialized high-tech investigators if the suit takes you far from home, not to mention additional travel and phone expenses during the investigation. Having an agency do a preliminary investigation can save you much money, time, and the expense of locating, much less hiring, the same level of legal and technical expertise.

Another reason for first pursuing complaints through federal and state agencies is that the agencies can order restitution and may be able to proceed against a foreign defendant on your behalf.[5] In many cases you could be made whole and not have to worry about how or where to bring a civil action. In addition, the perpetrator could be subject to fines, injunctions, IRS investigations, and/or prison, in addition to having to make restitution to you and others similarly situated. Now that's getting even!

On the other hand, if the defendant strikes a settlement with the agency, you *may not* be able to use it to support your case, especially if the defendant pleads no contest (*nolo contendre*) or gets the record sealed. This is another reason to see an attorney before taking action on your own, especially if it appears the damages are going to be significant.

Intentional Misinformation: Fraud Actions

To summarize:

- Get an attorney. Expect to bring in all of your records, including the "terms and conditions" and disclaimers of the offending Web site.

- You will need much more information than indicated here. This is just an overview and is not legal advice. You will need to weigh your options, such as paying an up-front fee or contingency, filing a class action or individual suit, going to the agency first, or having an attorney contact the person posting the misinformation.

- Remember that people who act as their own attorneys have fools for clients—because they most often lose their cases. If you or your company have been seriously harmed, you cannot afford not to get an attorney.

Countering a Cybersmear of Your Company

What if you or your company is targeted by a revenge Web site or malicious postings of misinformation on the Internet? You'd be in the same pickle as United Airlines was in 2000. According to the World Organization of Webmasters (WOW) Newsletter of December 2000, unhappy customers apparently targeted United with a rogue site.

According to WOW, Untied.com, United Airlines' most heavily trafficked rogue site to date, is run by Jeremy Cooperstock, a professor at McGill University in Montreal. After experiencing what he thought to be unacceptable service from United four years ago, he sent a letter of complaint. The first letter got no response; a follow-up brought only a form letter. After that, he launched Untied.com, a popular forum for disgruntled airline passengers. It gets close to 20,000 visitors per month and has been written up in the *Chicago Tribune*, the *Wall Street Journal*, and *USA Today*, among others. In addition to posting unflattering news about United and customer complaints, the site enables visitors to submit an anonymous online complaint form, which the Webmasters then forward to UAL's customer relations director and CEO.

According to *The Economist* (April 24, 1999), "The misinformation, disinformation and rumors posted daily on Internet Usenet groups and World Wide Web pages cost corporations money. A company can spend millions of dollars trying to repair its reputation in court, for example. Everywhere you look in cyberspace, disgruntled consumers, interest groups, and competitors are bad-mouthing some company. Sears, Roebuck and Co., General Electric Co., AT&T Corp., MCI Communications Corp., Kmart Corp., and Wal-Mart Stores, Inc., have all been hit. Companies that fail to monitor Internet traffic may be headed for a public-relations disaster."

As *The Economist* astutely lays out the territory in that same article, "The falsehoods fall into four principal categories. Intentional fraud— as in the Bloomberg case (wherein a former employee posted a false press release, allegedly from Bloomberg, to affect the price of a particular company's stock)—seems to be relatively rare. Malicious gossip is far more common: Mean fictions that once would have circulated in a small group now spread across the world instantly through forwarded e-mails and newsgroups. Pop singer Mariah Carey has been a frequent target. ... Then there is slovenly reporting, which happens because the standard of accuracy on the Internet is low, while the speed of dissemination is high. Lastly, there are 'Chinese whispers,' which make the Internet such a perfect vehicle for urban legend. Somebody puts something on the Internet, and, somehow, as it is spread it turns into something else altogether."

Vigilance in checking the Internet for reputation-damaging libelous postings is as much an imperative as checking for press clippings from newspaper and magazine articles about your company. The Internet can reach millions of customers and potential business partners. Monitor your company and product names on the Internet, familiarize yourself with the newsgroups, mailing lists, Web sites, and chat rooms that discuss your organization and its products, and know how and where to seek recourse should you be maligned.

If you or your company is the victim of a libelous smear, there are a number of useful, proven tactics you can employ. One is to ignore the site. It may get so few visitors in any month that it just isn't worth the trouble. On the other hand, a carefully drafted letter to the site's owner can be effective.

First, ask the owners of the site to remove the offensive material. You may also wish to request that they post a retraction. Send a private e-mail and be polite in your request. Document all communications. If you can prove your innocence and veracity to their satisfaction you will have won half the battle. It's possible that misinformation or a product from your company really harmed them, so you may consider compensating them to the extent that they were in fact harmed and find out why their complaints were never addressed by your company in the first place. A local dealer, customer complaint "800" line operator, or "write the Webmaster" representative may have failed to handle a valid complaint, been rude or unsympathetic, or just failed to listen and/or investigate. Alert *all* employees of the risks of misinformation, arrogance, failure to respond to complaints, etc. Point out the costs to the company when misinformation, deceit, or fraudulent information appears on the Internet, i.e., the costs the company incurs in investigations long after the complaint first comes in, the costs of litigation, and the costs of public relations repair. Check out the World Organization of Webmasters Newsletter for December 2000 www.joinwow.org/newsletter/16/in for more details.

Once you have resolved the problem, let the customer know the steps your company is taking to prevent the same thing from happening again.

Go to the ISP of the perpetrator and request the removal of the offending posting under the Communications Decency Act. Notify your own ISP, the government, and self-regulation groups that are (or might be) in an oversight position with the perpetrator. While a customer cannot hold ISPs responsible for every Web site or posting, an ISP is liable if it fails to respond to or investigate alleged copyright violations, libel, and other defamatory or trade libel incidents that have occurred on their service and been brought to their attention. In some cases, an ISP will cut service to a customer who is a recurring source of problems and complaints.

If the posting is to a Usenet or other news group, post a message yourself to set the record straight. Deny the false accusations. These groups can self-police their members. If they believe you, they will challenge anyone who reposts the false information. This tactic worked years ago for Tommy Hilfiger against misinformation about an alleged appearance on the Oprah Winfrey show that never occurred, as described by Steve Ulfelder in *Computerworld* (July 14, 1997).

Consider creating a link from a banner on your Web site to counter damaging misinformation on an offending site, with appropriate facts and contacts for the media. In other words, take your case to the court of public opinion. Post your response on the same Usenet newsgroups or thread-postings on LISTSERVs where you find the misinformation. The truth will set you free, at least some of the time.

If your company has done nothing wrong and the Web site won't retract or remove the libelous material, check your company's insurance policies for Internet risks coverage or a duty to defend against this type of business risk. If you have threatened suit, follow through with the promise. File suit, go for a cease-and-desist order or an injunction. However, since the issues involve free speech, don't pin all your hopes here. If nothing else, a lawsuit might deter the next Web-skilled person considering a revenge site. Of course, this is only in the case that the alleged cybersmears are in fact false.

The Internet court of public opinion is also an opportunity to confess. If those posting the revenge Web site are correct, inform your customers of the misinformation or lack of information your company is responsible for and the remedies it is providing. Ford and Bridgestone used their Web sites in this manner following the Ford Explorer tire fiasco. Be sure to include the steps your company will take to make sure it never happens again. A public apology with true contrition and significant action may stop or slow the bashing, if not turn the tide of public opinion altogether.

Remember, if you have been seriously harmed, see a lawyer who has experience with these types of cases. He or she should be versed in the remedies available, and have experience in pretrial procedures, such as establishing jurisdiction over a defendant who may not reside or operate in your state.

Government Agencies and Nongovernmental Organizations

General Sites

Organizations that certify or uphold standards for reliability of information, honesty of the Web site provider, and/or work to protect a searcher's privacy:

- Better Business Bureau (www.bbbonline.org): Reliability Certification for businesses and consumers. Privacy Certification (including kid's privacy)

- BBB Wise Giving Alliance (www.ncib.org/standards/cbbbstds.asp): Standards in Philanthropoy

- TRUSTe (www.truste.org): Privacy standards for Web publishers and Web users

Government Agencies (Many with Online Complaint Forms)

- Commodities Futures and Trading Commission (www.cftc.gov): File a complaint at www.cftc.gov/cftc/cftccomplaints.htm).

- Federal Trade Commission (www.ftc.gov): Complaint form (www.ftc.gov/ftc/complaint.htm) or call 1-877-FTC-HELP (TDD 1-202-326-2502).

- FBI Internet Fraud Complaint Center (www1.ifccfbi.gov/index.asp): Complaint form (www1.ifccfbi.gov/strategy/howtofile.asp).

- Food and Drug Administration (www.fda.gov/opacom/morecons.html).

- U.S. Department of Justice (www.usdoj.gov/criminal/fraud/Internet.htm).

- Internet fraud section, Internal Revenue Service (www.irs.gov): Regarding charities, see www.irs.gov/exempt/display/0,,i1%3D3%26genericId%3D6867,00.html.

- Internet Fraud Complaint Center (www.ifccfbi.gov).

- National Association of Attorneys General (www.naag.org).

- National Association of Secretaries of State (http://nass.org): Listed by state at www.nass.org/sos/sosflags.html. Find your state's site and look for its complaint form.

- North American Securities Administrators Association (www.nasaa.org): For a complaint form, click on Enforcement, then Cyberfraud.

- Securities and Exchange Commission (www.sec.gov): For complaint form, go to www.sec.gov/complaint.shtml.

- List of state agencies regulating charities (www.ncib. org/links/index.asp): Find your state's site and look for its complaint form.

- U.S. Postal Service (www.newusps.com): Complaint form at www.usps.com/postalinspectors/fraud/MailFraudComplaint. htm and http://new.usps.com/pdf/ps8165.pdf, but don't forget you can go to your local Postmaster.

Industry and Self-Regulation Agencies

- Alliance for Investor Education (www.investoreducation.org/index.cfm).

- Better Business Bureau (www.bbb.org): Complaint form at www.bbb.org/bbbcomplaints/Welcome.asp. For a state-by-state listing of private and government agencies supervising or otherwise involved with nonprofits, go to www.give.org/links/govregs.asp.

- Commodity Futures Trading Commission (www.cftc.gov): Reparations request form at www.cftc.gov/proc/pcdform30.htm.

- Electronic Frontier Foundation (www.eff.org).

- Internet Fraud Council (www.internetfraudcouncil.org): Complaint form at www.internetfraudcouncil.org/ifcc.htm. Or phone (888) 848-6907.

- Internet Nonprofit Center (www.nonprofits.org): What to do if you suspect wrongdoing by a nonprofit at www.nonprofits.org/npofaq/16/06.html. How to help the Attorney General Handle a Complaint at www.nonprofits.org/npofaq/17/00.html.

- Investor Protection Trust (www.investorprotection.org): File complaints at www.investorprotection.org/complaint.htm or call (703) 276-1116.

- National Association of Securities Dealers (www.nasd.com/ secindrg/default.html): Complaint form and instructions at www.nasdr.com/2100.htm or www.nasdr.com/2150.htm; dispute resolution at www.nasdr.com.

- National Charities Information Bureau (www.ncib.org).

- National Coalition for Prevention of Economic Crime (www.ncpec.org).

- National Consumer's League (www.fraud.org): Includes a link to "How to Report Fraud." This organization also battles telemarketing fraud.

- National Fraud Information Center (Internet Fraud Watch) (www.fraud.org): Report Internet fraud incidents at www.fraud.org/internet/intset.htm or call (800) 876-7060.

- National Futures Association (www.nfa.futures.org): File a complaint at www.nfa.futures.org/basic/report.asp.

- National White Collar Crime Center (www.nw3c.org/ home.htm).

- Philanthropic Advisory Service is now the BBB Wise Giving Alliance, which certifies charities and handles complaints. Complaint form at www.give.org/inquire/index.asp.

- State offices for securities complaints (www.investorprotection. org/guide2.html): Find your state on the list, click on it and look for a complaint form on that site.

References

1. See www.ftc.gov/ftc/action.htm for an enumeration of investigations and other options for pursuing consumer complaints.

2. See www.ifccfbi.gov and also Christine Winter, "Groups to Share Mail, Net Gripes; Cyberspace Complaints to be Added to Database," *Sun-Sentinel,* May 11, 2000, p. 6B.

3. See "One Cover or Many?" *Reinsurance Magazine,* (June 1, 2000, pp. 16+). The author describes two types of e-commerce risk: "The first stems from carrying information on the Internet, giving rise to exposures such as liability to a third party for the infringement of intellectual property rights; misuse of statutory information, breach of confidence or infringement of privacy; the transmission of a virus and cyber-vandalism—where a Web site is fraudulently altered. Second, there are the risks of undertaking actual business transactions." This is in addition to traditional publisher's liability, crime-related risks, and/or business interruption by fraud or hackers.

4. See Randy B. Holman, "Global Reach: E-Commerce may be an economic boon, but it comes with its own set of risks and boundaries ... or lack of them," *Verdicts & Settlements,* January 7, 2000.

5. See Michael Schroeder, "Fraud Charges are Brought Against Touters Using the Web," *Wall Street Journal,* September 7, 2000. Among a number of other SEC actions, the article notes that "The SEC also is bringing more cases against foreign nationals who target U.S. investors." The article proceeds to discuss the cases of German residents who, among other things, "agreed not to violate U.S. securities laws, to disgorge their profits plus interest, and to pay a civil penalty of $50,000 each" following an SEC investigation.

6. In cases such as spamming and other direct unsolicited commercial communications, consider contacting the sender's ISP. It can get the offender's service cut off or limited to small mailings. See *CompuServe, Inc. v. Cyber Promotions, Inc.,* 962 F. Supp. 1015 (S.D. Ohio 1997), *Cyber Promotions, Inc. v. America Online, Inc.,* 948 F. Supp. 436 (E.D. Pa. 1996) and *CompuServe, Inc.,* 962 F. Supp. 1015 (S.D. Ohio 1997).

What a Tangled Web We Weave

Barbara Quint and Anne P. Mintz

As we hope we've demonstrated in the preceding pages, the Web has become tangled, weaving a curse as well as a blessing. The blessing: As Anne sat in her office in New York City the day of the destruction of the World Trade Center, it was possible to e-mail all her family and friends that she was unharmed and able to get home safely. The Internet was the vehicle by which her colleagues could communicate with her even though all the phone lines were jammed. It was the means by which media librarians all over the world helped each other over the next weeks with information queries, providing links to important sites that could provide quality information, debunk rumors, and look up old information for each other in print publications (history did *not* begin with Nexis).

The curse (as we alerted you in Chapter 5 about charity scams on the Internet): Within 24 hours of the destruction of the World Trade Center in September 2001, Scambusters posted a warning to Internet novices to beware of charity scams, particularly for the American Red Cross. The deception on the Web occurs exponentially faster than what we have experienced in the past, and makes us more vulnerable to unverified information. Even as we try to get this book to the publisher for final production, the news keeps providing example after example of Internet postings designed to misinform, mislead, or misdirect the sincere seeker of information.

But it doesn't stop there. Suddenly, it seems there are a number of Web sites that think Anne needs Viagra. She's been getting solicitations to purchase it since she started checking out some Web sites that Susan Detwiler mentioned as she researched her chapter on medical misinformation. She's gotten a lot of unwanted e-mail on sales opportunities since visiting the Web sites Lys Chuck and Carol Ebbinghouse told her about as she fleshed out those chapters. She's gotten a lot of investment "advice" since looking at some of the Web sites Helene Kassler mentioned in the course of her research. We edited out a lot of those sites to make sure we don't exacerbate the problem while documenting it. Don't worry if you check out the sites in the Webliography—they are quality sites we want you to use.

In considering the curses of the Web, what stands out is the broad spectrum of the deception. Medical, business, e-commerce, privacy, charitable contributions; these are just the tip of the iceberg. Many people using the Internet don't have research backgrounds or training in research methodology and run into problems because they are relying on anonymous sources of information without ways of evaluating what they are finding. We really need those filters called editors, publishers, teachers, and librarians to help ensure the quality of the information we are exposed to. The Internet has launched us into another realm entirely, with self-publishing made so easy a child can do it.

In the *New York Times* (September 9, 2001), James Grant concluded his op-ed piece "Sometimes the Economy Needs a Setback" with:

> The financial historian Max Winkler concluded his tale of the fantastic career of the swindler-financier Ivar Kreuger, the "Swedish match king," with the ancient epigram "Mundus vult decipi; ergo decipiatur": The world wants to be deceived; let it therefore be deceived. The Romans might have added, for financial context, that the world is most credulous during bull markets. Prosperity makes it gullible.

Grant might well have been describing the Internet. A certain economic prosperity over the course of a decade made it possible for a large percentage of the American population to purchase computers and get hooked up to the Internet. Without that prosperity, the development of services and applications would have taken longer to ripple out to the general public and perhaps more quality controls and safeguards would have been built in. But we were technologically prosperous and we certainly have shown ourselves to be gullible. Deception and gullibility predate the Internet by thousands of years. As we hope you've learned from reading this book, the new technology just puts that deception and gullibility into overdrive.

You might think that the editor and authors of this book want you to believe you are innocent victims of powers beyond your control. This could not be farther from the truth. We wrote this book to empower you to take charge of the Internet you encounter. As a last topic of endeavor, we want to alert you to your own responsibilities as Internet nomads and information seekers. You are certainly not the root of the problem, but some of your research habits can turn you into your own worst enemy.

Here are some of the pitfalls that you could create for yourselves and how to stay out of them:

1. Wimbledon or Ping-Pong?

Know the game you're playing, the level you're playing at, and play by its rules. All too often we start searches with grand and glorious plans to gather all the relevant information on the broadest range of subjects and end up limping off the Web with just a few pieces of data. Then we try to convince others and ourselves that the tiny packet of information retrieved meets our originally stated specifications. In the course of the search, as we move from dreams of status as a final round player at Wimbledon to the reality of a quick game of table tennis with our 10-year-old nephew, we revise the rules of the game. The field of dreams shrinks from Center Court to the size of a Ping-Pong tabletop. The powerful netting of a tennis racket is diminished into the small, flat surface of a Ping-Pong paddle.

There's nothing wrong with revising your search goals as long as you realize that you have done so. Scaling back a project can represent a prudent use of time and resources, but you should tell everyone involved of the shift the search has taken. If you are sharing the results with clients, friends, or colleagues, you should make sure that they know the reasons and scope of the retreat. If you tell them that the little bit of information you found was perfect, exactly what you wanted all along and they believe you, they may toss away sources they gathered independently to meet your original specifications.

When the stakes are high, it might be a good time to bring in an expert searcher, who may be able to come up with a compromise solution that gets you more of what you wanted originally.

2. The Tick-Tock Block

Back in the Stone Age era of online searching (the distant 1980s and 1990s), all online searching was on expensive proprietary commercial online services, services usually pricing their services by connect time. This pricing structure gave professional searchers a permanent nervous tic and effectively kept the rest of the intelligent universe from signing up. Every search became a race to find the right information before the clock ate up all the budgeted search funds. Web searchers do not bear the psychological scars of that kind of pricing structure, but the clock still ticks.

When you're tired of doing something, you don't do it well. Often you let time warp your judgment. You fall into the Wimbledon/Ping-Pong syndrome and overhype the value of whatever information you have found. You throw your hands up in the air and maintain that the information doesn't exist. You sigh in discouragement and admit defeat. STOP! Don't let the clock tick louder than your good sense. One of the greatest virtues of Web-borne information lies in its 24/7/365 availability. Tomorrow is another day and later tonight is a good time, too. Take a nap. Let your creative subconscious do some work. Then later or tomorrow go back to the project and review your results and strategy. Most likely new ideas will have emerged and search angles have opened up that will seem so obvious you will wonder how you could ever have missed them. As you grow more experienced, you may even learn to build in these kinds of delays and learn to search in stages.

3. Defensive Documentation

When it comes to documenting search results, wise searchers get in the habit of seeking out Web site documentation and maintaining records as good as those of the best Webmaster. The bigger the outfit behind a Web site, the more misleading sloppy Web site management can make their data, specifically because users expect big outfits to conduct more professional and competent Web efforts and often trust these Web sites more than they should. Horror stories abound. Once, on the Web site of a newspaper publishing chain that owned over 120 newspapers, a collection of press releases appeared that hadn't been updated in six months. Having a slow news year, are we? Large companies or institutions often are slow to fully adjust to the Web. Whole divisions or subsidiaries may not remember to keep the Webmaster informed and the Web site fully informative.

On the other hand, small outfits owning handsome, well-structured Web sites may not supply full contact information, e.g., omitting a street address for regular mail delivery. Call us info-bigots, but we don't place much trust in the reliability of any operation that won't tell you where it operates. Even a telecommuter operating from home who doesn't want any foot traffic could have a post office box. If you have any serious business to conduct with a company or government agency or institution of any kind, get the address and phone number. Check their press releases and other news announcements. Scan for the dates on whatever you find. Know when the site and the pages you used were last updated.

Make copies of whatever seems relevant to you and annotate those copies with the date you downloaded material. When you write reports on your Web research, make a point of including the last date you checked the URL in your descriptions of Web sites. If you handle a lot of URLs on a regular basis, buy some software to help automate the checking process. Professional documentation procedures not only protect you from charges of inaccuracy, they subtly remind colleagues, family, or friends with whom you share the material, that all good Web research requires a critical eye to check and double-check the quality of results.

4. The World Wide Un-Web

The Web is wonderful. The Internet is marvelous. Digital data is super. But at any given moment for any given question, the right answer may lie in other formats. Dare we say it? The answer could lie inside a journal article, a newspaper column, a print index to specialized subject matter, or even this book! It could exist within the ear-to-ear database of an expert only a phone call away.

One dramatic example of the pitfalls awaiting those who rely on online sources is the death of a 24-year-old woman in Baltimore in June 2001. As part of a study on an asthma drug she was given an inhalant with the chemical hexamethonium that caused a fatal reaction. Subsequent research by medical librarians turned up evidence from the 1950s warning that inhaling the drug could lead to death. It is not clear if the medical researchers on the project used one particular database that might (or might not) have led them to this information. Lesson: The most important information you need may not be online at all, or may not be available widely due to cost. Even expert researchers need to be reminded of this on a regular basis.

Sometimes such answers are not only better, but faster and cheaper. After you've spent an hour—or two or three—tracking through the endless wastes of the Web, you may come to dream of the simplicity of the perfect reference source in print or the exhilaration of asking another human being a question and getting an answer tailored to yourself.

Of course, alternative formats for information have different problems requiring evaluation by the critical user. Print takes time to produce, time may render content out of date and of limited utility. On the other hand, the sheer publicity built into the process of publishing material can provide and support reviewing of information. Peer-reviewed journal content, letters to the editor, footnote citations in more current work, these all represent a kind of verification process for printed information. However, to make that process work, you have to follow up on those leads. You must check the correspondence columns in issues appearing after the one containing your critical article. You must conduct a forward search in the citation indexes and then scan promising journal articles.

Personal contacts with experts have little external verification built in. No one knows what you asked. No one knows what the expert thought you meant by what you asked. No one heard the expert's answer directly. Take detailed notes on any such expert inquiries. You will need the documentation for your own records.

The bottom line is the Web cannot prevent sloppy research techniques and weak search strategies from getting us into trouble. The Web cannot prevent us from hiding the weakness of our searches under exaggerated claims and misrepresentation of the relevance and accuracy of search results. The Web cannot prevent us or the people with whom we share data from getting in a whole mess of trouble when we don't follow wise procedures and apply critical judgment.

In other words, not even the Web can keep human nature from being human. But if the Web can't achieve that noble goal, each of us can every time we go onto the Web. We can work at doing it right. We can keep ourselves honest. We can allow for human nature, both in judging the offerings of Web site owners and in examining our own consciences as Web searchers. With that approach and the information provided in this book, we hope that the guidelines we've given you to avoid the potholes, wrong signs, and unmarked detours along the way provide you with good directions for a safe journey.

Webliography

This is not a complete listing of every Web site in the book. It is a selection of the sites mentioned that may help the reader with obtaining quality information and assistance while using the Internet.

Chapter 1: Web Hoaxes, Counterfeit Sites, and Other Spurious Information on the Internet

Adbusters
www.adbusters.org/spoofads

The Centers for Disease Control and Prevention
www.cdc.gov

The Computer Incident Advisory Capability
http://hoaxbusters.ciac.org

Don't Spread that Hoax
www.nonprofit.net/hoax/default.htm

Hatchoo
www.hatchoo.com/parody/index.html

National Fraud Center
www.fraud.org/welmes.htm

The Onion
www.theonion.com

Quackwatch
www.quackwatch.com

Register Web Sites
www.register.com

Urban Legends
http://urbanlegends.about.com/library/blhoax.htm

Chapter 2: Charlatans, Leeches, and Old Wives: Medical Misinformation

AltaVista
www.altavista.com

Alzheimer's Disease Education & Referral Center
www.alzheimers.org

Dairy Management, Inc
www.whymilk.com

Dairy Management Inc.
www.butterisbest.com
www.dairyinfo.com
www.dairynutrition.com
www.extraordinarydairy.com
www.ilovecheese.com
www.milkinfo.com
www.nationaldairycouncil.org

Google
www.google.com

Hardin Library
www.lib.uiowa.edu/hardin/md

Health on the Net Code
www.hon.ch/HONcode/Conduct.html

Healthfinder
www.healthfinder.gov

Healthweb
www.healthweb.org

Hi-Ethics
www.hiethics.com/Principles/index.asp

HotBot
www.hotbot.com

Internet Healthcare Coalition
www.ihealthcoalition.org/ethics/code0524.pdf

International Medical and Dental Therapy Hypnosis
www.infinityinst.com

MD Anderson
www.mdanderson.org

Medics Index
www.medicsindex.org

National Dairy Council
www.familyfoodzone.com

National Dairy Council
www.nutritionexplorations.com

National Dairy Promotion and Research Program
www.ams.usda.gov/dairy/ndb.htm

Pauling Therapy
www.paulingtherapy.com

The Pew Internet & American Life Project
www.pewinternet.org

SearchPointe
www.searchpointe.com

Tetrahedron Incorporated
www.tetrahedron.org

University of Iowa, Virtual Hospital
www.vh.org

University of Pennsylvania, Oncolink
http://oncolink.upenn.edu

Urban Legends
urbanlegends.about.com

Urban Legends Reference Page
www.snopes2.com

Chapter 3: It's a Dangerous World Out There: Misinformation in the Corporate Universe

Network Solutions
www.networksolutions.com/cgi-bin/whois/whois

SEC Internet Fraud and Avoiding Investment Scams
www.sec.gov/consumer/cyberfr.htm

Chapter 4: Internet Users at Risk: The Identity/Privacy Target Zone

2600 Hacker Quarterly
www.2600.com

Anonymizer.com
www.anonymizer.com

Apache Software Foundation
www.apache.org

Cheskin Research
www.cheskin.com

CP Systems
www.cps.com

Docusearch
www.docusearch.com

iMarketing News from the Mill Hollow Corporation
www.dmnews.com

Internet Security Systems
www.iss.net

Journal of the American Bar Association
www.abanet.org/journal

MIT Distribution Center for Pretty Good Privacy
web.mit.edu/network/pgp.html

Nua, Internet consultancy
www.nua.ie/surveys

Privacy Times
www.privacytimes.com

RA Security
www.rsasecurity.com

SecurityFocus.com
www.securityfocus.com

Spector Software
www.child-monitor.com/spector

TSS catalog by Surveillance Solutions.com
http://shopping.epix.net/cgi-bin/surveillancesolutions/index.html

Chapter 5: Brother Have You Got a Dime? Charitable Scams on the Web

American Institute of Philanthropy Charity Rating List
www.charitywatch.org/list.html

Changing Our World Inc./Blackbaud Inc.
www.internet-fundraising.com

Charitable Choices
www.charitablechoices.org

Council of Better Business Bureaus Foundation

> Standards for Charitable Solicitations
> www.give.org/standards/cbbbstds.asp

> Where to find local offices
> www.bbb.org/bbbcomplaints/lookup.asp

Reports on specific charities
www.give.org/reports/index.asp

Public and private organizations assisting consumers and business
www.bbb.org/library/subpages/linkssubpg.asp

Guidelines for business giving
www.bbb.org/library/pubpages/bizpage.asp

Links to other resources
www.give.org/links/index.asp

Dollars for Scholars
www.dollarsforscholarsne.org/dfsdev14.htm

Give.org has merged with CBBBF Philanthropic Advisory Service

GuideStar Database on Nonprofit Organizations
www.guidestar.org/index.jsp

Idealist and Action Without Borders
www.idealist.org/beth.html

Internal Revenue Service
http://apps.irs.gov/search/eosearch.html

Internet Nonprofit Center
www.nonprofits.org

Minnesota Council on Foundations: links to useful sites
www.mcf.org/mcf/links/nat_phil.htm

National Center for Charitable Statistics (Urban Institute)
www.nccs.urban.org/990

National Fraud Information Center
www.fraud.org/internet/intset.htm

Netaid
http://app.netaid.org

Online Shopping: names of organizations on the sites
www.igive.com
www.4charity.com
www.greatergood.com

Chapter 6: Welcome to the Dark Side: How E-Commerce, Online Consumer, and E-Mail Fraud Rely on Misdirection and Misinformation

Cole, Raywid & Braverman Internet FAQs
www.crblaw.com/faqs/faqs.html

Consumer Sentinel Database
www.consumer.gov/sentinel/index.html

Federal Trade Commission Home Page
www.consumer.gov

Internet Fraud Watch
www.fraud.org

Internet Scam Patrol
www.scampatrol.com/index.html

Internet Scambusters
www.scambusters.org

Official Internet Blacklist
www.blacklist.com

Quatloos
www.quatloos.com

Real Scams
www.utexas.edu/courses/kincaid/avab766/scamz.html

US Dept. of Justice, Criminal Division
www.cybercrime.gov

The World Wide Scam Network
www.worldwidescam.com

Chapter 7: Make Sure You Read the Fine Print: Legal Advice on the Internet

Ballard Spahr Andrews & Ingersoll LLP
www.virtualchase.com/quality/checklist.html

Council for Better Business Bureaus Foundation
www.bbbonline.org

Findlaw
www.findlaw.com

FreeAdvice.com
http://freeadvicelive.com/live.htm

Martindale-Hubbell Directory of Lawyers and Law Firms
www.lawyers.com

National Law Journal
www.nlj.com

TheLaw.com
www.thelaw.com

TRUSTe
www.truste.org

US Law.com
www.uslaw.com/ask-a-lawyer

West Publishing Directory of Lawyers
http://directory.findlaw.com

Chapter 8: How to Evaluate a Web Site

Bibliography on Evaluating Internet Resources
www.lib.vt.edu/research/libinst/evalbiblio.html

Brandt, D. Scott. Evaluating Information on the Internet
http://thorplus.lib.purdue.edu/~techman/evaluate.htm

Checklist for Evaluating Web Sites
http://www.library.wisc.edu/libraries/Instruction/instmat/
webeval.htm

Criteria for Evaluating Internet Sites
http://library.webster.edu/webeval.html

Criteria for Evaluation of Internet Information Resources
www.vuw.ac.nz/~agsmith/evaln/index.htm

The Effects of Margins on Legislative Drafting
www.aallnet.org/products/crab/margin.htm

Evaluating a Site
www.2learn.ca/evaluating/evaluating.html

Evaluating Internet Sites
http://cii.vcsu.nodak.edu/classroom/evaluating.htm

Evaluating Quality on the Net
www.hopetillman.com/findqual.html

Evaluating the Quality of Information on the Internet
www.virtualchase.com/quality/index.html

Evaluating Web Sites
www.lib.lfc.edu/internetsearch/evalweb.html

Evaluating Web Sites: Criteria and Tools
www.library.cornell.edu/okuref/research/webeval.html

Finding Quality Information on the Web
www.library.wisc.edu/libraries/Instruction/instmat/webtips.htm

Free Pint
www.freepint.co.uk

The Good, The Bad, & The Ugly or, Why It's a Good Idea to
Evaluate Web Sources
http://lib.nmsu.edu/instruction/eval.html

How to Evaluate a Web Page
http://manta.library.colostate.edu/howto/evalweb.html

ICYouSee: T is for Thinking
www.ithaca.edu/library/Training.hott.html

Librarians' Index to the Internet
http://lii.org

Libraries of Purdue University. (Anyone can (and probably will)
put anything up on the Internet)
http://thorplus.lib.purdue.edu/~techman/eval.html

The Scout Report
http://scout.cs.wisc.edu

Usable Web
http://usableweb.com

The Virtual Chase, A Research Site for Legal Professionals
www.virtualchase.com

Chapter 9: This Is What I Asked For? The Searching Quagmire

Steve Lawrence & C. Lee Giles
www.wwwmetrics.com

Greg Notess
www.notess.com

Chapter 11: Getting Mad, Getting Even, Getting Money: Remedies for Intentional Misinformation

Council of Better Business Bureaus Foundation complaint form
www.bbb.org/bbbcomplaints/welcome.asp

Federal Trade Commission complaint form
www.ftc.gov/ftc/complaint.htm

Internet Fraud Complaint Center
http://www1.ifccfbi.gov/index.asp

National Association of Securities Dealers complaint program
www.nasdr.com/2100.htm

National Consumer's League National Fraud Information Center
www.fraud.org/info/repoform.htm

Network Solutions on behalf of the U.S. Department of
Commerce
www.internic.com

North American Securities Administrators Association
www.nasaa.org

Register.com
www.register.com

Sane Solutions, LLC
www/checkdomain.com

Securities & Exchange Commission
Complaint form
www.sec.gov/complaint.shtml

Contributors

Stephen E. Arnold

Steve Arnold has more than 20 years' experience in online information. In addition to helping develop ProQuest's ABI/INFORM and Business Dateline, and the Gale Group's General Business File, he was one of the founders of The Point (Top 5 percent of the Internet). He provides professional services to organizations worldwide. The author of five books and more than 40 journal articles, he is involved with several Internet-centric search-and-retrieval services including Talavara and Kendara as well as a major initiative for the healthcare industry. He was also involved in the planning of President Clinton's Web portal for U.S. government information.

Steve received the 1998 Thomson/Online Award for his article on push technology. In 1989, he received the ASIS/Rutgers University Distinguished Lectureship Award. Selected Web-related projects can be reviewed at www.arnoldit.com.

Lysbeth B. Chuck

Lys Chuck, an information resource and database expert, has over 20 years' experience as an information professional and consultant in the field of library and information sciences. She was the first Director of Research for *Investor's Business Daily*, represented LexisNexis in the information professional community, and worked with the *Los Angeles Times* designing and implementing adult-education courses in database research, and managing changes in TimesOnline, the newspaper's electronic morgue.

Lys is a founder and senior partner of Corporate Questions & Answers (CQ&A), an information management consultancy in Los Angeles. She frequently lectures at UCLA's School of Education and Information Sciences, and serves as the co-chair of the Southern California Online Users Group (SCOUG), a 20-year-old professional organization comprised of leaders in the online information industry. She is the e-commerce columnist for Information Today's *Searcher* magazine and also writes regularly for a number of corporate internal publications and Web sites.

Susan M. Detwiler

With more than 25 years' experience in health and information, Susan Detwiler is uniquely positioned to cross-pollinate each industry with insights from the other. She frequently consults to information and medical companies on resource content and quality. She is author of several studies on the quality of health information on the Internet, including *The Medium Isn't Getting the Message*, and is a frequent speaker on medical and health information topics. In 2001, she was asked to testify before the White House Commission on Complementary and Alternative Medicine on the dynamics of online health information. She is author of *Super Searchers on Health & Medicine: The Online Secrets of Top Health and Medical Researchers,* and writes regularly for the *Medical and Healthcare Marketplace Guide*, as well as several information industry journals. The originator and now Editor of *Detwiler's Directory of Health and Medical Resources,* she also participates in the industry as a member of the Medical-Surgical Marketing Research Group, of which she is Past-President, the Association of Independent Information Professionals, the Special Libraries Association, and Midwest Healthcare Marketers Association. More information about her is available at www. detwiler.com.

Carol Ebbinghouse

Carol Ebbinghouse is the library director of Western State University, College of Law. She serves on the board of directors of the Western State Law Foundation, and chairs the Library and Technology Committee. She is also on the board of the Southern California Association of Law Libraries and is an appointed member of the Copyright Committee of the American Association of Law Libraries.

As the International Business Law Services' database specialist, she is responsible for policies/procedures for writers, indexers, classification specialists, business librarians and editors, and negotiates licenses with worldwide commercial database services and information aggregators.

Prior to her present position with Western State University, College of Law, she held law library management positions for both law firms and universities. She has a vast anthology of publications to her credit. She has been a regular contributor to *Searcher* magazine for more than 10 years, and has many other articles to her credit in publications such as *In Brief, Marketing Library Services, AALL Spectrum,* and *Research & Education Networking.* Carol has a juris doctor degree from Southwestern University School of Law and a Master of Science degree in library science from the University of Kentucky.

Susan Feldman

Sue Feldman is Director of the Document and Content Technologies Program at IDC, a Boston area-based technology consulting and analysis firm. The software research program she leads tracks, analyzes, and forecasts markets and trends in Web content management, search engines and other information retrieval technologies, metadata extraction, information processing and management, enterprise information portals, and document management. Before coming to IDC in 2000, she spent 20 years as President of Datasearch, an independent information consulting firm where she consulted on search engines and digital libraries to clients such as the U.S. Senate, the Illinois State Library, H.W. Wilson Company, Manning and Napier Information Services, and the Institute of Physics. Datasearch also conducted usability tests for information systems.

Sue is the author or editor of numerous articles and books about the Internet and information retrieval technology for which she has won several national and international awards. She wrote the chapter on search engines for the 1999 volume of the *Encyclopedia of Library and Information Science* and was the first editor of the IEEE Computer Society's *Digital Library News.* A former president and charter member of the Association of Independent Information Professionals, she is also a member of the Association for Computing Machinery and the American Society for Information Science.

LaJean Humphries

La Jean Humphries is the Head Librarian at Schwabe, Williamson & Wyatt, a regional law firm based in Portland, Oregon. She received an MLS from San Jose State University and was previously employed in public, school, academic, and special libraries. A past president of the Oregon Chapter of Special Libraries Association, she has taught Legal Research Internet classes and given presentations at her firm and for many outside groups such as the Institute for Paralegal Education, Lorman Education, and the College of Legal Arts (Portland State University). She is a member of the Special Libraries Association, American Association of Law Libraries, and the American Library Association.

Helene Kassler

Helene Kassler has seven years of experience in competitive intelligence, including serving as Library Director and Research Analyst at Fuld & Company, a leading competitive intelligence consulting firm. She has been featured in numerous magazines and the book *Super Searchers Do Business.* Her extensive writing on the topic of competitive intelligence research on the Internet has garnered two awards. She also contributed the chapter "Information Resources for Intelligence" for the book *Millennium Intelligence.* Most recently, she served as Director of Competitive Intelligence Applications at Northern Light, where she was responsible for competitive analysis. She also contributed to Northern Light's functionality for competitive intelligence research and helped develop RivalEye, the company's competitive intelligence research tool.

Elizabeth D. Liddy

Dr. Elizabeth D. Liddy is a Professor in the School of Information Studies at Syracuse University and Director of its Center of Natural Language Processing, where she directs $2,000,000 in government and commercially funded research into the applications of Natural Language Processing-based information technologies. Her research has been continuously focused on applying linguistic theories and technologies to improving information access since her dissertation research in 1988 that won three prestigious international awards for pioneer work in the successful application of linguistic theory to information retrieval.

Liz's research agenda has been continuously supported by both government and corporate funders for a total of 35 projects. Her federal funders include the National Science Foundation, National Institutes of Health, Department of Defense, National Imagery and Mapping Agency, and NASA. Corporate sponsors have utilized her software in a wide range of both internal and external applications to improve knowledge capture from textual data. Her research has resulted in 75 professional papers and hundreds of presentations, both here and abroad. Additionally, she is the inventor on seven patents in the area of Natural Language Processing.

In the School of Information Studies, Liz teaches courses in Information Retrieval, Natural Language Processing, and Data Mining.

Anne P. Mintz

Anne Mintz currently holds the position of Director of Knowledge Management at Forbes Inc. She is responsible for negotiating license agreements with online services to include Forbes content and is part of the team that prepares the magazines for electronic redistribution. She is also responsible for overall online and Internet training within the firm and oversees the Forbes Inc. information center and index. Prior to Forbes, she was the Manager of Library Services at Lazard Freres & Co., a major New York investment bank.

She has written a number of award-winning articles on various issues in the information industry. She regularly presents papers at information industry-related conferences and meetings on topics such as quality control in database production, information liability and malpractice, and the vagaries of locating full text articles online. From 1989 until the school closed in 1992, she served as an adjunct lecturer at the Columbia University Graduate School of Library Service, teaching courses in bibliographic and nonbibliographic online databases.

Paul S. Piper

Paul Piper is a librarian for the Western Libraries at Western Washington University in Bellingham, Washington. He received his MLIS from the University of Hawaii, Manoa, and proudly tells everyone that he was lucky enough to take every class Carol Tenopir and Péter Jacsó offered. He has worked in libraries for 16 years, including the Missoula Public Library, the University of Montana Mansfield Library, and the Western Libraries. Paul has also worked with humanitarian and education nonprofits as a Web designer, information specialist, and writer. He is interested in the Internet both as an information resource as well as an influence on popular and world culture.

Barbara Quint

After completing her MLS graduate work in 1966, Barbara Quint went to work at the RAND Corporation, where she spent close to 20 years, almost all of it as head of Reference Services. In the course of that employment, she began her career as an online searcher. As the founder of the Southern California Online Users Group (SCOUG), she began her role as a "consumer advocate" for online searchers everywhere, a role that led her to leave familiar library work and become a leading writer and editor in the online trade press. In 1985, she began editing *Database Searcher* for the Meckler Corporation, which led in 1993 to her current position as editor-in-chief of *Searcher* magazine for Information Today, Inc. She has also spoken often at national and international meetings, writes the "Quint's Online" column for *Information Today*, and operates her own information broker service, Quint and Associates. She is the subject of the recent book *The Quintessential Searcher: The Wit and Wisdom of Barbara Quint* (Information Today, Inc.).

INDEX

A

Aastrom Biosciences, 62
ABA/NBA Lawyers' Manual on
  Professional Conduct, 162
Abacus, 90
Abbey, Gardy, & Sauitieri, 81
Abbott Labs, 56
Abortionismurder.com, xix
About.com, 20, 35–36
accidents, disinformation and, 1
accounts. *See also* bank accounts
  fraudulent creation, 87
  takeover, 87
accuracy, 165
Action without Borders, 240
Acxiom, xxii
Adbusters, 16, 235
addresses. *See also* e-mail addresses
  charities, 101
  collection, 90
  false returns, 133
  identity theft and, 93
  online directory listings, 160
  pharmacy practice sites, 46
  physical, 143
  validity and, 80
adult services, 129. *See also*
  pornography
advance fee schemes, 115–116, 129,
  133
advertising
  banners, xxiii, 154, 158
  branded responses, xxiii
  counterfeit sites and, 2
  deceptive, 123–124, 175–177
  FTC complaints, xxiv
  objectivity and, 168–169
  online legal advice, 151

paid placement as, 176
site evaluation and, 171
on Web sites, xviii
advocacy sites, 173
affinity marketing, 79
agents, 79
AIDS misinformation, 11, 35
AIDS Myth Site, 11
AIDSFACTS.htm, 16, 170
Airport scanning devices, 92
Allen, Paul, 66
allergies, 37
Alliance Against Fraud in
  Telemarketing & Electronic
  Commerce, 116
Alliance for Investor Education, 226
AltaVista, xxiv, 64, 175–176, 236
alternative medicine, 36
alumni lists, 38
Alza Corporation, 56
Alzheimer's disease, 39
Alzheimer's Disease Education &
  Referral Center, 44, 236
Amazon.com, 65, 78, 166
American-Arab Anti-Discrimination
  Committee, 66–67
American Association of Law
  Libraries, 163, 169
American Bar Association, 92–93,
  120, 239
American Board of Medical
  Specialties, 30
American Cancer Society, 173
American Dairy Association, 26
American Dietetic Association, 27
American Express, 90, 94
American Institute of Philanthropy
  (AIP), 101, 105, 239
American Jewish Congress, 66

C

F

N

O

R

S

More CyberAge Books from Information Today, Inc.

Net Crimes & Misdemeanors

Outmaneuvering the Spammers, Swindlers, and Stalkers Who Are Targeting You Oline

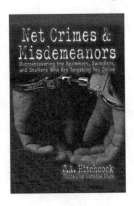

By J. A. Hitchcock
Edited by Loraine Page

Cyber crime expert J. A. Hitchcock helps individuals and business users of the Web protect themselves, their children, and their employees against online cheats and predators. Hitchcock details a broad range of abusive practices, shares victims' stories, and offers advice on how to handle junk e-mail, "flaming," privacy invasion, financial scams, cyberstalking, and indentity theft. She provides tips and techniques that can be put to immediate use and points to the laws, organizations, and Web resources that can aid victims and help them fight back. Supported by a Web site.

2002/384 pp/softbound/ISBN 0-910965-57-9 $24.95

Naked in Cyberspace, 2nd Edition

How to Find Personal Information Online

By Carole A. Lane
Foreword by Beth Givens

In this fully revised and updated second edition of her bestselling guide, author Carole A. Lane surveys the types of personal records that are available on the Internet and online services. Lane explains how researchers find and use personal data, identifies the most useful sources of information about people, and offers advice for readers with privacy concerns. You'll learn how to use online tools and databases to gain competitive intelligence, locate and investigate people, access public records, identify experts, find new customers, recruit employees, search for assets, uncover criminal records, conduct genealogical research, and much more.

2002/586 pp/softbound/ISBN 0-910965-50-1 $29.95

The Invisible Web
Uncovering Information Sources Search Engines Can't See

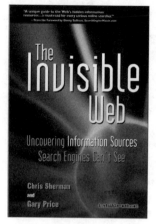

By Chris Sherman and Gary Price

Most of the authoritative information accessible over the Internet is invisible to search engines. This "Invisible Web" is largely comprised of content-rich databases from universities, libraries, associations, businesses, and government agencies. Award-winning authors Chris Sherman and Gary Price introduce you to top sites and sources and offer tips, techniques, and analysis that will let you pull needles out of haystacks every time. Supported by a dedicated Web site.

2001/450 pp/softbound/ISBN 0-910965-51-X $29.95

Electronic Democracy, 2nd Edition
Using the Internet to Transform American Politics

By Graeme Browning
Foreword by Adam Clayton Powell III

In this new edition of *Electronic Democracy*, award-winning journalist and author Graeme Browning details the colorful history of politics and the Net, describes key Web-based sources of political information, offers practical techniques for influencing legislation online, and provides a fascinating, realistic vision of the future.

2002/200 pp/softbound/ISBN 0-910965-49-8 $19.95